A Paradigm for Looking:
Cross-Cultural Research with Visual Media

A Paradigm for Looking: Cross-Cultural Research with Visual Media

Beryl L. Bellman
Bennetta Jules-Rosette

University of California, San Diego

ABLEX PUBLISHING CORPORATION
Norwood, New Jersey
1977

Ablex Publishing Corporation
355 Chestnut Street
Norwood, New Jersey 07648

ISBN 0-89391-002-3
Printed in the United States of America

Contents

Preface

This is a study of the introduction of media to two African communities: a traditional rural village at the Liberian–Guinea border and a shanty town compound on the outskirts of Lusaka, Zambia. Both of us have conducted several years of sociological research in the field settings, and at various times in our work we asked informants to videotape or film different kinds of social interactions, palavers, and rituals. When we independently analyzed these materials, we found not only that they contained information which contributed to their analysis, but which actually influenced the direction taken by such an analysis.

We were both confronted with similar problems: How could the tapes and films be considered as descriptions from an informant's perspective? What was an informant–cameraperson attending to while filming, and what were the effects of the media on the interactions recorded? After many discussions we recognized the need for writing this book to both present and analyze a method for treating informant-made visual materials. We believe that the methodology we developed and discuss here can be adapted for the analysis of any production, whether it be a home movie or an informant-made film in different contexts and culture areas. These materials should be of interest to scholars using visual media in social science research, analyzing research in the home mode, or studying the effects of media on social and technological change.

We would like to suggest a useful procedure for reading this work. Chapters 1 and 2 provide the theoretical and methodological background for analyzing materials. Chapter 6 assembles the implications of this analysis and points to areas for future research. These chapters may be read separately as a unit and they offer an overall context for data. Chapters 3 through 5 contain detailed presentations of our hypotheses about mediated accounts and of the data collected in two field settings. These in-depth presentations will give the reader the required information about the background of our informants, the structure of our respective research designs, and the processes of field observation and media use in each setting. It may be helpful to refer to the theoretical portions of the book while reading these chapters and then move forward to our comparative analysis in Chapter 6.

The two field investigations extend far beyond the purview of our present conclusions. Bellman continued his research on Kpelle secret societies and rural community life at the same time that he introduced video recording. Jules-Rosette's study is part of a larger field project to investigate religious factors in urban social change, and was initially intended to provide a visual survey of a Zambian urban community. The data presented here, therefore, touch upon many areas that go beyond the interests of this book. The contents of each tape and film (e.g., secret society rituals, palavers, syncretic ceremonies, and confessions) are topics which we have dealt with in separate publications.

Our task here is quite specific: (1) to analyze how the ways in which informants learn to use visual media reflect already existing communicative conventions within each group, (2) to examine the structure of the media forms as statements about the settings in which they were recorded, and (3) to explore how the format and manner by which content is segmented reveals the structural properties of each group's cognitive system. In fulfilling this task we suggest a phenomenology of filmmaking and an ethnography of mediated communication.

BERYL L. BELLMAN
BENNETTA JULES-ROSETTE
La Jolla, California 1976

Acknowledgments

We owe an intellectual debt of gratitude to Harold Garfinkel and Aaron V. Cicourel, whose studies of the practices which constitute everyday interaction and of verbal and visual modalities have inspired our work. In each of our studies, there were numerous people both in the field and during the analysis who contributed to the investigation. In the Kpelle study, some of these include Joan Logue, Harold Miller, Hope Adler, and Marylyn Bellman. We also wish to thank the Hon. A. M. Briggs and Mr. Bai T. Moore of Monrovia for their assistance and interest in the work, and the staff of Curen Hospital in Zorzor for permitting us use of space to recharge batteries and show the video tapes while in the field.

For the Zambia project, we wish to thank the members of the Apostolic Church of John Maranke and the residents of Marrapodi compound in Lusaka. We also thank Christopher Bagley and Peter Hayward for their role in the Lusaka field research, filming, and later analysis. We specifically wish to thank Mr. Arthur Winston Lewis of the American Cultural Center for use of the Center's media equipment and screening facilities, and Dr. Mubanga E. Kashoki, director of the Institute of African Studies of the University of Zambia, for his support and interest in the project.

The research on the Bapostolo reported on in this book was supported in part by grants awarded to Bennetta Jules-Rosette from the Social Science Research Council, the Academic Senate of the University of California, San Diego, the Ford Foundation, and the National Institute of Mental Health, Grant #451440.

Several persons have ably assisted in the preparation of this manuscript. They include Christopher Bagley, Colleen Carpenter, Edythe Hosenpud, and Peter Hayward. Most of all, we thank the people of Sucromu and Marrapodi for their participation and encouragement throughout the studies.

B. L. B.
B. J.-R.

To the people of
Sucromu and Marrapodi

1

Perception as Lived Experience: Do They See it Differently?

Africa is no longer isolated. The influence of media extends to many towns and villages across the continent. In most areas radio broadcasts are frequent, and in some, television can be seen. Yet in other parts, media are just beginning to make an impact. We combine the results of two independently conducted studies to analyze the effects of media on culture and, conversely, the effects of culture on media. In the one case, video, and the other, film was introduced to different African communities. Through the first study, video was brought to a relatively traditional Fala Kpelle community. The Kpelle are subsistence agriculturalists living in the tropical rain forests of West Africa. Sucromu, the town where the research was conducted, is considered to be one of the most conservative villages in its clan and is widely known as a major center for the Poro and Sande and other subsidiary secret medicine societies. Beryl Bellman first lived there from 1967 to 1969, at which time he conducted ethnographic and linguistic research focusing on their secret society complex, cosmological beliefs, shamanistic practices, and social structure (see Bellman, 1975b). During the summer of 1973 he returned to conduct the research that is reported here. He has since returned to the field four times for follow-up work.

In contrast to the Kpelle, the Bapostolo, to whom film was introduced, are largely an urban people cross-cutting ethnic lines in Central Africa. They are an indigenous African church established in 1932 by John Maranke, a muShona prophet. As the church grew, it spread as far north as the Zaire Republic encompassing several different tribes. Bennetta Jules-Rosette first worked with the church in the West Kasai Province of Zaire in 1969 and 1971–1972 (see Jules-Rosette, 1975a). She joined the church and, in addition to an ethnographic and historical study, made a film of their major rituals. During the summer of 1974, she returned to initiate a community study encompassing the Maranke Apostles and several other independent church groups located in the Marrapodi

1

compound of Lusaka, Zambia. In 1975 she returned for a six-month follow-up study. In contrast to the single Kpelle village, the Apostolic community involved in the study included two major subgroupings of the church, one in the West Kasai and the other in Lusaka. These subcommunities considered themselves part of the larger Maranke church and had an overlapping but distinctive ethnic composition.

Both Bellman and Jules-Rosette became apprentices in a variety of their communities' work and ritual activities. This apprenticeship served as a resource for their respective analyses and provided a perspective from which they interpreted ceremonies and daily events in each setting.

We are dealing with communities that differ radically from each other in their relation to media. The Kpelle provide data on a community's initial contact with a visual medium. Although they had had some exposure to photographs before, most had never seen a motion picture and no one had ever seen television. Their contact with other media was also minimal. Shortwave radios were common, but due to the community's location near large sources of iron deposits the reception was, at best, poor. Recently, tape recorders have made their appearance but are mostly novelties brought up-country by returning labor migrants. Since the cost of batteries is prohibitive for most members of the town, tape recorder use is severely restricted.

Literacy is growing among the younger members of the town, but the large majority of adults can at best only sign their name or make a distinctive mark. Three of the seven informants participating in the project were able to write.[1] The other four spoke only Kpelle and were not literate. In contrast, the Maranke Apostles, or Bapostolo, had developed considerable sophistication with writing and used the Bible to convey a collective image to outsiders. All of the informant filmmakers had at least a primary school education, and two out of the three were literate in at least one European and several African languages. Many Maranke Apostles had had contact with film before, albeit intentionally restricted, and had even incorporated the tape recorder into a great many of their rituals both as a recording device and a stimulus for performance.

Our respective materials provide two kinds of data. First, they are informants' accounts mediated by the particular technical constraints of filming or videotaping, and second, they are recorded documents of face-to-face interactions. The two are closely related since understanding the former provides a method for

---

[1]Although the Kpelle are traditionally nonliterate, there have been serious efforts to introduce English literacy by the central government and through the efforts of the Peace Corps. Many persons between 7 and 25 years old have had some exposure to schooling. The average public school near Sucromu teaches up to the sixth grade. In the sixth grade, students take an examination to qualify for the next level of school in the market town. Most students in the Sucromu school leave before the sixth grade. Most elders in the community have no facility whatsoever with writing.

There has also been an attempt to introduce a phonetic alphabet for writing Kpelle by members of a local missionary group. The project failed to attract the attention of members of the community.

analyzing the latter. How a member–cameraperson attended to a given recorded interaction and a description of his background knowledge of the situation and its participants is relevant for an analysis of a given setting.

In dealing with our materials, we reject the concept of the neutral observer. No matter how "disinterested" the observer filmmaker or videoist is in the events taking place, he perceives them from an intentional perspective located in the "here and now" of the recording situation. Attempts to construct an objective ethnographic or documentary videotape or film must be viewed as the cameraperson's and editor's interpretation of objectivity. This involves as much choice and discrimination between essential, tangential, and irrelevant events as does the making of a film or tape with a definite or obvious message. In this regard, we agree with Saul Landau that "cinema verité does not exist."[2] Not only do some elements in the setting change to accommodate the presence of the camera, but the cameraperson throughout the process of filming or taping makes definitive choices of what to shoot, when to turn the camera on and off, and where to use zoom, pan, dolly, crane, and follow shots. These decisions, whether they are made for aesthetic considerations or to posit a particular feature of the setting, are intentional choices.

Although the presence of a camera does affect some features of a recorded setting, it is surprising how little members actually do engage in posing and performance when they are deeply engrossed in an activity such as a ritual, game, or palaver. When posing or performance does occur, these practices demonstrate properties of the social setting that the participants have chosen to emphasize. Similarly, a member's discrimination between what is recordable and what is insignificant, either while operating a camera or by offering criticism in a viewing situation, also demonstrates features of the situation that are important to him. This is particularly relevant in view of the description of social facts offered by Garfinkel (1967) as "an ongoing accomplishment of the concerted activities of daily life, with the ordinary, artful ways of that accomplishment being by members known, used, and taken for granted" (p. vii). During such instances of posing and performance or during a member's criticism, the various properties that constitute the methods and practices for producing a social fact become objects of his immediate concern. He must reinterpret what is taken for granted in order to discriminate between what he wants to see presented and what should remain hidden.

While we carefully distinguish between video and film as separate media throughout our discussion, there is a strong similarity between our materials. First, the bulk of the materials was obtained by informant camerapersons taping or filming within the context of some naturally occurring activity. These materials contrast with films and tapes made by American researchers in the same

---

[2]Saul Landau made this statement during a discussion following the showing of his film *Jail* at the Conference on Visual Anthropology held at Temple University, 1974.

settings. Second, both sets of materials are in what is sometimes referred to as "real time," since they were not edited by either the informants or ourselves. Finally, they differ from tapes or films by recorders who intend to later edit their various shots in a setting quite apart from the interactional context.

Although the intentional project of a recorded event is also a feature of the latter kind of editing situation, it is accompanied by post hoc formulations, by either the cameraperson or editor, of what the interaction was all about. Situated formulations or accounts of an event during its course, which our data contain, are by their very appearance different. They constitute a set of as yet unfulfilled expectations whose meaning can be immediately reinterpreted for the exigencies of the situation. Post hoc formulations, on the other hand, draw upon a retrievable and complete history. The events that editors recognize as part of that history, their order and arrangement, are intentionally documented to the process of making sense in the editing room for the production of a finished, coherent, and aesthetically pleasing film or videotape.[3]

Our materials, however, do contain a particular kind of editing process. The informant camerapersons edited in-camera by using the techniques of turning the camera on and off, zoom (in and out), dolly (toward and away from the action), pan (horizontal and vertical), tilt, follow shots, narration, and various combinations of the above. We are therefore extending the concept of in-camera editing to include not only the cameraperson's selection of shots but also the techniques used to produce them. Each of them also knew that there was a limited time on the battery (there was no electricity in either of our field settings) and amount of tape or film in the camera.[4] Consequently, they had to choose carefully within the context of an event which occurrences were significant and which were nonessential. Their use of these editing techniques marked the incidents chosen as significant. For example, in one of the Kpelle research tapes, a high ranking member of the Poro (men's secret society) priesthood recorded an important ritual of the Sande (women's secret society) and its Zo (priestess-leadership). The tape, which is approximately twenty-five minutes long, has eighteen recognizable segments. Each is, in turn, segmented by different camera techniques that serve as markers to show particular actors, follow central action, study interesting movements, display instruments, exhibit important medicines, and point out significant periods within a given occurrence (or segment). We will analyze this tape later. In it, the cameraman used in-camera editing techniques in

---

[3]The question of intentionality has been a major concern since Brentano's first postulation that all perception is perception of something. Husserl, Merleau-Ponty, Heidegger, and Ricoeur are among many who have written extensively on the subject. Our use of the term draws upon that literature and refers to consciously intended actions and those reflexive to the personal biography of the cameraman and his acquaintance, comprehension, and attention to the historicity of events and persons that make up the event recorded.

[4]This is an important feature in the production of both sets of materials. It will, consequently, be discussed later.

consistent, intentional, and meaningful ways. Thus, his use of zoom differed from his use of dolly, his use of horizontal pan differed from vertical pan, his use of follow shots differed from centering.

Since it is our belief that from the producer's perspective these editing devices segment a recorded interaction into meaningful units or tape-film components, we will henceforth refer to them as *cademic markers*. We use the term ''marker'' to denote that the devices mark out the tapes and films into their composing segments. The concept of ''cademe'' is borrowed from Worth and Adair (1972) in their study of 16 mm films made by Navajo living on an Arizona reservation. They defined a cademe as ''that unit obtained by pushing the start button of the camera and releasing it, producing one continuous image event'' (p. 89). We extend the definition of a cademe to include in-camera editing techniques and their respective variations. Our concept of cademic marker refers to the location of meaningful camera techniques in the analysis.

Worth and Adair's basic unit of analysis differs from ours in that they are concerned primarily with edited footage and the way it was put together. They refer to the segments of edited footage as ''edemes.'' Their informants used camera techniques in meaningful ways, but they differ from the ways our informants utilized them because they involved the cameraperson's implicit knowledge that the later cutting process would be the primary editing device. However, our informants knew that the tapes or films would consist only of what was produced during the event. Thus, although Worth and Adair's informants filmed in continuous sessions, their project with the camera, as an organizing principle, was different.

The Navajo filmmakers' use of camera techniques produced different meanings and visual effects than similar techniques accomplished in our informants' materials. This is particularly evident in the film made by Johnny Nelson entitled *The Navajo Horse*. He shot one horse from different perspectives, interspersed with long shots of a group of horses dashing across a field, to mark the start of a Squaw Dance ceremony. Included in that montage were shots taken the day after the ceremony that were spliced together with the original shots. The filmmaker wanted the audience to perceive that the shots taken of one horse from various close-ups were views of several different horses and that both days' filming had occurred at one time.

Although the film incorporated some of the same techniques used by our informants, they were conceived of in the future perfect tense. That is, the filmmaker had an idealized notion of the type of events he wanted to film. The completed film was a fabrication of that idealized perception rather than a recording of the event as a naturally occurring and ongoing activity. He and many of the other Navajo filmmakers had already organized their scripts, selected their locations, and planned their shots by the time they picked up the camera. In contrast, our informants knew beforehand only that a particular event was about to take place and that they would have a limited amount of tape or film and time on the battery to record it. Consequently, in order to show different perspectives for an event, they had to move with the action as it occurred. Their use of intentionally applied camera techniques was, therefore, conceived in the present tense. Their spontaneous recording in the setting also differed with respect to the technological constraints of filming and taping, respectively, such as changing film cartridges or tapes and the variable time lapse involved in switching the camera on and off.

The Navajo films were members' idealizations of what the filmed events and situations should look like. Our informants' tapes and films differ in that they are productions made according to the members' background knowledge of the ordinary sequencing of occurrences that constituted the actual events as they took place. They represent what Schutz (1964a, pp. 20–21) suggests is the participant's knowledge that the scene can be reproduced ("I can do it again") and its corollary, "what comes next?" Thus, the Kpelle cameraman interacted with the events of the Sande ritual so that he would be in the appropriate position to record what he *knew* was about to happen next. This knowledge was composed in part of the following features:

1. His possession of surface structural descriptions or rules constitutive of a folk taxonomy for kinds of rituals and ceremonial events.[5]
2. His knowledge of the normative serial order of occurrences for the kind of ritual he was taping: how interruptions are made, new personages introduced, themes changed, improvisations introduced, and rest breaks taken.
3. His knowledge of circumstances that normally elicit the performance of rituals of that kind.
4. The historicity of events, interpersonal relationships, location settings, and personal biographies of all persons in the ritual he taped.
5. His rights and speaking prerogatives within the order of reality or *meni* that served as the organizational grounding for the ritual's performance.[6]

Hence, in order to tape a specific act, the Kpelle cameraman had to maneuver himself into a position that was best for taping from the desired perspective prior to its occurrence. A similar reliance on background knowledge about ritual format is evident in three major informant films of the Bapostolo Sabbath ceremony, or kerek, that will be discussed later. The format structure of the tapes and films in these instances reflects background expectations, and in so doing provides a visual accounting for them. This is not to say that there were no unexpected or unaccounted for happenings. Rather, as will be described later, the unexpected reveals itself in the visual account through such markers as abrupt transitions and the videoists' use of direct narration.

[5]We are using Cicourel's characterization of surface structural rules. He sees them as culturally specific meanings such as folk taxonomies, typologies, and the like. He contrasts these with deep structural rules, which are interpretive procedures for accomplishing surface structural descriptions. This position differs from that of Chomsky. For a discussion, see Cicourel (1972).

[6]The concept of *meni* or "orders of social reality" will be discussed in the following chapter.

It is necessary to examine the extent to which the various camera techniques and the way our informants developed in their use of them are typical of learning to make films or videotapes in any culture. Implicit in this is the assumption of linguistic and behavioral universals. In the same manner that it is held that all languages share common phonological, syntactic, and semantic properties, it is an accepted position that there are a limited number of tasks that one can perform with a camera. The total amount of all camera techniques provides a kind of etic system into which all movements with a camera can be coded.[7] It is assumed that anyone who first picks up a camera will encounter the same difficulties in acquiring expertise. Hence, each of the tapes and films have that "project one" look about them. The problems, for example, of centering the field, making smooth transitions from one action to another, focusing the camera, and holding it steady are the same for the Kpelle as for the Bapostolo, the Navajo, or the beginning student in any university film or video program.

There are major problems in the above assumptions. They require a reexamination of the theories of language used to describe film. As Cicourel (1974) pointed out, the so-called universals of the linguist are "normative constructions." Those concepts allow the researcher to locate noun phrases, phonemes, morphemes, and the various transformation rules in all languages. In order to proceed with an analysis, however, the investigator necessarily relies on his intuitive knowledge of his native language and applies that knowledge to the array or strings of sounds that he identifies in the particular languages studied. In other words, he indexes the sounds into objective glosses belonging to the closed scientific community recognized and taken for granted by the linguist. Hence, the field worker relies "so heavily on his nativeness that it is not always clear whether one can claim he is developing a 'general theory' of language or syntax that is not culture-bound, given that the researcher's native knowledge is treated as the primary resource for the formal rules derived" (Cicourel, 1974, p. 106). Cicourel exemplified this by asserting that:

> Anyone who has done field research with children and adults in his own and foreign communities will recognize the difficulties of locating phonetic representations for many sounds. We utilize phonetic categories as normative rules that we force on materials. By incorporating scientific knowledge into our everyday use of language as well as our teaching children how they are to represent themselves through sound patterns, the linguist ignores the interaction between what is learned normatively and what is claimed as linguistic universals or an acquisition device. (p. 106)

The process of coding the sounds of a language into a set of phonemic representations can be extended very easily to the recognition of different camera techniques. In a single segment of film or tape, several perceptible movements of the camera can be noted. Most often, however, the procedure is subsumed with a

---

[7]By "etic," we mean a so-called objective notational system that can be used to describe meaningful features of a given culture's system. This idea is borrowed from the linguistic notion of the relation of phonetic notation to the study of phonemes. Its extension outside of language to other domains of behavior was first suggested by Pike (1964).

single gloss such as vertical or horizontal pan. The most significant movement that operates to define the segment is a normative construction of the film or tape analyst. That recognition leads to his ignoring all other camera movements. When the latter are particularly apparent, the analyst considers them to be mistakes or difficulties encountered by one who is just beginning to use a camera. The recognition of what constitutes a given technique is the analyst's own recognition made without reference to the cameraperson. This line of reasoning is particularly apparent in Western film primers in which students are exhorted to make camera movements as unobtrusive as possible through minimal panning to follow activities and the selective but emphatic use of zoom and facial close-ups.

Since it can be argued that a cameraperson learns how to make a tape or film from others who have expertise, his instruction consists of obtaining competence with a shared filmic language. It is assumed that the audience will respond to this language in a predictable way. For example, Whitaker (1970) suggested that if there were two different shots, one of a small cottage, then a dissolve to an elderly man reading a book in a den, it is interpretable by the audience that "there is a cottage and within it is a man reading a book" (p. 132). If, on the other hand, the shots were reversed, the interpretation would be "there is a man reading a book about a cottage" (p. 132). Hence, the properties of the first shot or sequence predispose the viewer to read the second shot in a predictable way. This, Whitaker calls a predispositional montage. Johnny Nelson, the Navajo filmmaker, used the same concept when he made his film of the running horses.

The question still remains as to whether filmic language is universal. Although the Navajo informants employed the above technique, Worth and Adair present strong evidence to suggest that placing together segments does follow, at least in part, the syntactic structure of the Navajo language.[8] This suggests that there are different kinds of perceivable messages being communicated by the arrangement of the shots. We will explore this point again shortly.

We have thus far presented two levels of film perception corresponding to the phonological and syntactic properties of language: the recognition of camera technique and the arrangement of shots to form a single montage. The analysis of both necessitates the indexing of elements from a particular display into the normative constructions or objective glosses of the analyst's own filmic language. The substitution of the world is perceived on tape or film into the descriptive system of the analyst cannot be taken for granted.[9] We do not dispute that there may be common features in languages and in the production of tapes or films. Rather, we want to explore, without the prejudice of predicated universals, the content and format structure of our respective materials.

[8]Their hypothesis that Navajo linguistic categories affect other communicative forms is linked in turn to the Whorf-Sapir hypothesis that language conditions cultural experience (see Whorf, 1956).

[9]This substitution is part of the more general question as defined by Garfinkel as the substitution of indexical expressions for objective expressions: that is, the problem of how speakers (and auditors) recognize the particulars from some display of the world as features of an analyst's model, whether lay or professional (see Garfinkel, 1967, pp. 4–7).

CULTURAL EXPRESSIONS OF TIME AND SPACE

Experimental studies have demonstrated the influence of environment and learning on perception. For the most part, these studies have concentrated on the perception of depth, contour, and color and have been less concerned with motion (Segall, Campbell, & Herskovits, 1966, pp. 49–68).[10] Discussing some of these experimental findings with regard to film is almost tautological, since the film image is itself a visual trick created by the rapid movement of still frames across an alternately light and dark screen. Furthermore, except by inference, these findings have not provided basic descriptions of perception and attention in natural settings. Participants in a setting attend to it selectively and reveal their orientations in ongoing and subsequent accounts of the scene (cf. Cicourel, 1974, pp. 141–171).[11] Visual accounts are products of overlapping interactions: those between the photographer or cameraman, the persons filmed, whether posing or not, and the filmmaker and audience viewers (Byers, 1964; see also Sudnow, 1972).[12] Our major concern in discussing informant-made materials later will be with the process of initially filming a scene.

An overview of some of the assumptions behind much of ethnographic filmmaking is essential to an understanding of the special position of informant-made materials. Ethnographic films have conventionally sought to uncover aspects of one culture or setting by using techniques superimposed from another. The underlying assumption, as already mentioned, is that there exists a universal grammar of film and that the cameraman employs this to filter rather than interpret events. Both the experimental and conventional ethnographic approaches to the cross-cultural study of visual materials raise the following questions: (1) Do members of different groups literally see that world differently? (2) Do differences in verbal communication imply differences in the uses of film? (3) What inferences can be made from findings about patterns of object perception for the filmic interpretation of a given setting?

In order to answer these questions we must first examine informant-made productions in relation to other types of ethnographic films. These are cinéma verité and interpretive film practice. Through the use of a version of the subject's or outsider's perspective as a point of departure, cinéma verité claims to present a

---

[10]Although the authors summarize experimental results from studies of color perception, contour distinction, and two-dimensional and three-dimensional color optical illusions, only a few of these experiments deal with the perception of motion. Even in the case of one such experiment, Allport and Pettigrew's work on the rotating trapezoidal illusion, the results are more relevant to the study of depth than they are to the study of motion per se.

[11]Cicourel stresses that the researcher's assessment of a scene is similarly based on his memory of it and therefore his selective attention to the original scene combined with his selective attention to the visual account when he reviews a videotape of the same scene.

[12]Both Byers and Sudnow emphasize that photography should be regarded as an interaction between the subject and the photographer in which both mutually create the split-second display that will be recorded by the camera.

"naturalistic" or "realistic" report of a scene. However, this claim relies on the assumption that a universal film grammar is achieved and viable and that the filmmaker's independent perspective can or should be masked as a feature of reporting. Jean Rouch's films represent one of the approaches to cinéma verité that has been used in African settings. Rouch's method, however, has been a source of controversy among some cinematographers (MacDougall, 1969)[13]:

> *Jaguar* and other films by Rouch have been criticized for mixing fact and fiction, and for presenting Rouch's feelings about Africa rather than Africa itself. There is no doubt some truth in this, as there is in Flaherty's case, yet it is also true that Rouch has done more than any other ethnographic filmmaker to try new methods and infuses his films with the spirit of their subjects. (p. 22)

It is a "sense" or "spirit" of realism that Rouch, who in his earlier films hired actors to portray current social attitudes, strove for and that, in various ways, characterized the cinéma verité tradition. By contrast, interpretive film practice goes a step beyond Rouch and is more systematic in its attempt to capture the essence and aesthetic of a particular setting and culture. Interpretive filmmakers, for example, the Rundstroms, consider their practice as a way to "present to the viewer the filmic experience of being in the world," in their case, the world of the Japanese tea ceremony (Rundstrom, Rundstrom, & Bergum, 1973; Bergum, 1974).[14] This approach is basically the work of the visual ethnographer rather than the member–cameraperson. However, according to the technique proposed by the Rundstroms, it requires the ethnographer's intimate familiarity with the events filmed and their background. In a discussion of film and ritual, the Rundstroms outline their basic research process and assumptions (Rundstrom *et al.*, 1973, pp. 26–31). They stress the importance of selecting a "naturally" bounded activity, in this case a ritual setting, as the topic for filming. The limitations of the activity itself point to a structured relationship between time and space during the progression of the activity. The format of the structured activity also provides a basic format or structure for the film. Like cinéma verité, the effort in interpretive film practice is to preserve the "sense" of the "real time" activity, in this case, by following its thematic progression.

A critical innovation of interpretive practice is the recommendation that the cinematographer become a participant and/or apprentice in the activity filmed. Before making their film *The Path,* the Rundstroms acquainted themselves with many available aspects of Japanese culture, learning the proper practices of dining, the tea ceremony, and Japanese stick fighting or Kendo. They state: "This apprentice perspective gave us the physical and emotional dimensions of the color, action-flow, and tensions of the ritual" (p. 27). Going beyond the

---

[13]MacDougall evaluates Rouch's approach as a "unique kind of experimentation" in the field of ethnographic film.

[14]These authors argue that it is the task of ethnographic film to create the reality of a cultural world for the viewer. Bergum in particular argues that his sense of cultural immersion can be created by the ethnographer's subtle manipulation of the dimensions of time and motion in filming.

cinéma verité tradition, they tested this strategy of observing participation by developing photographic projective interviews that were administered to both the tea master and local members of the Japanese American community. These photographs furnished the filmmakers with specific information about the exact progression of the ceremony, its dominant symbols, and its aesthetic dimensions. For example, a salient relationship was found between the Japanese ideogram *do,* meaning path or way, and the ritualized progression of the tea ceremony.

Other events, objects, and sequences that were particularly meaningful to participants or to persons who presumably shared a Japanese cultural aesthetic were also observed in this way. The overall result of this interpretive strategy is a documentable procedure for creating an ethnographer's account of a naturally bounded event that claims to preserve cultural sensitivity and the depth and subjectivity of those who participate in it.

Implicit in the interpretive approach is the assumption that the ethnographer can discover, through photography, images and sequences that are "psychologically real" to participants in the event (Burling, 1964).[15] From the photographic elicitation, montages for the film were carefully planned utilizing "master sequences" capturing the essential actions of the ceremony and close-ups of its dominant symbols. Thus the cinematographers attempted to tap or simulate "native" experiences and to present them in an interpretive manner by modifying a standardized film grammar to fit the requirements of the ceremony filmed. For example, a selection of camera angles was planned showing the tea ceremony from the approximate direction of each of the participants, with close-ups of its most essential actions and symbols. However, the Rundstroms never explicitly assert that it is identical with or entirely within the idiom of Zen practitioners or, more generally, those who share certain aspects of Japanese culture. Instead, participants' responses to visual cues were used to inform the ethnographer's aesthetic reconstruction of an event. The result might be compared to English versions of haiku poetry that preserve some stylized conventions yet still remain translations and adaptations of the original art form.

This in-depth ethnographic approach acknowledges and plays upon the assumption that film presents the viewer a mediated account of events rather than a copy of a consensual reality. This assumption may be viewed in terms of a basic phenomenological thesis (Brinkley, 1971)[16]:

> In a fundamental sense, it is only when we 'bracket' the 'facts' of film experience, when we suspend our thesis that the facts make up the total reality of film experience, that we become

[15]Burling emphasizes that semantic terms isolated in deriving "native" taxonomies should be tested as to whether or not they make sense to users. Only if they do, he argues, should the claim be made that they can be used to make valid inferences about cognitive processes. The Rundstroms employed photographic elicitation to isolate sequences of ceremonial actions that were meaningful or in Burling's terms "psychologically real" to participants.

[16]Brinkley stresses that we must look at the ways in which sense is made of motion and attributed to the visual image in order to understand film.

open to the moving image as a phenomenon of consciousness. The moving image has its life not amid the abstractions of quantified space and clock time, but in the fullness of lived, concrete spatiality and temporality. (p. 5)

The distinction between standard or objective time and lived time is used to achieve the rhythms and effects of a cultural aesthetic. Nevertheless, it is also assumed that the underlying dimensions of this distinction can readily be tapped. In music, standard or objective time (e.g., the rhythm in which a piece is played) can be contrasted with inner time or the flow of the music that is meaningful to those who listen and play (Schutz, 1964b; Gurwitsch, 1964).[17] Contrasting time dimensions are present in all mediated communications. In ethnographic film, this contrast is complicated by the differences among shared interactive time in the natural setting, the inner or subjective time of participants in the setting, the structure of "real time" film, and the results created in an edited version. As indicated earlier, this is also influenced by the technological constraints of filming.

This subjective approach to ethnographic filming suggests an attempt to reflect the internal flow of an actual setting and to use various camera techniques to highlight aspects of time flow and spatial arrangements in the film image. Under the assumption that film is a verisimilitude rather than a copy of subjective realities, time and space are manipulated to simulate the experience of participants.

Thus, we may summarize the following requirements as characteristic of interpretive film practice: (1) the analysis of a naturally bounded setting, for example, a ceremony or work setting; (2) the cinematographer's apprenticeship or immersion in that setting; (3) the systematic elicitation of informant responses to the sequencing and aesthetic components of the setting; and (4) the attempt to mirror or closely follow the dominant symbols that participants recognize as meaningful aesthetic features of the setting through film. According to this definition, perhaps Mead and Bateson's *Trance and Dance in Bali* was the most significant forerunner of interpretive film practice.

SOME GENERAL FEATURES OF INFORMANT-MADE FILMS

The method of elicitation that formed the background for projective interviews was based on ethnographers' photographs (Collier, 1957).[18] While the intent was

---

[17]Both Schutz and Gurwitsch describe the distinction between objective musical time, or a shared standard time, and the inner duration of a musical piece for both players and performances.

[18]In experiments in Acadian and Navajo communities, Collier used a photographic battery to elicit respondents' descriptions of settings and relevant persons in the community. He found that ethnographers' presuppositions before photographic elicitation and the actual descriptions varied substan-

to uncover responses of the subjects whose familiar environment was photo-graphed, those subjects were not given a camera. As mentioned earlier, Worth and Adair used informant filmmaking to examine how members of a group viewed and structured their world through visual images. Rather than assume that film grammar could be modified to capture another aesthetic, Worth and Adair (1972, p. 45) penetrated to the heart of the question by testing its universality.[19] They hypothesized that regarding film as if it were a language might lead to the conclusion that a "deep structure" or underlying basis for the assembly and use of images could be located. From this structure, culturally varying film grammars would be generated. Thus, the language of Navajo films would be based on a shared syntax and way of interpreting film codes. The film or basic linguistic structures would then in turn explain basic cognitive processes. They also postulated that the ordering of images both in filming and in editing would be influenced by existing narrative styles. For example, the importance of walk-ing in Navajo myths and legends is paralleled by a preference for walking shots in many of the films (Worth & Adair, 1972, pp. 144–148). As a part of Navajo narrative format, walking is transposed into the overall structure of the edited film and to the individual camera units.

The strength of Worth and Adair's argument relies on the meaningful use of walking as part of the visual account in the edited product. The analogy drawn between meaningful film and linguistic units ultimately relies on an idealized, syntactic view of language on one level and an assumption of the comparability between narrative form and visual assembly and display on another. While the concept of deep structure points to the surface variations of everyday language (or languages) and their ambiguities, as applied by Worth and Adair to visual materials, the notion ignores everyday usage in favor of stylized form. Rather than viewing the camera unit as an intentional act, comparable to an utterance, it is ultimately analyzed in terms of its role and usage in the final product. The intended use of film grammar and the ambiguities inherent in this usage are overlooked in favor of categorizing "cademes" in terms of these idealized re-sults.

Although Worth and Adair deal with the informants' "filming behavior," their biographies, and their avowed interest in shooting and organizing sequences in certain ways, their rationale of the units of analysis selected is not entirely conducive to an analysis of the "pragmatics" of film (Worth & Adair, 1972, p. 42). In this sense, Cicourel's (1974) suggestions with regard to a developing generative semantics that clarifies practical language use could be applied to their

---

tially. Although Collier's primary aim was to acquire substantive information about the community, his methods also required him to compare the results of visual in contrast to verbal elicitation procedures.

[19]Worth and Adair pose the question of whether or not there can be considered to exist a "universal film code or grammar upon which different cultural styles of filming could be seen as variations."

underlying assumptions about visual communication. He states[20]:

> Logical frameworks are subdomains of everyday language which have been cleansed of difficulties that would confound the correspondence theory necessary for idealized outcomes. Therefore, grammatical or logical utterances retain their rule-governed structure because they have been cleansed and divorced from their occasions of use, and other particulars about the biographies of the participant, the features of the setting tacitly taken into account, the reflexive thinking and use of talk, and so on. For the linguist, the book he is now reading is proof that language behavior can be understood independently of the occasions that produced it. The speaker–hearer (linguist, logician) can consult his own speech for evidence that his enterprise is a success because his mastery of the formal normative framework becomes a referential scheme or system of general rules to justify claims that utterances he produces or those of native informants can be described with reference to these rules. (p. 109)

In a naturally bounded sequence such as the recording of a ritual, it is indicated in our materials that informant conceptions of the ceremony's basic format influence the structure of their visual accounts. This paralleling of film and ritual formats, including a marked emphasis on song, took place in Bapostolo informant filming. However, while the format influenced the ordering of events, it did not determine the film grammar used to present them. Beyond the technological constraint of breaks between the three-minute Super 8 films, the camera units used relied heavily on the informants' relationship to a given scene. Thus, informants' biographies cannot simply be summarized prior to an analysis of their films since, in both ritual and everyday interactions, who they are influences their access to the scene for filming and the very conventions that they employ.

While interpretive practice is concerned with uncovering and simulating informants' visual accounts of social scenes, these very interpretations are contained in the informants' films. Yet it may be premature to use these films to investigate how members of a group structure events in their environment without examining filming in more depth as an interaction and an immediate act of interpretation. On the other hand, the fact that filming is regarded as a situated activity does not mean that it lacks aesthetic and symbolic conventions, some of which may be culturally shared. By looking at film uses in member-selected settings, it is possible to locate properties of the interface between perception and symbolic conventions. Rather than discrediting the aims of either interpretive film or of the basic Worth–Adair method, we are suggesting that elements of each can be expanded upon by concentrating on how informants use the camera in the initial phases of filmmaking.

Visual elicitation studies, chiefly using still photographs, point to further uses of informant-made films. Although Collier (1967) and Bateson and Mead (1942) did their own photography, they suggest that detailed visual studies can be

---

[20]The analogy between verbal and visual communication must be drawn very carefully, however. Equating film grammar strictly with formal linguistic rules and film statements with speech acts masks some of the crucial differences between the two.

applied to substantive areas (see also Mead & MacGregor, 1951). Both of these studies were concerned with capturing events and behaviors in "natural" settings and explaining the attitudes and behaviors of their subjects—by elicitation in Collier's case and research analysis for Mead and Bateson. Collier suggests that photographic elicitation can be used to uncover informants' conceptions of an entire community and its social organization. By showing to subjects photographs of households, places of work, and selected central areas within the community, he was able to gather detailed descriptions and comparisons of social groups and activities. Informant-made films have a similar potential for showing the ethnographer overall views of selected activities in the community, particularly when the film is used to record naturally occurring activities rather than staged events.[21]

THE KPELLE VIDEOTAPES AND BAPOSTOLO FILMS

The tapes and films described in this book are the result of our respective efforts to teach informants how to use media. As ethnographers we wanted records of numerous situations which would have been recorded differently if we had been the camerapersons. We also realized that our informants possessed an idea of what-comes-next during such occasions that better enabled them to follow the course of events and to discriminate between central and peripheral activities to record. Had we been the camerapersons our productions would have reflected our apprenticeship to those settings.

We recognize that the presence of media had its effects both on the informant–camerapersons and the situations recorded. However, we do not want to simply make that assertion without fully understanding the nature of those effects, nor do we believe that they invalidate or significantly alter the fact that each tape and film represents a study of the recorded situations from an informant's perspective. A large portion of this monograph is directly concerned with this issue.

Since the contents of our materials were composed in the context of ongoing social situations, their analyses offer descriptions not only of the events themselves but also of what members find as significant in them. These attended-to properties constitute the field of consciousness within which members make their judgments, discriminations, choices, and interpretations of events. The analyses of the tapes and films, consequently, provide new data for understanding the structure of our informants' cognitive processes.

[21]Contrast this finding with Worth and Adair (1972, p. 48). Worth had given 16 mm cameras to a group of young black students in Philadelphia and found that they preferred filming staged activities in other neighborhoods to daily life in their own. This was not the case for our informant–filmmakers.

In the following chapter, we describe our methodology for discovering what our informants were doing when they made their recordings. In Chapter 3, we briefly summarize some of our previous findings about the structure of our respective groups' verbal accounting practices. Then in the next two chapters we analyze our materials, making use of those findings to show how they lead to the location of our various camerapersons' intentions in composing their tapes and films.

2
Some Methodologies for Understanding Media

The studies presented in this chapter demonstrate a methodology for analyzing informant-made media materials. In so doing we do not advocate that informant-produced films or video tapes are necessarily "better" than those made by an experienced ethnographic or documentary filmmaker because they are made by members. The subtleties of expertise with a camera take many years to acquire. Yet, after only a short period of instruction with a camera (especially with the instant replay facility of video) it is possible to make aesthetically pleasing and intentionally directed productions. Informant films, however, may not be the best procedure to employ if an educational documentary is desired. These films or tapes have a different value. They are, as already mentioned, a special kind of member's account, specifically a visually mediated one.

Our project in this book is to develop a set of practices for analyzing those accounts and the informant cameraperson's intentions in recording them. The analysis of format structure and an understanding of why and how an informant recorded what he did provides access to the content of the materials. By format structure we mean the structural arrangement of cademic markers in a tape or film. Although it is possible to view the materials solely for content without attention to format structure, a wealth of material would be overlooked. In making a tape or film the cameraperson assesses what the sense of the situation is within the context of the production setting. We intend to show how the camera techniques used, length of shots, and actions focused upon are ordered by the cameraperson's recognition of that sense.

Our investigations are not just replications of the Worth–Adair (1972) study mentioned in the first chapter. We are not attempting to reveal some underlying deep structure that generates both the informant's native language and the format of his media productions. Although this may be possible, our interest rather is to locate what a cameraperson was doing when he or she recorded an event. We take as a resource the structure of the informants' verbal accounts. We are not attempting to prove that the structure of the media productions is the same as that of those accounts. Instead, verbal accounts provide us with a method for looking at the media productions. Our major assumption is that once an informant learns how to handle a camera with reasonable facility, he will think about what he shoots before and during a recording. The productions as accounts are similar to an informant's telling the ethnographer what is happening in a social interaction while it is occurring. The format structure of a tape or film is an artifact of that telling.

THE UNITS OF ANALYSIS

We have developed a set of procedures for deciding whether at any given time a certain camera movement was accidentally produced or intentionally used to give a certain visual effect or is the result of the cameraperson's response to the events on camera. For instance, in the Bapostolo materials the informant–camerapersons often panned past an object and then returned to it after a brief pause. The effect was that of hesitation with the camera. The question arises whether this was intentional or the result of too fast a pan movement. Again, in those same materials during films of rituals the informants kept the camera level and never tilted up to include a subject's face in the visual field. We can ask whether this was caused by the position the cameraperson took during the event or by the intentional act of not looking up into the subject's face. In the analysis presented in Chapter 6 the argument is made that these were intentionally applied camera techniques and thus can be treated as cademic markers.

  We have also devoted attention to determining whether a certain movement of the camera is a single marker or an embedded property which, along with other camera movements, constitutes a different marker. For instance, in Chapter 5 it will be shown that several Kpelle camerapersons used the combinations of horizontal pan and tilt in a consistent way to segment content during the course of an event or interaction—as opposed to turning the camera off while changing position, which segments an event both in content and time. The former marker is composed of several movements, each of which accomplishes different effects when it appears alone than when it appears together with the other movements. Before discussing what the above methods are, it is necessary to begin by examining the problem of logging our tapes and films.

THE PROBLEM OF LOGGING AS A THEORETICAL
ISSUE

At first glance, how to go about logging tapes and films recorded by informants seemed unproblematic. When we first looked at our materials, we were quite excited by the wealth of information they contained. As Collier (1967) has pointed out, each visual image contains an immense inventory of both cultural artifacts and proxemic relations between persons filmed. The films and tapes permit us to examine events and see phenomena which as participant–observers we overlooked or relegated at the moment to a nonessential status. In order to deal with the films and tapes as data concerning social interactions we first had to set about the long task of logging the various events that occurred on each tape and film.

Initially we took for granted that all we had to do was look at each frame and write in a notebook an inventory of what we saw. As soon as the work began, however, we realized that the transcripts we were making were very much our interpretations of what was occurring. Hence, we decided that we had best find a way of justifying those formulations. We realized that we could not even take the visual image for granted. For instance, when Bellman first showed one of the Kpelle video tapes to his sociology class he was astonished to find that no one in the room saw what he was describing. The tape showed an infant being force fed some wet rice by his mother and two other women. The class heard a baby cry but was able to locate where he was on the monitor only after Bellman put the tape on still frame and pointed to the child.

In our analyses we did not want to use the position, too often cited, that we could see what was in our materials because we were ''there'' and ''parties to'' the events recorded. Instead we were confronted with the question of how it was that we knew what was occurring, and whether that ''knowing'' was the same as a member's or participant's understanding of what was taking place. We realized that we were using an implicit theory about what was going on when we made our formulations. We saw ourselves in danger of constructing what Garfinkel and Sacks (1970) have called ''anthropological quotes.'' They characterized that procedure as the following:

> The anthropologist proceeds to rewrite the texts [in this case the tapes and films] as a report using a procedure that he calls 'writing.' A prevailing task that is done by writing is to propose an account of what his natives, in the language *they* talked, will be treated as actually and not supposedly having been talking about, given that the anthropologist cannot and will not say finally and in only so many words what they were really talking about. In this fashion he reports to colleagues that they talked in this way, definitely. So, for example, he cites the natives in their native terms and treats those terms with the device of a 'glossary.' That is to say, he recommends to colleagues that *he* will mean by *his* translations of natives' terms what the natives were really talking about, that he will treat the natives and their practices as final authority for, although what those might consist of beyond what he has written, he cannot say and says that he cannot. The writer means what the native really means, given that the writer elects to be cautious in specifying in just so many words 'what the native really means.' This further 'what the native really means,' which is incorporated into the report as the professional's paraphrase of native informants' reportage, is glossed over the report as it is available in an actual occasion through work of professionally unspecified methods of authorship and readership. (p. 365)

Both of us could make the argument that our particular field methodologies (apprenticing ourselves into the societies we investigate to discover experientially what it is to be a member) permit us to "speak" for the "natives." Such a position, however, would, as the quote implies, only gloss what we are doing. The fact of our apprentice membership in our respective societies provides a resource for our interpretations but cannot constitute their methodological basis. Yet, we do not claim that anyone who sees our tapes and films, even if they know our analytical procedures, could make the same analysis and state the same findings as we do. We do not make the same claim as Moerman (1972), after giving an extensive analysis of Lue conversation, that "It is possible to subject entirely public data of actual social interaction to explicit analytic procedures without either reliance upon private or conventional knowledge about such things as culture, class, role, motive, etc. or assumptions that some actual data are less informative than others (pp. 206–207).[1] We are thus caught in between. Neither, on the one hand, do we claim that analysis should be based solely on introspective procedures (although introspection contributes to the analysis) (cf. Moerman, 1972) nor, on the other hand, do we argue for the positivist hope that wholly "objective" procedures can be found that would be used to analyze any interactional data.

Our project of logging did not come before our analysis but made direct use of it. Consequently, we each decided that before analyzing the various interactions recorded in our tapes and films we would make the [doing of logging] a phenomenon for investigation.[2] The studies contained in this monograph are the result of that decision. We, of course, make constant references to the content of our material but we cannot do real justice to it. We intend, therefore, to proceed with such analyses in different contexts. Our task here is to make explicit the assumptions used in doing a transcript, and to offer a set of general procedures for working with any informant-produced films and tapes.

The transcripts developed for our respective studies contrasted in their format and organization. These differences did not reflect mere notational or aesthetic decisions on our part. In Chapter 5, Bellman elected to combine several markers in his left-hand column. Consequently, he transcribed "zoom in and all the way out" or "on/off and mid zoom" as two related markers and part of a single camera "message." On the other hand, Jules-Rosette chose to separate each movement in the left-hand column (e.g., full zoom in/zoom out) and to designate

---

[1]Both authors were able to apprentice themselves to various individuals in the societies they studied. Jules-Rosette became a high ranking member of the Bapostolo and is considered by many in the church to be an important and respected official. Bellman joined three of the secret societies in the Poro complex and studied medicines in two of them to eventually acquire the society power object (*ngung sale*). A feature of such a methodology is the ability to ask questions of informants within the situational context where such questions are appropriate. Both Bellman and Jules-Rosette have discussed their respective field techniques extensively in other studies.

[2]An example of the introspective approach is the work of Carlos Castaneda (1968). In each of his books he relies solely on his own experience with a Yaqui brujo. In no case does he claim nor manifest interest in objective verification of the information he presents.

the changes in content accordingly. Her next step included timing some of the movements (e.g., pause and hold) and finding other distinctive features based on their structure as well as the contents of the tapes. Although both of our approaches were intended to examine the structure of the markers in relationship to the structure and content of the event, Jules-Rosette was also concerned with using her transcripts to highlight individual markers for comparison across the informant and student groups.

In Chapter 1 we mentioned how different camera techniques can be treated as cademic markers. However, the recognition of a camera movement or technique does not necessarily render it a cademic marker. Rather, its appearance indicates that it is a candidate for being considered as one. We do not claim that a syntactical description of camera techniques is possible without reference to what is being focused on by the use of that technique.[3]

The meaning of a camera technique is found by analyzing what it is doing there on a tape or film at a particular time. We cannot say that a dolly as a cademic marker is contrasted to zoom by presenting some minimal pair. In linguistics such pairs are used to identify phonemes. For example, the bilabial voiced plosive /b/ is opposed to the bilabial unvoiced plosive /p/. For those phonemes such minimal pairs as "pat" and "bat," "pill" and "bill," and "bar" and "par" are easily recognized. On the other hand, we know that in Kpelle /kp/, pronounced like the "p" in stickpin, and /p/ are separate phonemes. In English they are both allophones of the same phoneme.

The minimal pair linguistic analogy cannot be translated to filmic language, since it is impossible to determine whether certain camera movements produce wholly different meanings in relationship to the same movements in other contexts. Yet we have already determined that certain camera movements in concert with others are used consistently to produce similar visual effects. For example, the Kpelle technique of using tilt embedded in pan to segment content can be contrasted to turning the camera off and changing positions. Nevertheless, we cannot claim that these are minimal pairs.

In our analysis we essentially agree with Metz (1974, pp. 151–152) that there are no phonemes in film. Individual shots are more comparable to simple declarative sentences because they are composed of a variety of camera movements. The scene communicates more than a word. It tells something in itself even though it follows a series of shots and prefaces others. An analysis of camera techniques and the identification of cademic markers does not yield a filmic language system. Rather, the markers are tied to the content of the production and provide a means to interpret it. Nevertheless, we can make cross-cultural generalizations. A comparison of Kpelle, Bapostolo, and American filmic tech-

---

[3]Contrast this approach with that of Christian Metz (1974, pp. 149–150) in film language. In his structural analyses, he divides events into episodic sequences and then segments them into meaningful filmic chains of shots.

niques will be given in Chapter 6. That comparison will not show that the Bapostolo films differ from the Kpelle tapes as Bapostolo grammar differs from Kpelle grammar. Rather, it will be demonstrated how the films and tapes differ from each other in (1) how the structure of Bapostolo accounts differ from Kpelle accounts, and (2) the interaction of the two groups of camerapersons with the phenomena they recorded.

The latter attends to the experience of the camerapersons and their relationship to the recording situation. For instance, in the Kpelle tape, recorded by a member of the Poro priesthood of a ritual of the Sande or woman's secret society, the cameraman used zoom in a cautious manner. Instead of dollying or walking up to certain ritual acts, he zoomed in on them. A similar shot was taken by Joan Logue when she later taped a portion of the ritual. She felt at ease moving in close to the action and then zoomed in to record the expressions of the dancers and those attending the event. The priest, on the other hand, was constrained by his being a male priest taping a woman's ritual. Several of the medicines used during the event have the effect of causing elephantiasis of the scrotum if a man gets too close to them. Consequently, men keep their distance from the Sande medicines and often during the production of a woman's ritual intentionally walk in another direction. When the Poro priest taped the Sande dance, the feature of maintaining correct proxemic distance was salient. Thus, although a slight movement toward the dancers at various points within the ritual would have permitted a "better" viewing of the action, the cameraperson kept his distance. The fact that Logue is a woman did not give her special rights to move in on the action. The ability to walk up close to a Zo during a ritual is a sign of strong position and power even for members of the society. Logue's ability to move in on action was more the result of her being a stranger to the community and Kpelle culture in general. Her use of camera technique in part reflected her naiveté. The Kpelle cameraperson's techniques, on the other hand, were directly affected by his "knowledge" of what a man's position should be during events of that kind.

The use of camera techniques, therefore, tells a great deal about the phenomenon filmed both from their selective attention to and avoidance of the events recorded. This is directly translatable to our own film experience. Recently we assigned the project to our sociology classes of photographing various situations and taking detailed field notes of the entire event as a social phenomenon. The students were able to discriminate immediately between those situations in which taking pictures was almost expected and those in which several students even maintained that they had to force themselves to take out their cameras. In addition, they found that the type of camera used often significantly affected the responses of those photographed. The presence of a cheap Instamatic was much less intrusive than a Leica or Nikon. In several cases the expensive camera elicited a great deal of posing. This was expressed by one student who interchanged between a Nikon and an Instamatic. She maintained that when she used the former her subjects would try to assume "natural poses" and were almost constantly aware of her presence. When she took out her Instamatic, however, they would usually ignore it. With the Nikon her subjects responded to her as an "experienced" and "obviously knowledgable" photographer even though she was relatively inexperienced in her use of it. The Instamatic shots were treated as "home photographs" or "tourist pictures." As a result the student claimed that she was able to take more candid or natural shots with the Instamatic. Experienced photographers, of course, have developed a variety of procedures to take photographs of naturally occurring events. The student's impressions are not necessarily relevant to such professional work. On the other hand, they do reflect that there are definite subjective responses to different kinds of photographic instruments.

The cameraperson is also affected by the particular camera that he uses. When an expensive camera is used, his choice of subject matter often concerns the attempt to be "aesthetic" rather than just get the image. When motion pictures are taken, whether video or film, the cameraperson often becomes visibly upset when his subjects show attention to the camera. This is exemplified in the case of another of our students who made a videotape of people picking up luggage in the San Diego airport. He panned the room until he located someone interesting to record. He then stayed on his subject until he had picked up the luggage and left the baggage area. That portion of the tape, consequently, was filled with back and forth pans and follow shots. When later a subject noticed the camera and waved at it, the cameraperson immediately shut it off and turned to the other side of the room. He found a new subject and turned the camera on again. This avoidance of subject was a constant theme in many of the student videotapes. Other students filmed subjects from the back and attempted to avoid eye contact with them for the same reasons. The search for "natural" shots, therefore, led to a great deal of in-camera editing and selective attention to various aspects of this recording setting.

The most obvious difference between an informant's verbal and mediated accounts is that in order to take a picture a cameraperson must address the technical problems of camera use. He must locate the correct f-stop, get the picture in focus, hold the camera relatively steady and upright, and pull or push some mechanism to make a recording. The variety of ways of making a sound or signaling with nonverbal or kinesic movements is manifestly greater. If any of the formal procedures of camera use are incorrectly carried out the image will either not appear or be hardly recognizable. Hence, we can expect that all media productions will contain many of the same features. We have already discussed how combinations of camera movements significantly differ between cultures. Although we are not addressing ourselves to professional filmmaking in this monograph, it can be pointed out that even within the Western tradition of making movies films from different countries are easily recognized. Foreign films differ from American films more than just by the languages used to make them. Even films made in non-Western countries for local viewers differ from those directed to an American–European audience. Consider especially films made in India for the general public and those (such as films produced by Satyajit Ray) that are made for export. The exported films attempt to use filmic traditions developed through the course of Western filmmaking. The former, on the other hand, are often quite tedious for Western audiences to watch. The plots are hard to recognize, the action often seems disjointed, and the camerawork looks odd.

At various times in our respective field investigations we have gone to the cinema in the African countries where we lived. Attending neighborhood movie houses or the occasional films shown in market towns are usually experiences. The audiences tend to pay more attention to the action than to the plot. Occasionally, when films are shown in the up-country market towns or migrant camps, the reels are shown in the wrong order without really being noticed. The content is overlooked in favor of the event of watching the film. This does not mean that persons from non-Western countries are incapable of viewing our media productions. Western films are quite popular and the more (Western) educated persons in those countries respond to them in a way much as American audiences would. Our assertion is that the process of Western education provides a context of meaning for interpreting these films. Learning how to read or even listen to a Western account of a plot gives instruction in how to look at a Western film. The non-Westerner uses that knowledge when he views them. He learns a set of expectations about what constitutes a Western account. For instance, the Kpelle make extensive use of parables and dilemma tales in presenting information. In order to interpret a fellow associate's account or narrative, Kpelle auditors selectively attend to the talk as *pointing to* meaning rather than directly presenting it. The logical progression of a narrative is therefore different from that of Western accounts. Similarly, Jules-Rosette found that Bapostolo instructions on how to interpret church rituals and regulations were at first perplexing. The same informant would often contradict himself as well as others in the group. When she later could point out the discrepancies to her informants, they saw all the accounts as being internally consistent. She consequently discovered that there were definite procedures for listening to such talk. Applying these techniques helped her to function as a member in a variety of complicated Apostolic rituals.

When our different groups of informants viewed Western films without knowing how Western plots are structured, they interpreted meaning from their own language system. As a result the content or message of the films was missed. We found the kinds of reactions to Western cinema which we briefly characterized above. On the other hand, when informants with exposure to Western education viewed them, they were able to attend to their content. That attention, however, still differed significantly from that of members of our own society.[4] Although they had a methodology for understanding the productions, it does not necessar-

---

[4]This is, of course, a general observation that would be subject to further in-depth investigation on the format structure of Western media and its influence upon audience response and perception.

ily follow that they viewed them as our filmmakers intended them to. To do so would require the same kind of attention as it would to listen to Western narratives. At any given time, such viewers had two sets of interpretive methodologies and could switch from one to another as easily as they could change languages. The effort involved in studying a Western film is similar to that of listening to a Western narrative. For those with considerable exposure to Western education the task is easy, while for others the difficulties of communicating in a second language are salient.

Implicit in the above is the recommendation that if videotapes or films are to be used, a presentational format can be developed that has communicative effectiveness for the particular cultural group. This is true not only for distant cultures but also for cultural groups within our own society. A great deal of research is currently taking place on how to present information in textbooks for different cultures in American communities (cf. Bellman, 1974b, pp. 22–27). This has generated a strong interest in the particular syntax and structure of semantic domains of Black English, Chicano Spanish, and Puerto Rican Spanish. It is the finding of those investigations that information must be presented using both the semantic structure and syntax of the respective dialects. In a like manner, if films and video are to be used to communicate with nonliterate peoples (or partially literate in our society) the order of presentation of information, the dialect used, and the length of shots employed should be directed to the particular population. Our media productions have been so dominated by the market economy that they are almost exclusively directed to the "mass" culture. Even experiments with new programming that are taking place on public television or public access on cable tend to replicate the format structure of commercial television broadcasts. It is our hope that the procedures we have developed will contribute to new research on developing productions that can better communicate with particular communities.

We have addressed ourselves in the above discussion to the formats of presentation rather than to camera techniques. We do not claim that the particular techniques our informants have used in our respective studies constitute a separate filmic language. Rather, they should be considered our informants' experiments with the camera to present information in a "meaningful" way. Different camera techniques than those employed by our informants may be used to convey the same information or new information in their filmic language. Their techniques instead provide us with data regarding how they segment events and arrange them in their accounts. For example, the Kpelle use of tilt embedded in horizontal pan to segment content provides an insight into how the cameraperson interpreted the phenomenon he recorded.[5] We do not claim that it is the only

---

[5] At the present time the Poro and Sande of Sucromu are conducting the last initiations for ten years. Bellman is currently working with his informants on recording various filmable aspects of those rituals and bush schools. In contrast to the study reported on and analyzed here the present project involves his informants editing tapes to produce programs on those activities.

or best technique to achieve that effect. We assume that as our informants acquire more expertise with the camera they will develop more sophisticated techniques to accomplish the same effect. It is, nevertheless, a finding that our informants used certain techniques in consistent ways to achieve specific effects. Thus, the identification of those techniques and an explication of the ways our informants used them provide new data on the camerapersons' cognitive system.

In our efforts to transcribe those techniques, we had to separate format structure and content. This led to different transcription techniques. In Bellman's palaver tapes and Jules-Rosette's confession films, the dialogue and outcome are as important as what we see. These scenes can be segmented into narrative units based on what is said. Hence, we decided to transcribe camera movements and context in separate columns. This permitted comparisons among transcripts of diverse settings. When Yeshaie's filming techniques in the confession sequence were described, camera movements were separated from content and the dialogue was handled as part of the ethnographic notation about the event. This allowed comparison between Yeshaie's and the American films of the confession sequence while still providing for analysis of the content.

Placing dialogue within the description of the event made the films and tapes of ritual and walkabouts, in which talk was sporadic, analytically comparable with events in which narrative was central.[6] This transcription format also facilitated contrasting aspects of informant and Western visual productions by emphasizing the process of recording. However, neither the structure of the event nor the interaction between camerapersons and subjects was necessarily included in these transcripts. Had we dealt exclusively with the correspondence between shot and content, it would have been necessary to summarize a collection of shots in relationship to each scene (cf. Metz, 1974, p. 71).[7] This approach does not portray the movements of the cameraperson and his communication with the persons filmed. For example, in his Marrapodi walkabout, Yeshaie began to talk to a young woman in front of one of the church households. She approached him, and he followed her with the camera as she came closer. Then she leaned over a fence and craned her neck toward Yeshaie as he swung the camera to the left, continuing to talk with her although he left her out of the picture.

A contrasting interaction transpired between Chris, the student videoist, and the workers at a Marrapodi smithing shop. As he began the videoing, the workers became increasingly aware of his presence. Within a few minutes, one of them began to feign hammering a thin strip of tin and the other two workers stopped altogether and froze for the camera. Although the workers' activities are described in the transcript, it is difficult to include the effects of Chris' presence and

---

[6]In this way, comparability was established for the materials in each of the studies. The reader is referred to Appendices A and B in which transcripts for the respective studies are presented.

[7]Metz states: ''Just as the word 'but' never expresses the idea of the adversative as such, but always an adversative relationship between two realized units, a forward dolly expresses a concentration of attention, not on itself, but always on an object.''

the subtleties of the interaction within our notation system. These behaviors, however, are no less important simply because they have not been covered within our transcripts.

The question arises whether there are definite procedures for locating cademic markers that can be used by anyone looking not only at our materials but any media productions. Cademic markers are second-order analytical devices since they are themselves the products of an analysis. Although we differed in particular ways in our location of markers, we make the following recommendations for anyone attempting to employ our concepts:

1. Make a transcript of the content of the production.

2. Then, make a transcript of all camera techniques and movements without seriously attending to what is occurring in the production.

3. Discover which techniques found in the second step appear to be associated with events that were located in the first step.

4. Record which techniques were used by the cameraperson as responses to his interaction with the event (e.g., dollying or moving away from the action as it moves in on him).

5. Record which techniques were used to posit acts embedded within events (e.g., in the Sande dance tape the cameraperson pointed out the entrance of the male priests or *Zo* into the ritual area by slightly tilting the camera up and narrating what was occurring into the microphone).

6. Record which techniques were used to terminate an event (e.g., shutting off the camera, fast pans away from the previous action, down tilts, and fast dollies to new locations).

7. Record which techniques were used in variation with other techniques. Note what was occurring in the event to discover if the difference was the result of the cameraperson's reaction to some action (e.g., the Poro priest's use of zoom rather than dolly when the Sande priestess danced with a medicine bundle on her head).

8. Keep a note book on all decisions made throughout the analysis and explicate reasons for the choices made.

Although we have presented the methodological procedures in a cookbook fashion these steps will be a problematic concern for each analyst. That is why we have suggested keeping a notebook of the analysis and treating it as similar to field notes taken during the recording situation. Somehow the analyst will make choices as to what constitutes an event and what are embedded events within events. Those decisions are reflexive to the analyst's own membership in the recording session or to events of the kind that were recorded. In a large sense the list of analytical procedures is open-ended. The methods used must be designed to handle the data rather than the other way around. Too often in behavioral science research, data are ignored because they cannot be treated with the methodologies advocated by a single discipline. In an attempt to emulate the methods of the physical and natural sciences we have often sacrificed interesting data because they could not be dealt with by the available analytical models. We can take the position of many analysts of social interaction who have produced voluminous works on conversational structures but never have presented an explicit methodology for inspecting a quantity of data (Sacks, 1972, pp. 31–74; Schegloff, 1972, pp. 75–119). They advise those who want to form such analyses to simply study theirs. We, on the other hand, have presented some basic steps for looking at a tape or film. However, the most substantial of our methodological procedures are to be found in our respective studies. We consequently recommend that the reader refer to our respective investigations and extrapolate from them those procedures which are relevant to other data.

3
The Ethnographic Settings

Before analyzing our materials, it is necessary to discuss briefly how our informants give verbal accounts in natural settings. This chapter is divided into two parts. First, we present various techniques Kpelle speakers use to organize and interpret talk both in daily interaction and within the restrictive settings of secret societies. Then, we present the narrative structures used in Bapostolo rituals, visionary descriptions, and testimonies. The reader will note that there is a difference in emphasis in each of our descriptions. The difference reflects the specific nature of the respective analyses. In Chapter 4, we will show that in the Kpelle tapes the cameraperson's structural position in the social setting, his speaking prerogative or right to talk within it, and his intentional interests in the recorded event are observable in the content and format of each tape. Thus, the ethnography of the Kpelle given here emphasizes how such concerns are member-recognized properties for both producing and understanding talk. The analysis of the Bapostolo films in Chapter 5 shows, through a comparison of informant and American ethnographic productions, how each is structured by the particular stylistic conventions of normal talk for each cultural group. The description of the Bapostolo presented below, consequently, emphasizes the variety of verbal styles and conventions used in Apostolic ritual and secular interactions. The two ethnographies also differ in the attention that is given to the social context in which accounts are given. The section on the Bapostolo is heavily concerned with the structure of accounts in ritual settings. It is shown how this structure influences mundane conversations. In both mundane discourse and ritual talk, there is a heavy reliance on the management of a variety of vernacular languages, which is best shown in the analysis of ritual narratives. These narratives provide the framework within which other Bapostolo accounts are given. Religious membership is the organizing principle for all social relationships. The Kpelle, in contrast, are members of a traditional rural community that is politically separated from neighboring towns, but in alliance with them through a complex network of secret societies. Although Sucromu is a renowned medicine town and a sacred Poro center, there is an integrated relationship between the secular and religious components of the community. Sacred concerns cross-cut both domains and define the structure of power relationships in all social interactions. Hence, the description of the Kpelle takes equal note of conversational structures within secular settings and the secret societies.

In order to describe the narrative practices of the Kpelle in our study it is necessary first to present an ethnographic sketch of Sucromu, the community in which the video research was conducted. This is important because the Kpelle have a variety of strategies for giving accounts in different kinds of social situations. They recognize that all situations are organized according to one of a number of possible structural arrangements for kinds of social situations which they refer to as *meni*. These arrangements or *meni* are identifiable as transcendent to any particular occasion, and each has its own status and time structure. When Kpelle speakers give accounts, they organize them by using a strategy appropriate to their recognition of the kind of *meni* that serves as the meaning context for talk done in the setting. Those strategies are more than simply deciding on what to say and when. They include the manner of presenting information and the logical arrangement or progression of ideas. Since the various kinds of *meni* directly refer to the town's political, familial, farming, and religious institutions, a brief discussion of them is pertinent. We shall then discuss some methods speakers and auditors use for locating which kind of *meni* serves as the organizational basis for an interaction. Finally, we shall present a short description of the kinds of account strategies and the methods necessary to interpret meaning that are appropriate to certain *meni*. It is beyond the scope of this discussion to even attempt a detailed analysis of these issues. Rather, the presentation here is meant only to point out certain findings which have been addressed more rigorously elsewhere.[1]

Sucromu is the last Kpelle-speaking town in Liberia, bordering on Loma country (see Fig. 1). Fala, the dialect spoken there, is known as ''cut'' Kpelle because most speakers are also fluent in Loma and use it in the market and at migrant labor camps to distinguish themselves from speakers of the four other dialects of Kpelle spoken in Liberia. Sucromu is one of five towns that compose the Vavala clan, but it also has close family and ritual connections with different Loma communities in the area. The recognition of clan affiliation was imposed by the central government after the area was pacified. However, the member towns in the clan do recognize a history of association and in several cases refer to one another as *kala tano* or ''one family.'' In addition to belonging to a clan, Sucromu is part of a larger Paramount Chiefdom. Again, this was a structure

---

[1]A detailed analysis of these methods is found in Bellman (1975b). The description presented here summarizes several of the arguments presented in that investigation.

FIG. 1   A typical patrilocal quarter in Sucromu. Several different house types are represented here. (Photo by H. Adler)

imposed by the Monrovia government and is used primarily for governmental and tax matters.[2]

Originally Sucromu was two towns, Sucronsu and Twasamu, that joined together during wars with the Loma. Each town still maintains its separate identity as a moiety by observing separate food taboos or *tinya,* and by making sacrifices to its respective sacred mountain. The people of Sucromu believe that when a man dies, his spirit goes to the mountain of his ancestors, where he joins them in a patrilineally organized spirit village that parallels the social organization of the living community.[3] The two moieties or *taa* are in a mother's brother–sister's son (*ngala-maling*) relation to one another. Sucronsu is *ngala* (mother's brother) to Twasamu and is where the Poro and most of its major supporting secret societies are located. Twasamu, on the other hand, selects the town chief and is known as the owner of the land.

[2]These larger political units also operate to adjudicate disputes between towns and function as an appeals court for anyone who disagrees with a judgment made by the town's secular ruling structure. Appeals from the secret society courts are sometimes handled by a district commissioner but are mostly taken to agents of the Ministry for Local Government. Such appeals are costly and consequently rare.

[3]This description is relevant only for Sucromu. Other Kpelle towns have their own descriptions for what happens after death. They all, however, share the belief that ancestors are active in the affairs of living persons. The sacred mountains of Sucromu contribute to its reputation of being an especially powerful medicine town.

Both *taa* are divided into patrilocal compounds or quarters called *koli*. Each quarter is a corporate patrilineage ruled over by a senior male or quarter chief (*koli kalong*) and respected elders. Marriage is polygynous. When a man decides that his son is of age, he presents him with a dowry to purchase his first wife. This woman is usually selected before the son's birth and represents an alliance between the father and a man of equal or greater status from another lineage. After the marriage, the first wife, as the head wife, helps her husband select his other wives and then rules over them. Often, men from poor families become the lovers of a rich man's wives. The women usually confess the lovers' names, after which the men are obliged to work on the husband's farms for several years. After a specified time the women are free to marry their lovers. In many cases, especially when the husband is rich and powerful, a lover may elect to remain under the husband's authority in return for his protection and the ability to farm on his lands (Gibbs, 1963).[4]

Each quarter is strictly exagomous and keeps a separate food taboo. This is in contrast to the Tototaa Kpelle, described by Gibbs, where *koli(s)* are simply convenient living compounds (cf. Gibbs, 1965).[5] In Sucromu the quarters, like the moieties, are in a *ngala-maling* relation to one another. Consequently, the members of the various quarters have different formalized ways of behaving toward each other.

Residence is patrilocal with the practice of alternative avunculocality. Persons living in the latter arrangement take a subordinate position to the patrilocal residents and do not participate in their quarter sacrifices on the sacred mountain. One quarter, Zoman of Sucronsu *taa*, is the patrilineage from which the hierarchy of Zo (priests) for the Poro society are recruited. Its members claim to have come from Guinea and to be one family (*kala tano*) with the Poro Zo quarters in other towns, whether they be Kpelle or Loma.[6] The principal family of Zo, from Zoman *koli*—the actual members of the Zo hierarchy—live in avunculocal residence in the main *ngala* (mother's brother) quarter of Sucromu, Yamii *koli*. It is in this latter quarter that the Poro fence is located. The family of Zo live next to it, and are responsible for its maintenance.

Sucromu has both a secular and sacred political structure resembling more Harley's (1941) description of Mano social organization than Fulton's (1972) account of the Tototaa Kpelle.[7] The secular ruling structure is composed of the

---

[4]Gibbs considered this to be a kind of marriage among the Kpelle. There are some accounts of powerful chiefs in the past who were reputed to have several hundred wives. Each wife took a special lover who in return for having both sexual and domestic rights to the woman, owed allegiance and work to the husband.

[5]In that study he maintained that the Tototaa Kpelle quarters have very few corporate functions. Quarters in Sucromu, on the other hand, separately manage cooperative work projects, settle disputes, and allocate farming lands.

[6]In Sucromu, the Zo are considered to originally have come from Guinea, and established their rule throughout Kpelle country. The Zo, nevertheless, recognized that the towns are "owned" by the chiefs and members of the secular ruling structure.

[7]The Mano live on the other side of Kpelle country, approximately 150 miles from Sucromu.

various quarter chiefs, a quarter headman from each *koli,* respected elders, and the town chief. These individuals usually operate independently of one another, hearing palavers mostly of a minor nature such as abuses and name confessions (adultery cases). The town chief primarily presides over palavers concerning arguments between persons from different quarters, while the quarter chiefs handle within-quarter disputes. Most matters heard by them are open to the public. The quarter headman's responsibility, in addition to hearing some palavers, is to collect the yearly hut taxes and turn the money over to the central government.

The sacred ruling structure is headed by the hierarchy of Zo for the Poro Society. The Zo are all ranked according to the order in which they take new initiates into the bush. The number two Zo of this hierarchy is called the "government Zo" and is responsible to the central (*kwii*) government. In addition, he functions as the society's and the Zo hierarchy's corporate representative. Either he or one of his fellow Zo sit in in all secret society matters, even though all activities are under the Zo of the particular society. If there is a dispute between two societies, the "government Zo" usually adjudicates. The Poro Society, as a political body, is concerned with in-town fighting, murder, violation of a girl before puberty, breaking of medicine laws, and land disputes between towns. Prior to government control, before two towns would enter into open warfare, the palaver would be discussed by members of the Poro leadership of both towns. Today, such matters are still discussed in this way, but overt warfare is prohibited.

There are eleven ranked secret societies in Sucromu, including the Poro and the Sande. The highest is the Balasilangamu. This society is composed of the Poro Zo and other persons who, according to the society's "crier," " know themselves" and "put their whole interest in the medicines." It is called together only for the most important medicine matters and upon the death of a member. The Poro, or Porong, is also called the Ngamu Society. Membership is restricted to males. Initiation involves being symbolically killed by the ngamu or masked dancer, living in an age-set community in the forest (traditionally for four years, but today, under government regulation, no more than a year and a half), and being brought back to life by the coming out, or rebirth ceremonies. The leadership of the society, as mentioned earlier, is the caste of Zo from Zoman quarter who live avunculocally in Yamii *koli.*

Inside the Ngamu Society is the Ngamunea, or ngamu's wife's society (see Fig. 2). The Ngamunea is the so-called dancing devil that makes a yearly sacrifice for the protection of the town and dances at major town celebrations. Membership is restricted to men, but women and noninitiates are allowed to witness the dancer perform all the sacrificial rites. This is in contrast to the ngamu dance which can be seen only by Poro members.

The Sande is the women's society that parallels the Poro. All women are required to join. Initiation involves living in a female age-set community for three years after the Poro, or men's bush school, is finished. When the Sande is

FIG. 2 The Ngamunea or Dancing Devil of the Poro Society. This is the only devil that nonmembers are permitted to see. It performs for major celebrations, funerals, and makes a special yearly sacrifice for the town. (Photo by C. Hirsch)

in session, it is responsible for the moral well-being of the community as a whole. Anyone who commits a major crime during that period is tried before them under the supervision of the Poro Zo. Within the Sande is the Zohii society, which is the women's equivalent to the Balasilangamu. Membership is matrilineally recruited, as are the female Zo positions in the Sande itself.[8]

There are also a number of other secret societies that serve the Poro and Sande

[8]The Kpelle maintain that medicine power (*kasheng*) is either inherited or learned by joining one of several secret societies. One can become a Zo of a society by learning its medicines and purchasing the societal power object or head of the medicines. Those that do so, however, must have a large corpus of inherited medicines to back up their claim to power. When medicines are inherited, they are transmitted from father to son and mother to daughter.

by protecting the bush schools and town from various malevolent spirits. These include the Snake Society (protection from both actual and spirit snakes), Iron society (protection from water women and other kinds of evil *jina* that appear to people in dreams), the Lightning Society (against lightning and persons and spirits that control it), Mina (horn society which protects the town from witches), and the Moling (ancestor society that protects the town from evil dead spirits).[9] In addition, the latter two societies function as the young and old men warrior societies, respectively. Each of the societies also operates as a mechanism for holding discussions that need to be kept secret or treated with special discretion.

ON THE LOCATION OF MENI

Speakers in our culture normally structure their verbal accounts linearly according to the arrangement of those events in time. Likewise, listeners respond with the taken-for-granted assumption that if they were present in the setting described in the account, they would have experienced the same ordering of events and would consequently report on them in the same way. The Kpelle practice of talking and interpreting talk has a somewhat different character. Their methodology for these procedures can only be mentioned here with the observation that a full explication requires more than a single analysis. In another study, Bellman described how Kpelle speakers talk while at the same time recognize that they practice secrecy of *ifa mo* (literally, "you cannot talk it") (Bellman, 1975b). That recognition concerns ways in which speakers recognize their speaking prerogative and right to talk with a given social interaction.

Once a participant in a social situation achieves his right to talk, he structures his account not only by recognizing the historicity of events but amends them according to the *meni* that provides the meaning context for the interaction when he presents his account. Those amendments are often so marked that many Western observers are astonished by the liberties taken by Kpelle speakers when narrating what happened in some past situation which they both shared. Their astonishment and frequent complaints should not be dismissed merely as ethnocentric bias. What is of interest is that while those observers consider Kpelle accounts to be factually "untrue," Kpelle listeners are able to interpret

---

[9]These spiritual enemies against which the secret societies provide defense are well specified in Kpelle lore. The water woman or mammy water is a mermaid spirit that is considered to cause certain kinds of mental disorders and to lure people with promises of wealth. Belief in it is found not only in Liberia but throughout West and Central Africa. The *jina* or dream spirits include a variety of other personages, male and female, that are said to attack or attempt to gain alliances with living persons (cf. Welmers, 1949). While Welmers has argued that the Mina society's primary function is to impress women with how brave the men are, it also has specific functions for the Poro and Sande Societies and for the community. Among their responsibilities is to guard the Sande bush school and protect the community as a whole from *wulu nuu* dream spirits.

what occurred with such facility that other Kpelle who were also present at the event being recalled find no fault or need to add to the speaker's descriptions.

This points to the existence of different procedures for interpreting Kpelle accounts so that the meanings understood are the same, for all practical purposes, as those intended by the speaker. We assert that those procedures also provide a way to understand what a Kpelle videoist was thinking about while recording an event. His structuring of the tape and selection of what to emphasize involve the same kind of logical operations as he uses for structuring a verbal account and deciding what are significant items to mention.

When a Kpelle speaker talks, he is careful to correctly evaluate his speaking prerogative within the social situation. If he should incorrectly assess his right to talk, he could be recognized as violating the secrecy law or challenging those others in the gathering whose right to talk is greater than his own. It often happens that a speaker may be unable to talk in one kind of situation whereas in another, in the presence of the same participants, he has that right. Likewise, his speaking order in the situation also varies according to the *meni* that provides the organizational basis for the occasion. Hence, different situations give rise to different social structures. It is for this reason that we refer to situations as being organized by what Kpelle call *meni* which we freely translate as orders of social reality. The latter terminology is borrowed from Alfred Schutz to show that not only does each *meni* or order of reality have its own social structure but that it is recognized by members to be transcendent to its appearance in any particular social interaction (cf. Schutz, 1964a, pp. 229–234). Consequently, speakers have ways of discovering which kind of *meni* obtains at a given time and are able to name them when called upon.[10]

The reflexive character of the structure of power relationships to various orders of social reality is illustrated in the case of a palaver that occurred within the Snake Society (Kali Sale) between the Zo and many of its leadership. An almost universal rule in the secret societies along the Guinea coast is that nonmembers are prohibited from entering into a society medicine house or fence. If someone should enter by mistake, he is held before the membership and usually forced to pay a large fine and then, if possible, made to join the society. On one occasion when the Snake Society met, the Zo demanded that a young woman who was not a member enter the medicine house and cook the societal meal. She did as he asked without question. When the society members entered the house, they saw

---

[10]There are occasions where *meni* are explicitly named. One such is in response to a question salutation which is given as part of normal greetings. Whenever people meet each other for the first time in the day, enter into a house, meet each other on a path outside of town, or enter into a medicine fence, they ask the question *ku meni naa* (what is the *meni* there?). Normally, the reply is *meni nyaw fe zu* (there is no bad *meni* in it), but when someone is being intentionally excluded from a scene the organizational *meni* is named. A collection of such *meni* names includes the *meni* for all secret societies (Poro meni, Sande meni, Gbo meni, Gbo Gbling meni, Mina meni, etc.), kala meni (family business), kuu meni (cooperative farm society business), etc.

her there preparing the food but said nothing. After the girl finished cooking, the Zo told her to take a portion of the food and leave. As soon as she left, the activities of the society gathering continued. It was not until the following morning that the members held the Zo responsible for violating his own society's law. The palaver hearing took place in the society under the authority of the head Poro Zo.

This palaver is important to the present discussion for, when the girl was in the medicine house, among the members present was her father who, in spite of the fact that his daughter was in danger of being held responsible for violating a major society law, did nothing. He took this tactic even though if he had spoken up at the time of the violation, he would have had nothing real to fear from the Zo challenging him to a medicine duel since it was common knowledge that he was a high ranking member of the Poro Zo hierarchy and the number three man in the Snake Society's leadership. If he had spoken against the Zo at the time of the violation and as a consequence been challenged to a duel, he could have held his own. Nevertheless, he chose to recognize the presence of the Snake Society order of reality as organizing the setting, and thereby his place in the structure of power relationships relative to such situations, viz., the third man under the Zo.

The morning after the incident, however, was a different matter. The head Zo of the Poro Society was asked to chair the palaver. This meant that the order of reality operative at the time was that of the Poro. This latter society is recognized by everyone to be the head, leader, and owner of all other societies in town. Consequently, each society recognizes its place somewhere in a subservient position to it. When, therefore, the members of the Snake Society spoke under the authority of the Poro Zo, they assumed their speaking prerogatives as ordered by the arrangement of personnel indigenous to the Poro. Thus, the girl's father was able to speak in the new setting from a different speaking position than he held the previous day. Within the Poro order of reality he spoke as a member of the Zo priesthood which was by definition a higher position than the Snake Zo held in such situations. If he had spoken at the time of the violation, he would not only have usurped the Snake Zo's authority in the Snake Society order of reality, but also have challenged his position as the Zo. However, when he spoke against the Zo the following day, he was able to hold him responsible for violating a major societal law while at the same time maintaining the structure of power relationships (speaking prerogatives) and thereby the integrity of the Snake Society.

In spite of the fact that the speaking prerogatives of the other members of the Snake Society relative to the Snake Zo did not change in the new order of social reality, they were, nevertheless, also able to reprimand him. This was because, as mentioned earlier, persons having the highest speaking position always speak last. In so doing they render judgments taking into account all the talk that preceded their own without having to necessarily recognize the positions of the previous speakers relative to one another. For instance, in the palaver under discussion, the head Poro Zo listened to the accounts of all the Snake Society members without necessarily having to consider the fact that they held lower order speaking positions than the Snake Zo. The Snake Zo was unable to challenge any of the members since they were speaking at the Poro Zo's request and thus were under his authority. They were, in a sense, speaking from the latter's corporate position relative to the Snake Zo rather than as regular members of the Poro. If they, instead, spoke from their normal Poro speaking positions, most would have been inhibited from talking since the Snake Zo also possessed a high speaking prerogative in that society by virtue of his interest in its medicines and his active participation in its activities.

There was, nevertheless, a speaking sequence structure in the setting. The members still had to evaluate their fellow members' speaking positions to decide on what to say and when to talk relative to one another. That assessment was made according to the speaking order indigenous to the Poro even though the discussion concerned events of the Snake Society. Consequently it was the head Poro Zo who was the final speaker and was able to make the formal interpretation of the events that occurred the previous day. That formulation, once made, could not be opposed since to speak after it would not only contest that account, but also be a challenge to the head Poro Zo's position within the Poro order of social reality.

This palaver structure also obtains outside the domain of society activity. Even in the most secular of matters an adjudicator need only regard those accounts which he considers relevant to the formation of his judgment. The other parties in the palaver must speak strictly according to the speaking sequence structure belonging to the particular order of reality in that interactional setting. Each of the speakers, however, does not necessarily have to attend to what the previous speakers said. Instead, what is important is who talks after whom. In this way testimonies often appear disjointed and difficult to understand to an outsider (cf. Cole, Gay, Glick, & Sharp, 1971). A speaker may relate a parable or give evidence which has little to do with what the previous person said. The discussion was the form of a two-party conversation between the adjudicator and each of the speakers in turn. The necessity of the speakers to pay attention to the order in which they speak has very little to do with their assessments of the truth or falsity of each testimony, but rather with their location of the status hierarchy of personages within that order of reality.

In the following chapter we discuss three palaver tapes made by the same informant videoist. It is shown how each of the tapes reflects the structure and the relative position of the cameraperson's ability to maneuver the camera, and his selection of shots reveals his recognition of each of the palaver setting's *meni* and his place within it. This is not to argue that the *meni* determined what he was able to do. Rather, the cameraperson, as a participant–member in each situation, was engaged in the ongoing accomplishment of its organizational *meni*. In the same way that talk "is a constituent feature of some arrangement of activities in order to produce a descriptive account of those same arrangements,'' the mediated account is a mundane or constitutive property of the recorded event.[11] In the tape when the cameraperson was not a participating member (i.e., neither witness, adjudicator, nor "interested" party) to the palaver, he assumed a position in the court as an observer and shot about the room, in marked contrast to the other palaver tapes he made in which he was a member. The tape represents more his presentation of what a Kpelle case ideally looks like than an actual accounting of the case recorded. In his other two palaver tapes he stayed with the testimony and kept track of relevant personnel throughout the proceedings. We will discuss the tapes in the following chapter; the issue at the moment is simply to point out how the cameraperson's recording practices are themselves constitutive of the *meni* he recognizes as organizing the recorded situation. This makes understandable also those instances when the videoist (or filmmaker in Jules-Rosette's study) created a filmmaking order of reality and took liberties of movement that would not normally be accorded to him as a regular observer.

TOWARD AN ETHNOHERMENEUTIC OF KPELLE NARRATIVES

It has already been mentioned that Kpelle speakers often take great liberties in amending their descriptions of historical events. Listeners interpret those accounts by reciprocally recognizing with the speaker the setting's organizational *meni,* and attending to what the speaker's amendments accomplish within the narrative. It is not necessarily a significant concern that the events recounted are logically coherent or factual. Cole *et al.* (1971), in their psychological study of Kpelle cognitive processes, encountered the same phenomenon. They conducted a variety of learning experiments comparing American and Kpelle subjects which showed significant differences in the way the two groups recalled objects from memory, attended to various object displays, and solved problems. In one set of experiments they found that the Kpelle treated verbally presented syllogisms as debatable arguments, rather than having single solutions. This practice of evaluating verbal problems exists not only in the artificial situation of the experimental setting but also during the most mundane events of daily life. The Kpelle consistently approach problems as if their solutions are problematic and reflexive to the particular *meni* which serves as the basis for the interaction.

In the next chapter the two transcripts of Kpelle palavers each contain a series of parables which act to terminate testimony and offer judgments. According to Gay and Cole (1967), this practice is carried out in order to invoke a cultural

---

[11]The concept of reflexivity of talk is a major concern of many phenomenological sociologists and ethnomethodologists. Garfinkel extensively analyzed it as a formal property of practical reasoning, and Cicourel discussed it as an invariant property of interpretive procedures.

rule.[12] The specific rule communicated, however, is not solely the property of the meaning context provided by the interaction in which it was produced. Kulah (1973) recently showed how numerous parables are used in a variety of different settings to intend quite different meanings. He does argue, however, that each exists within a certain semantic domain so that there are possible sets of parables available for any occasion. Yet, to understand its meaning in any particular conversation necessitates the same kind of practices used to interpret the amended versions of historical accounts.

In the more acculturated Kpelle communities the prominent use of parables, dilemma tales, and amended versions of historical events is referred to as "deep Kpelle." Often the children of Kpelle migrants who have not been raised in traditional communities express great difficulty in understanding up-country conversations even though they are fluent in the language. Even in the traditional villages speakers will often use "deep Kpelle" as a way of excluding others present at the interaction setting from the conversation. Bellman has several transcripts of such parable use in which conversationalists use a series of parables or disjunctive accounts. The speaker is often interrupted and has his sentence completed by another conversationalist, while others present have no idea what they are talking about. The use of parables, however, is not solely used as a membership exclusion device. They are often presented in mundane discourse with the assumption that most of the listeners understand their intended meaning. For example, in a palaver whose full transcription is presented elsewhere, an elder was testifying before the leaders of the Paramont chiefdom that the town chief had an historical right to his position (Bellman, 1975b). The following is an excerpt from that testimony:

> FLINGAI: Let Kaboku come as a witness.
> KABOKU: What did you people call me for?
> FLOMO: Muwulu said that his parents gave him this land, is that true?
> KABOKU: What my father told me about this land business is that they took white cloth, kola, and white chicken and gave the land to Chief Vallai's fathers. He told me all these stories when I was young. If you go to someone and sit on his foot anywhere you go first of all you travel . . .
> SEVERAL PEOPLE TOGETHER: Ohhh, we are not here for that!

To understand Kaboku's use of the parable "If you go to someone and sit on his foot . . ." requires a detailed analysis of his position in the dispute and of the structural relationships existing in the town. What is important here is that the entire group present immediately saw Kaboku's use of the parable as a breach and interrupted his presentation. To a nonmember at the palaver Kaboku's statement was vague and even nonsense. Those present, however, saw it as introducing an interpretation of history which they did not want presented at the trial,

---

[12]Gay and Cole discuss what they considered to be the disjunctive nature of Kpelle palavers. Bellman (1975a,b) has shown that there is a definite structure to the talk and methods to interpret meaning within the context of different *meni* or orders of reality.

viz., that there was a distinction between the two moieties, Sucronsu and Twasamu, and that the former was mother's brother to the latter.

An example of the effective use of a parable is given in the following chapter in which an adjudicating Zo announced "the devil cannot chase the owl." The witness who was testifying immediately ceased his accounting and entered into joking behavior with the other members of the priesthood. To understand the Zo's statement requires not only knowledge of how such devices are used in talk, but also background information about the Poro society, its three masked devils or bush things (ngamu, balasilangamu, and ngamunea), the Mina Society, and a certain kind of manevolent dream spirit called *wulu nuu* or stick people.

The kind of interpretive methodology necessary to understand the intended meaning of such parables, dilemma tales, or amended versions of histories is demonstrated in the account that Torkalong, the blind Zo of the Iron Society, told Bellman about how he acquired his powers and became a Zo. That account and its analysis is presented in another publication (Bellman, 1975a). We will only summarize it here. Torkalong told Bellman that before he was born, his mother was upset because she had no male children. She finally decided to have intercourse with her husband's brother since, as a member of her husband's patrilineage, he had sexual rights with her. When she became pregnant, the husband was very upset and tried to kill her and one of her daughters. He was stopped by the townspeople, and shortly thereafter Torkalong was born. When he was about to be weaned, the husband set a medicine on him which caused his blindness. The mother's family made a medicine which killed the husband. After that Torkalong was not accepted by the husband's patrilineage and was considered an outcast. One night in his sleep Torkalong said that God spoke to him saying that everything would be all right. The next day the Iron Society came to Sucromu. The *faa sale* or spirit oracle of the society spoke directly to him. That was considered almost impossible since the *faa sale* can speak only to the Zo or priest of the society. Consequently, Torkalong was made a Zo of the society. He claims that from that time on whenever he needs to learn a new medicine, the societal spirit communicates with him in his sleep telling him which leaves to prepare and the methods to apply them.

Immediately after presenting the above account, Torkalong told a story about an orphan boy who was tricked by an opossum. The boy was accused of stealing kola nuts from a powerful chief. While he was asleep, the opossum put some of the stolen nuts in his hands. When he was taken before the chief for execution, an old woman intervened and asked that before the boy was killed he mind her unbeaten rice until she had finished grinding it. When the old woman had finished the rice, she gave a small portion to the boy. Just as he was about to eat it a cat approached him and said that if he gave him the rice, he would save his life. The boy agreed and gave the cat the rice. The cat in return gave the boy a dead rat. While the boy was lamenting, a snake came and told the boy that if he gave him the rat, he would save his life. When the boy gave him the rat the snake told him that the next morning he would bite the chief's favorite wife and that he would give the boy medicine to try to cure her. The next day after the snake bit the woman she died. Just as they were about to bury her the boy asked if he could try to cure her. The chief agreed and the boy cured the wife. The chief rejoiced and awarded the boy half the town. Torkalong then asked ''who is the main person responsible for this boy being a man today, the old woman, the cat, or the snake?''

What is significant about the first story or ''historical account'' of how Torkalong acquired his powers is that Bellman was well acquainted with Torkalong's older brother. The latter once even claimed in Torkalong's presence that he had taught Torkalong the Iron Society medicines and was responsible for his becoming a Zo. The question immediately arises whether Torkalong was lying in the first account or whether it needs to be interpreted in the same way as a parable. When considered as the latter, the presentation of the dilemma tale becomes significant. It provides the listener with an interpretive key to correctly understand what Torkalong was intending in his first account.

When Torkalong posed the question of ''who is the main person responsible . . .'' he was asking his listeners to correctly identify the *meni* relevant to the story and to his historical account. The location of ''main person'' within a social interaction is a location of *meni*. It is according to that identification that participants in a setting locate their speaking prerogatives and rights to talk. Concomitantly, that discovery provides the correct meaning context for interpreting and producing meaning within an interaction.

Both the riddle and story were dichotomized into two component themes: (1) those events which were descriptive of troubles, and (2) those which led to help and eventually to status and power. The first theme was represented in the riddle by the category set, those who cause the boy trouble, while in the story account it was in those events telling of Torkalong's father's malicious behavior. The second theme was represented in the riddle by the category set, those who made the boy a man today, and in the story by events that followed God's talking to Torkalong in his dream. The two accounts, consequently, expressed the same structural relationship:

trouble:help

| *Story* | *Tale* |
| father's actions/God's help | opossum's acts/women's help |

Thus, Torkalong's father's actions were to God's help in his account as the opossum's acts were to the old woman's help. Torkalong was able through the telling of the riddle to posit the above relationships between positive and negative events and explicate the member categories of the former (those that gave help). By establishing who the main person was in the riddle, he provided a methodology for locating the particular *meni* that governed his obtaining Zo powers. Since God was in the same structural position as the old woman, He was both responsible and the source of his powers. Hence, Torkalong's powers were based in God (*Xala meni*) rather than in the society.

We have now seen how *meni* provides the meaning context for Kpelle accounts. Its correct identification and the hearing of accounts as analogizing history rather than interpreting directly from the spoken text are members' methods for producing and understanding narratives. In the following chapter we discuss how in the Kpelle videotapes the reflexivity of meaning to *meni* and the structuring of shots as analogizing the cameraperson's definition of the situation are displayed. We will analyze the format of the tapes and their contents to locate which features of Kpelle verbal accounts are reflected in them. This includes an examination of the importance of speaking prerogatives within various *meni* to the cameraperson and his or her intentional positioning of the camera and use of technique during the course of taping. Consequently, we make constant reference to the materials presented in this section throughout the course of that analysis.

THE IMAGE AND THE WORD:
BAPOSTOLO NARRATIVE FORMS AND MEDIA

To understand how Bapostolo informants construct their films, a knowledge of the relationship between extant narrative styles and filming behavior is necessary. A verbal description of an event presented during or after its course summarizes or typifies the event and shapes the experiences described as they unfold (cf. Garfinkel & Sacks, 1970).[13] Verbal accounts are obviously mediated through linguistic conventions and styles. A visual account such as film provides another order of representation of a social scene and relies on its own narrative conventions (Jules-Rosette, 1976b).[14]

There are two major assumptions motivating this conception of narrative. First, the narrative structure of Apostolic ritual events closely parallels the structure of their verbal accounts, including visionary descriptions and testimonies. Second, the narrative structure of Apostolic verbal accounts provides a background for Apostles' filmed accounts of ritual and everyday events. These assumptions represent a methodological turn toward the structure of accounts rather

---

[13]Garfinkel and Sacks are concerned with the ways in which persons formulate conversations and social scenes during the course of talk. They state: "A member may treat some part of the conversation as an occasion to describe that conversation, to explain it, or characterize it, or explicate, or translate, or summarize, or furnish the gist of it or take note of its accordance with rules, or remark on its departure from rules" (p. 350). These formulations are accounts of the conversation presented during its course.

[14]Films and videotapes may be considered accounts of social scenes comparable to other conventional forms of verbal description.

than an analysis of discrete logical elements in communication (cf. Fabian, 1974, p. 267). These narrative styles emerge even more sharply against the background of contrasting assumptions (e.g., those of Bapostolo and American students) for organizing and presenting their accounts of a scene. The present analysis of narrative will serve as a background for understanding the way in which informants structure visual accounts. This approach also facilitates a comparison of cultural assumptions that form the background of the process of structuring communication.

Bapostolo narrative forms.   Narrative will be defined here as a form of communication that tells a story. Colby and Cole (1973) state that narrative structure reflects cognitive processes, for example, the strategies commonly employed by a group to solve problems.[15] For Colby, narrative is examined in terms of the smallest symbolically meaningful sequences of action (Colby, 1973; Colby & Peacock, 1973).[16] Although they use another approach, Colby and Cole concur with Labov and Waletzky (1967) that narrative can be divided into invariant structural units that are arranged differently in their presentation from one story to another.

The ritual of the Bapostolo is an African adaptation of certain Christian practices.[17] Bapostolo narratives take three major forms: (1) ritual language, including sermons, testimonies, song, and myths, (2) palavers and instruction sessions, and (3) visionary accounts and ordinary talk. There are occasions on which these forms seem to overlap, for example, in the relationship between palavers and ordinary conversation or the communications of lay speakers outside of ritual contexts. In each of these accounts, religious membership is a thematic concern for all Bapostolo participants. Each of these forms of communication is a *managed accomplishment* that relies on the sensitivity of all of the participants to cues given by others in a setting and on their awareness of what type of setting or order of reality has been invoked.

The Sabbath ceremony or kerek contains all of the basic features of Apostolic social organization. It is built around the core elements of prayer, preaching, and song (see Fig. 3). These elements form a larger narrative or action sequence, beginning with the invocation of the Holy Spirit and the angels to enter the place of worship through prayer and hymns and terminating with their departure, also signaled by a hymn. In the interim, the ceremony reaches a focal point or peak, developed by the alternation of preaching and song. Through song-chants, Apostles

---

[15]Colby and Cole analyze narrative in terms of its syntactic and sequential structure. On the other hand, Labov and Waletzky (1967) divide narrative into clause and phrase units that they analyze sequentially. For them, the narrative account relies on the syntax of the actual oral presentation.

[16]Colby segments narratives into "eidons" or classes of action that are structurally essential to the narrative's progression.

[17]For further descriptions of Apostolic ritual and social organization, see Barrett (1968) and Murphree (1969).

FIG. 3   The Apostolic men pray at the opening of a *kerek* worship service. Men pray facing east with hands up in praise. (Photo by R. Markoff)

enter into an ecstatic state and witness the presence of the Holy Spirit in kerek.[18] This peak is not formed by a progressive, linear increase in fervor or the calculated manipulation of the congregation that is occasionally evident in Western Pentecostal worship. By contrast, Apostolic worship has a "circular movement" in which members return to basic themes and intensify their ritual expressions through the alternation of activities. While the intensity of preaching inspires song, there is no guarantee that either activity will, in fact, reach a peak during the ceremony. As the song becomes a chant, its verses and, eventually, most of its words drop away, so that a humming sound is all that remains. Speakers following a chant will tie the original topics of the song into their sermon.

Within kerek, each speaker's or singer's "turn" and chance to obtain the floor may be viewed as the basic symbolically meaningful unit of action (cf. Sacks, Jefferson, & Schegloff, 1974).[19] The structure of preaching is open-ended and follows a ceremonial and aesthetic ideal that no gaps should occur in the flow of worship. Preachers work collaboratively with Bible readers to explain and ex-

[18]Elsewhere, the progression from discourse to song-chants in Bapostolo worship has been described in more detail (cf. Jules-Rosette, 1975b).

[19]Sacks et al. argue that turn-taking is a basic structural feature of conversation and is essential to various specialized speech exchange systems, for example debates and rituals.

pand upon the texts that they present. The transition from speaker to reader takes place on cue from the speaker.

Singers may interrupt at any time during this transition and at any break in the sermon. Their interruption constitutes a challenge to the mainstaged activity, and the speaker has the right either to continue his discourse or yield the floor. Therefore, for the most part, songs are not prescheduled. There are, however, two exceptions: the standard hymns introducing and closing the kerek as a whole and the moment at which the preacher gives the reader his first biblical passage.

Topics and themes developed across ritual activities are used to link one sequence of events to another. The initial sermon topic is presented by the speaker and outlined by the reader in the assigned text. The exegesis is closely timed so that the reading appears to be a continuation of the speaking. Through this process and through song, the topic may be modified or expanded. Church members feel no necessity for topic consistency from one sermon to the next. However, the intensity of worship tends to be cumulative across activities. Speakers and readers use the following techniques of topic development: topic definition, antiphonal presentation of texts, topic integration, and topic redirection by virtue of another ritual activity.

Topic definition.   Topic definition may take place through both reading and singing. Most commonly a topic is introduced in preaching and explained through Biblical reading and discourse. In the following exchange, reading explicates the sermon directly. The Sabbath is defined as Saturday and as the day that the original Apostles elected for worship.

Kananga, 1969
>   SPEAKER: ... Now that I have told you that we won't get rid of you, let me share this secret with you. Believe me, today is the real Sabbath. Listen and understand how Saturday is defined in the French dictionary.
>   READER: Saturday: the seventh day of the week, Sunday: the first day of the week.
>   SPEAKER: What should we believe? Your definition or Larousse's? Be attentive to this. Acts 16:13. Somebody asked me about this. Did the Apostles ever change anything when they were alone?

Antiphonal presentation.   The speaker and reader elaborate the topic together in a closely timed production. The pace increases as each echoes the other's statements. Eventually, the speaker and reader use incomplete sentences and each completes the other's last utterance. The two excerpts below suggest the gradual buildup of antiphonal preaching. In the first example, the speaker echoes the reader's statements with close timing.

Kananga, 1969
>   READER: ... Isn't there a balm in Gilead?
>   SPEAKER: Does the clinic have medicine?

READER: Isn't there a doctor?

SPEAKER: Isn't there a doctor?

READER: Why hasn't the daughter of my people been healed?

SPEAKER: I regret very deeply to see a big monument built and called a hospital. We witness every day a very disappointing fact. . . (The speaker's discourse continues.)

Kananga, 1969

The collaboration is intensified in this excerpt and the speaker completes the reader's verse in overlapped antiphony.

SPEAKER: God promised that He will satisfy you. How will He satisfy you?

READER: The eighth verse says that there will be a wide road—

SPEAKER: There will be a wide road—

READER: —and it will be called the Holy Road—

SPEAKER: —the Holy Road—

READER: —those who are not purified will not go through that road—

SPEAKER: —those that have not had the baptism of the water will not go through that road, except those that have been redeemed. . . .

Topic integration.   The speaker or the singer integrates elements of the previous sequence into his own, thereby facilitating the transition from one ritual activity to another. For example, a song may be used to elaborate upon a sermon. Similarly, in reinitiating discourse, the speaker may summarize and explain a song.

In this case, the song grows out of the themes implicit in the sermon and is, in turn, used by the speaker as a point of departure for discourse:

SPEAKER: . . . When our Kimbanguist brothers came, they read a letter to us and they showed us that everybody should know where he stands. . . .

SONG: I put my heart in God.
We are passengers, we are passengers.
We are not baptized from the cup.
We are song of Heaven.

SPEAKER: The singer just told us that you (nonmembers in the audience) are baptized from the cup. It's astonishing to see that such a big man can be put into a can like canned beef.

The song alone may set the tone for what is to come. Since singing is also considered a form of preaching, the singers may also cite verses and give moral instructions.

SONG: It is time to sing for our Lord
It is time to sing for Jerusalem

> We sing and ask for grace
> Come to song and the sound of the drum of life
> Cigarette smoking and alcohol keep you from God
> Come out of houses made of mud and ask mercy of God
> Our main preoccupation is to sing

SPEAKER: Life to you Apostles (ritual greeting). Looking at how we sing, it is not necessary that I do the Gospel. I do the Gospel only because I feel sorry for you. . . .

Topic redirection.   An alternative ritual event may change the topic and direction of the previous activity. This form of redirection, of which song interruption is the most common, involves the integration of prior topics and a change in their initial intent. Such redirection occurs through the gradual buildup of chants, characterized not only by the disappearance of song texts but also by intensity, glossolalia, rising pitch, and increasing syncopation. On the other hand, ordinary songs may redirect the substance of discourse without intensifying ritual activity. In the following excerpt, the speaker broadens his message because of the song.

Kananga, 1969

SPEAKER: Whenever you [the audience of outsiders] come here, you notice some difference between you and us. The difference is not only because we wear beards and gowns and canes. But the main difference resides in the symbols we have.

SONG: Our season has come before God
Those who are sleeping, get up
Those who are sleeping in alcohol
The drum calls us to life
It feels so good to observe the law

SPEAKER: Life to you Apostles. It is said that the time for Africans has come. It is a fact that God makes his plans without consulting anybody.

NARRATIVE FORMS IN ACTION

These excerpts demonstrate that narrative forms rely on their communicative context. When examined in terms of its structural properties, the kerek may be seen as the entrance of spiritual forces, the response given to these forces by the congregation, and their departure. However, the alternation of activities within kerek through these rhetorical devices complicates its progression. Discourse and song operate in different ways to build up a spiritual response.

Many Bapostolo sermons assume the following types of narrative themes or functions: a church member seeks spiritual inspiration, is blessed, and returns to everyday life with this blessing.[20] Alternatively, a member commits sinful acts and is condemned. These themes also occur in Apostles' accounts of religious experience and conversion. Rhetorical devices distinguish sermons from ordinary accounts and emphasize their major themes, including the specification of an audience, the invoking of an order of reality through discourse, and the unification of a group by the use of terms of reference.

The rhetorical greeting, "Life to you Apostles," sets off the audience of Apostles as those being addressed. The speaker informs the audience that what will follow is not intended for them. He states: "Looking at how we sing, it is not necessary that I do the Gospel. I do the Gospel only because I feel sorry for you [outsiders]." This comment also defines an order of reality, that of spiritual singing, as an event in which only members take part. It unifies members, referring to them as "we" and outsiders as "you."

Shifting between the terms of address in sermons and song is commonly used to intensify ritual activities and redirect topics. Every Apostolic song characterizes the community of believers or the outsiders. "We" verses proclaim the spiritual transcendence of members. "Our joy is in the Spirit of God. We are the light come from the Father." On the other hand, "you" verses exhort potential and wavering members to obey the laws and seek grace. "You who wish to pray, pray from this moment on. You who are taught to sing will inherit Heaven. You who are asleep, get up, you will miss Heaven."[21] Through these rhetorical devices, the focus of discourse and song moves from proselytizing to collective spiritual experience.

Collaborative preaching and song-chants are oriented almost exclusively toward members. A similar collaboration exists between the song leader who sings the lines of the verses and the responsorial chorus. Once the verses are established the singer may truncate them, allowing the chorus to enter at progressively earlier points in the verse. This truncation is one form of the fading away of song verses that leads to chanting. Observers have noted the almost hypnotic quality of these song-chants (Murphree, 1969, p. 107).[22]

Every aspect of narrative form in ritual has nonverbal correlates or kinesic properties. The use of rhetorical devices coincides with a speaker's orientation toward different parts of the audience. Collaborative preaching involves subtle cuing between the speaker and reader. The speaker may also emphasize passages by flourishing his staff, using emphatic hand gestures, or miming his message.

During kerek, a sacred path is formed between the separated rows of men and

---

[20]In his analysis of Russian folk tales, Propp (1968, pp. 25–64) described narratives "morphologically" in terms of their functions or a series of basic events involving the hero and others in the story. For Propp, these actions are invariant and cannot be defined apart from their place in the narrative.

[21]This song is a variation of the selection presented on pages 47 and 48.

[22]Murphree describes the singing accompanying exorcism as hypnotic. With the exception of a few special exorcism and healing songs, these song-chants overlap with those presented in the main kerek.

women, with men seated to the east and women to the west. Male prophets are seated to the north, facing inward toward the aisle. While the reader remains stationary, the speaker uses the entire aisle as a "manipulatory" area. The spatial extent of an environment used by the persons within it has been referred to as a manipulatory area (Schutz, 1964a).[23] The manipulatory area does not include an entire visual field. Instead, it consists of "those objects which are both seen and handled in contradistinction to distant objects which cannot be experienced by contact but still lie in the visual field" (p. 223). The manipulatory sphere of kerek is part of a larger ritual order of reality. Women cannot enter the sphere where men preach. Normally, speakers and readers do not occupy the same area. Similarly, a male singer challenges the speaker's position at the center of the aisle when he enters it to sing. The speaker performs ritualized blessings on entering and leaving the central area, considered to purify his "taking on" and "giving back" the ritual power associated with it. The singer asks rhetorical questions, generally to the men in the congregation, and attempts to elicit their full participation in the responses. Singers employ a similar technique by approaching parts of the congregation and urging members to sing along. The parallel between speakers and singers also illustrates that their activities are considered mutually exclusive, and the presence of any other person on the sacred path is considered a violation of the ritual order of reality.

It is, therefore, of particular interest that informant camerapersons created their own filmic order of reality, using the sacred path as a vantage point of filming. The filmic order of reality held in abeyance and reversed some of the ritual principles. Jérémie and his sound assistant were allowed to stand beside persons as they went through the prophetic examination and confession, events that were handled only by the candidate and a prophet or an evangelist. Jérémie and Ezekiel also entered the women's side of the sacred aisle (see Fig. 4). In fact, Jérémie filmed a large part of the kerek ceremony from the women's side. The only time that visual recording did not reverse ritual principles was during the kerek opening. Videotaping and filming of the hymn "Mwari Komborera" invoking the Holy Spirit into the place of prayer were not allowed. This restriction was imposed to assure that everyone present participated in this potent invocation.

Large segments of the informant-made kerek films consist of singing. In Chapter 5, we discuss some of the stylistic reasons for this choice. Jérémie followed the singer in the aisle, keeping his camera movements in rhythm with those of the filmed subject. He used panning to cover the congregation, particularly the women, and included very few shots of collaborative preaching. When the film was screened, members felt that the large amount of singing it showed was representative of kerek. On the other hand, when they saw videotapes made by an American student, they were surprised that his version of kerek contained

---

[23]Schutz limits the manipulatory area to objectives that can be seen and handled rather than including objects visible at a distance.

FIG. 4   Apostolic women interrupt to sing during *kerek*. Ezekiel took the license to cross over to the women's side of the sacred space while filming. (Photo by R. Markoff)

only preaching. One disappointed member reported that he had only come to the screening room to see himself sing.

Apostles refer to songs as "the food that we give to God." One prophet described Heaven as a place where angels sing all day with no other concern. When listening to audiotape replays, members often requested that I skip over the sermon and move to the songs so that they could join in with the tape. Singing predominates in all members' narrative accounts of the ceremony and is the key factor in evaluating whether a kerek achieves its spiritual goals. Its presence as an aspect of Bapostolo narrative style resembles the predominance of walking that Worth and Adair (1972, pp. 144–152) noted in Navajo films.[24] If singing is good, say members, the Holy Spirit and the angels have been contacted. Informant films follow the speaker's assertion that good singing makes the spoken Gospel superfluous for members. For example, Ezekiel made a three-minute film sequence of a kerek in which four out of the six cademes began with new songs.

[24]Worth and Adair noted what seemed to them to be excessive shots of walking in Navajo films. Upon closer examination, however, they found that walking is a meaningful feature of many Navajo myths and stories. Images of walking were a regular part of Navajo narratives in general.

In the other two, songs provided the background for talk. Singing in film invokes an order of reality meaningful to informants, for, they would argue, it is only those who have sung who can understand the ritual intent of kerek and the spiritual purpose of singing.

SOME APPLICATIONS OF RITUAL FORMAT OUTSIDE OF KEREK

While singing is the spiritual core of kerek and is viewed as a form of preaching, it is only in combination with discourse that it produces some basic elements that recur in other ritual contexts. A shortened version of kerek takes place at personal or home prayers, masowes or wilderness prayers,[25] and non-Sabbath services. The mere invocation of the term kerek, and, in particular, the singing of the "Kwese Kwese" or introductory hymn invoking the angels, creates that ceremonial order of reality.

While masowes or bush retreats open with a full kerek if several church members participate, these ceremonies vary in their adherence to full kerek format. Every evening, the Apostles of Lusaka crossed Chaisa compound to a vacant area near the railway. Some, still wearing overalls, entered the worship area directly from work. A baptist led the "Kwese Kwese" as the sun set. The men confessed first, followed by the women. Prayer and the closing hymn followed this masowe without intervening preaching. The basic features of kerek were sustained in what was essentially a confession ceremony. If members departed for the wilderness alone, they confessed beforehand to prevent the attacks of demons. Kabeya, an evangelist, related that he had witnessed his friend chased down a mountain by beasts because he had not confessed beforehand. The only ritual elements that remain in the individual masowe are prayers and songs of ritual invocation.

On the other hand, instruction builds upon the format of preaching. Lyson, an evangelist, asserted that all instruction should begin with the biblical passage Mark 16:15, in which Christ admonishes the Apostles to go into the world and preach the Gospel to everyone. He viewed this passage as the foundation of all other messages. Instruction is often conducted rhetorically. For example, Yeshaie, in a short play that he directed to instruct Americans about the Apostles, asked, "Is the baptism real?" He directed one of our group to find and explain the answer in Mark. He then elaborated on the importance of baptism. The collaborative reading format of kerek and the use of instructions based on rhetorical questions were combined to create Apostolic "theater."

Confession and prophecy are forms of instruction. They are also often part of a larger curing ceremony. Every confession begins with a standard formula: "I

---

[25]*Masowe* is a Shona term meaning wilderness. Apostles use it to refer to individual and group prayer retreats in the bush.

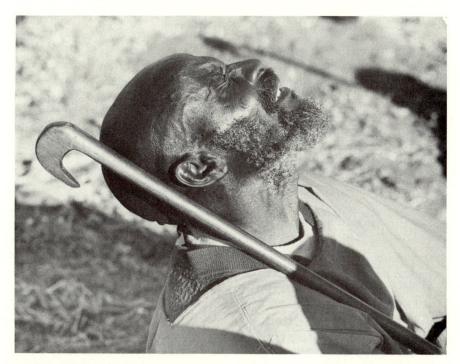

FIG. 5   An Apostolic prophet goes into trance prior to delivering an ecstastic message during *kerek*. The informant filmmakers considered the ecstatic states of song and prophecy as the keys to worship events. (Photo by R. Markoff)

stand before God to confess.'' The prophet helps members to determine confessable materials. He consults the Holy Spirit, speaks in tongues, and presents a message (see Fig. 5). The message may simply be a warning, for example, ''attach your feet,'' or do not travel. When Jules-Rosette was examined by the prophets, she was told to confess hidden anger, reciting the formula, ''I have too much cheek.'' In this case, once the formula was repeated, two evangelists absolved the transgression. Prophecies may also be made after kerek, to advise the whole congregation or to challenge specific church leaders.

Prophets are considered to speak on behalf of God. They cannot be challenged during the course of prophecy. The candidate merely answers ''Alleluia'' in assent, denies the prophecy, or briefly asks for more information. If a prophecy takes place in a home rather than a public setting, it is common for the prophet to ask the candidate whether he or she is satisfied with what has been said. Should the candidate refuse the prophecy, the prophet will either pray for more enlightenment or promise to return with further clarification.

Like singing, prophecy is considered an especially inspired communicative form. Prophets are careful to specify the order of reality under which they speak, distinguishing between personal opinion, dreams or visions, and true prophetic messages (cf. Fitzgerald, 1970, pp. 11–14).[26] It is a general feature of Apostolic speech to inquire about the auspices under which a given assertion is made. Thus, when expressing an opinion, a member may say ''this comes from me and not from God.'' When evangelist judges receive cases from prophets, they evaluate the possible orders of interpretation involved and their relevance for a public hearing. If there is a minor dispute, evangelists may decide that it does not constitute confessable material but instead should be resolved outside of church. In general, however, the prophet determines what is to be confessed and the evangelist attempts to reach a viable verdict that can be applied by the individual member (Murphree, 1969, pp. 106–107).[27]

PALAVERS, ADJUDICATIONS, AND INSTRUCTIONS

The palaver, or *tshilumbu,* is both a ceremonial event and a discussion of mundane matters. There are palavers of preparation or instruction and palavers of adjudication (*dare*). The preparatory palaver is held to discuss the order of speakers and organization of the larger ceremonies or to evaluate a concluded ceremony. The speaking prerogatives used in the palaver follow those of the main kerek. Highest ranking members have the final word. Unless a case is being adjudicated or a special palaver is held, women do not participate formally in the discussion. The palaver is a pivotal event that mediates between kerek as an order of reality and daily life. While the head of each congregation generally organizes weekly pre-kerek palavers, a *tshilumbu* may take place at any time for a discussion of organizational issues.

In a preparatory palaver, discussion of daily events is initiated by those who will participate in kerek. While the discussion appears to be unstructured, it is always monitored by the elder baptist or evangelist who selects the order of speakers and who speaks last. When Tshiambi and Nawezi, both head baptists, held palavers, they would make sure that any guest or outsider was seated immediately to their left, while the other members faced them with the highest ranking members to the far right and closer to the central table. The leaders would turn around the table to select the next speaker, usually by gesture or by giving them instructions on the subject matter to be discussed in the next kerek (cf. Faïk-Nzuji, 1970).[28]

---

[26]Fitzgerald stresses that the Ga spirit medium establishes a particular form of social reality when she speaks. This prophetic speech instructs others in their ritual obligations and serves as a form of social control.

[27]Murphree notes that a large number of the members accused of witchcraft confess rather than challenge the accusations. Confession without resistance takes place in the case of many other transgressions as well.

[28]The relationship of status to speaking prerogatives is reflected not only in palaver but also in the structure of traditional Luba riddles and proverbs. Faïk-Nzuji has collected several Luba proverbs that

In contrast to preparatory palavers in which definitive statements are made by the highest ranking persons, palavers of adjudication involve the arbitration of disputes by a group of several evangelist judges. These palavers begin with prayer and confession. The evangelists question those bringing cases and wait for them to testify before a final decision is rendered, often with the attempt to find a satisfactory compromise. Prophets may be called upon to present spiritual evidence in the adjudication. Thus, three orders of speaking take place: (1) the questions and renditions of the judges, (2) the confessions of the participants, and (3) the spiritual testimonies of the prophets. The focus of activity in a palaver of adjudication is between the evangelists and those who give testimony, though various judges may contribute to the discussion. Informant films of a confession stressed the activities of the prophets and of the members testifying rather than those of the evangelists and the audience. An excerpt from a *dare* case emphasizes the relationship between confession and prophecy.

Bocha, Rhodesia, July, 1974

Musumbu came before the evangelists. He was asked some questions and gave a fairly long reply. Kadima was called. He was sitting toward the back of the musasa (ritual enclosure). Three men were called to prophesy: two prophets and a baptist. The first prophet had begun prophesying in the space where Musumbu had been sitting. He said:

"I see a tug of war."
   Musumbu and Kadima answered, "Amen" as a sign of assent.
"In the middle, I see a woman."
   "Amen."
"Their argument involves this woman."
   "Amen."
"It is a case of adultery to be decided."
   To this they said, "No."

The second man, a baptist, came forward and stood near the chief judge. He prophesied as follows:

"I see the same tug of war between them. The baptist [Musumbu] wants the evangelist [Kadima] to obey him. The evangelist thinks the baptist hates him and does not want him in the church. He is accusing him of witchcraft. (Amen.) Why are they fighting? I see the baptist picking up sand and throwing it on people. He must be very careful not to follow behind people and worry about what they are doing but must look after his own affairs. For the evangelist, I see a blackboard with four things written on it. He agrees to the first three but on the fourth, he thinks they cannot agree. It is the same matter of witchcraft."

---

she analyzes in terms of their structure and content. The following is Jules-Rosette's translation.
Mmuntu kai
(What person)
Udi udia ne bakalenge banene ku mesa
(Eats with great lords at the table)
Kayi ubatshina?
(And doesn't fear them?)
Lujiji.
(A fly.)

A concluding discussion took place in which Kadima stated that Musumbu could not accuse a
baptist, an evangelist, and then a prophet of witchcraft. The evangelists tried to persuade
Musumbu and Kadima to reach an agreement. They reached the decision that the two should go
out for the night and think about their answers.

The order of speaking in all palavers affords a background for later accounts of
the scene. In a preparatory palaver, all persons present are given a chance to
speak. In a palaver of adjudication, the judges control the order of speaking in
that only those with relevant testimony step forward. The speaking order of
prophecies and confessions within the palaver is also controlled, while discussion
among the judges and between them and the parties follows a pattern similar to
an informal discussion.

Prophets are particularly important in providing spiritual evidence and validation for decisions made in adjudicative palavers. Just as singing is central to
members' descriptions of kerek, prophecy is the spiritual theme of palavers. The
evangelists speak last, presenting their negotiated conclusions. These are often
expedient solutions for closing the case. The final decision relies upon an agreement among the parties that cannot always be settled in palaver. The conclusions
presented in palaver take the form of instructions. For example, in the preceding
excerpt, the prophet states: ''I see the baptist picking up sand and throwing it on
people. He must be careful not to follow behind people and worry about what
they are doing but must look after his own affairs.'' The visionary account is
translated into an instruction about daily activities. The baptist is presumed to
know what the prophet is referring to and to be able to follow his suggestions.
The instruction itself provides a way of interpreting the entire palaver (Jules-
Rosette, 1974).[29] Kadima's claim of having been judged too harshly is implicitly
referred to when Musumbu is told not to follow others too closely. Palavers are
thus the occasions on which visionary decisions and biblical precedents are
applied to mundane events. They are the bridges between full worship and daily
activity.

VISIONARY ACCOUNTS AND ORDINARY TALK

Much of Apostolic talk contains visionary elements. They are especially found in
accounts of dreams, conversion experiences, and visions. The record of John
Maranke's own visions has provided the prototype for other Apostolic visionary
accounts (Maranke, 1953).[30] John's descriptions are also used to interpret the

---

[29]In this analysis, it is stressed that instructions rely on the context in which they are presented and
on the uses to which they are put. Both verbal and nonverbal instructions contain an element of
ambiguity which those that are exposed to them are expected to resolve.

[30]John recorded the visions that he received during the early years of the church in this booklet.
These visions were not intended to replace the Bible as the main sacred texts for Apostles. Instead,
they provided a record of John's early spiritual experiences and innovations. They also explained the
spiritual basis of Apostolic worship to other members.

Bible and to relate Apostolic figures, for example, John's spiritual ancestors to it. When interviewed, Apostles offered spiritual explanations for all answers, including their names. They converted "factual" queries into spiritual matters. The following excerpt from John's own visionary account is illustrative of this type of narrative.

John Maranke, August 5, 1935

(a) The Waking State:
It was midday when I had a prayer in the forest. The Voice told me to go home and lie on my bed, which I did. Later, the Voice told me to rise up and pray which when I did, I found that there was an opening in the roof of the house.

(b) The Ascent into Heaven:
Through the opening in the roof I could see a cart which had two wheels and it was being driven by two horses. There was a man in the cart and it was brought to my bed. The horses and the carts were moving in mid-air. The man in the cart lifted his hand and picked me up. . . .

(c) Heaven:
When we got near Heaven, the angel lifted a white long thing that I could not describe. The Heaven opened and we entered. This was the first Heaven and in it I saw nobody. We came to the second Heaven and the angel opened. We entered here and were taken in another cart that was driven by two horses. . . . When we came to the third Heaven, the angel produced a key with which he let us in. Here in the third Heaven we dismounted. . . . I spoke in all the languages of the earth and understood every tongue. I also spoke in some other languages which I was taught by the Holy Spirit. I strove to get in to the other angels but my angel forbade me.

(d) The Return:
After a time, the horse was brought and I was asked to ride. I rode on this horse, which was brown, and the Voice told me to go down with the horse. I argued that I did not want to go to the earth again. I was surprised to find myself on my bed again. (pp. 27–29)

The four parts of John's story resemble the progression of kerek starting from the waking state, moving to a spiritual transcendence that culminates in ecstasy, and then returning to the earth. This structure is also found in Ezekiel's film of kerek, in which he begins with men talking on the periphery of the ceremony and then turns the camera in for increasingly intense song-chants. While the songs themselves attempt to create and sustain ecstasy, many of the Apostles' verbal accounts end, as John's did, with an abrupt and perhaps unwanted return to earth. Apostles have incorporated this format into ordinary storytelling (cf. Doob, 1961, pp. 102–103).[31]

When Nyalongo, a mupostolo evangelist, described the dream that persuaded him to become an Apostle, he described the visionary experience as a rapid ascent to communicate with the angels and a return to the waking state with a definitive sign or message. The abrupt return to earth contained the account's validation.

[31]Doob makes a similar point in his discussion of African talking drums. Ashanti, for example, translate the tones of speech into drumming language. Similarly, Apostles translate the tones and topics of speech into songs. They also reverse this process and use the themes and progression of rituals in ordinary storytelling.

Nyalongo, Lusaka, 1973[32]

> Then I had a vision showing me other churches. First I saw the Catholics. They were a group of children playing with ''mud'' money. Next came the Salvation Army. They were very intelligent but also very proud. Then an angel told me, ''There are 9,999 churches already and one more is needed to make 10,000.'' As I awoke, I was hurrying to catch the 10,000. (pp. 116–117)

In contrast to John's and Nyalongo's descriptions of ascent to Heaven, accounts of combat and victory over Satan reverse this progression. Although one visionary sign appeared to Esthere, an Apostolic healer, in the waking state, she was reluctant to accept it. When a second sign appeared that directly affected her, she acknowledged its existence and changed her attitude.[33]

Esthere, Lubumbashi, 1972[34]

> While we were in the village, my husband became very ill with a stomach disease. [The first sign] The prophet said that he could be cured only if I were baptized. I argued that the Apostles could have my body, but they could not have my soul. When I approached the water and reluctantly entered it, a snake appeared out of nowhere. The baptist hit the snake and broke it into two pieces with his staff. I then said: ''Go ahead. Baptize both my soul and my body.'' I was finally baptized. (pp. 66–67)

These themes of salvation, conversion, and visionary experience emerged later if Apostles had a chance to edit their own films into coherent stories. Yeshaie's play, as well as Apostolic ritual in general, illustrates that Apostles dramatize these accounts in various ways and present their visionary experiences in ritual much as they do in outside descriptions of it. Stressing that these experiences must be explained to outsiders, Yeshaie created a dramatic format for this filmed account. This format drew on narrative conventions with which Apostles were already familiar for speaking with outside audiences. On the other hand, through his film of kerek that contained only singing, Ezekiel presented an account in which participating in a spiritual experience was more important than its explanation. Both interpretations were based on members' familiarity with the narrative structure of ritual, although they drew opposite conclusions from it when translating their experiences into visual accounts.

On a follow-up trip, Ezekiel edited his films. His editing was characterized by a series of jump-cuts. At first Jules-Rosette could not understand the logic of his organization. Finally, he stated that all events in his film, entitled *Baba Jacob's Journey,* were to be seen as examples of the fact that good Apostles pray on Saturday and other people do not. For Ezekiel, the temporal sequence of events was of far less importance than their thematic unity.

---

[32]Nyalongo's entire account can be found in Jules-Rosette (1975a, pp. 116–117).

[33]The format of Esthere's account of a combat against evil resembles many Apostolic confessions and conversion accounts. The initial reluctance that members attribute to themselves in these accounts sets them apart from John's original descriptions.

[34]See Jules-Rosette (1975a, pp. 66–67).

Repetition is a stylistic aspect of ordinary talk that also occurs in other informant films. In Tshiluba, repetition is often used for emphasis. Once a subject is introduced, it is constantly reemphasized to stress its importance. This style of presentation may seem more circular than direct to the Western listener. However, each time that a subject is introduced, it is handled somewhat differently. An interesting analogy might be drawn between verbal and visual accounts. Direct emphasis, like staring, and its filmic equivalent, the close-up, is often considered impolite, whereas repetition and indirect return to a topic present a point appropriately.

The selection of shots used in the informant films is a presentational strategy resembling the use of stylized argumentation in parables and stories. The use of repetitive panning links and emphasizes filmed subjects much as the use of innuendo does in parables. When parables occur within visual materials, they are not necessarily spelled out through camera movements. In this way, the organization of rhetorical strategies used in visual accounts appears to resemble that in talk.

Nawezi Petro, an Apostolic leader, called a small group aside to discuss his grievances with some other church members. He set the stage by describing all of the church members that had been witnesses to his dispute with the church leadership. Rather than present the accusation first, Nawezi named all of those present and thereby evoked the context of the dispute for those who already knew about it. He used a repetitive list and was aided by his wife Tshibola Marie who interjected names and repeated them for emphasis. Nawezi's return to the names on the list resembled the "repetitive" panning found in some of the informants' films. This style of presentation is common to many informal spoken Luba narratives that were recorded among the Bapostolo.

Nawezi Petro, Lusaka, 1974

NAWEZI:	Mbolela, Tshibuyi, ne ye Kasanda, Muteba Pierre,
	Ba'Kadima— (and him)
TSHIBOLA:	Kadiata Titus.
NAWEZI:	Kadiata Titus. Muamba malu a bungi.
	(He said a lot)
TSHIBOLA:	William. Ne Luka. Ne wewe ne Muteba,
	(and) (and you and)
	ne Kasanda—
	(and)
NAWEZI:	Ne Kadiata. Bantu ba Tshiaba, Tshiaba Daniel.
	(and) (The people of)
TSHIBOLA:	Tshiaba Daniel.
NAWEZI:	Mu— mu— muamba malu a bungi . . .
	(he— he— he said a lot)

FILM AND OTHER MEDIATED ACCOUNTS

When Apostles use film they are influenced by other communicative conventions. These communicative forms include the interactive strategies that are employed to present them. The status relationships so central to the organization of speaking prerogatives in palavers and kerek are reflected in the filming behavior within these scenes as well. The absence of face close-ups and shots from below are striking in Apostolic filming (Worth & Adair, 1972, pp. 152–162).[35] Yeshaie's first film of a confession ceremony cut off the candidate's head and focused on his torso and hands. Facial close-ups never appeared in the informant-made films, although Yeshaie's film of the market place, discussed in a later chapter, contained a few brief portraits. These observations are in accord with the Lulua conception of eye contact or the stare as bold (Faïk-Nzuji, 1970, p. 14).[36]

The repetition that occurs in Luba stories has its visual parallel in constant camera motion and the intentional use of panning. Ezekiel explained that since the 8 mm camera runs for only a short time, it was necessary to "get everything" by keeping it in motion. In his filmed sequences, Yeshaie used panning to establish a center of action to which he constantly returned. This indirect process resembled Nawezi's use of the list to set the stage for his story. They both used repetition to emphasize and provide a larger context for the scenes that they described. Both the verbal repetition and the panning stressed the importance of all of the participants to a given scene.

Two potential filming styles emerged in the informant accounts: the use of film to simulate experience and the use of film to communicate intended meaning to outsiders. Ezekiel's film creates a spiritual account of ritual that resembles that of the performance itself and of other visionary accounts. On the other hand, Yeshaie's play adapts the ritual format of preaching to an expedient and commonly known way of communicating a message to outsiders. Using media as a record is another variation of Yeshaie's approach suggested in Bapostolo audiotaping of ceremonies and palavers. In this case, the audio tape is regarded as an artifactual document of the event and, in certain adjudication cases, as a piece of evidence for the disputes.

CONCLUSIONS

A background of other forms of communication is necessary in order to understand informant-filmed accounts. At the same time, the purpose of resorting to

---

[35]Worth and Adair report a similar absence of facial close-ups in Navajo filming. Such close-ups were considered to be both strange and amusing.

[36]Faïk-Nzuji reports a Luba proverb about the "audacity" of the eye. The proverb remarks on the irony that the eye always follows others but does not allow others to approach it too closely.

informant films rather than, for example, interpretive film practice is to examine how visual representations are used to convey the intended meaning of events. The interpretive filmmaker extracts aesthetic conventions from other domains, for example, ritual, and applies them to filming practices.[37] However, informant films provide these very aesthetic dimensions as they occur and are interpreted in natural settings. Thus, the appearance of a ritual performance to an outsider as gradual and methodical may be just the opposite for the participant. On the contrary, an Apostle may perceive what seems to the outsider to be the drawn out repetition of chanting as a rapid and intensifying experience. The informant filming of this event would be characterized by rapid sequences, just as was Ezekiel's film of singing, whereas the interpretive version could not assure the portrayal of intended meaning as it was experienced.

On the other hand, specifying intended meaning may be problematic. Since many verbal and nonverbal conventions are not overtly taught, it is difficult to say whether they influence or are reflected in film. It is often impossible for informants to articulate the reasons for which they see a scene in a particular way. However, it is much easier for the ethnographer to survey a number of similar settings and isolate approaches to them that are assumed but not verbalized by participants. These approaches are, to a certain extent, the ethnographer's constructions of regularities across events. When the ethnographer wishes to convey a cultural similarity in communicative styles rather than the ways in which these styles are meaningfully used in a particular setting, participant films may not provide a viable method of presenting information. Analyzing film in the context in which it is produced offers the alternative of treating it on a par with other indigenous interpretations of social events. Both our analyses take the latter perspective. The Kpelle materials are analyzed with respect to the relationship between videotaping practices and the production of *meni* as a key to the study of cognitive systems. On the other hand, the Bapostolo materials are examined in terms of the comparison of narrative and visual styles as ways of making accounts.

[37]In this regard, Bergum (1974, pp. 8–9) presents the goal of interpretive film as cultural translation based on the ethnographer's observation of a series of events rather than the informants' own filmic rendition of them.

4

The Kpelle Tapes: Format and Content

Edmund Leach once apologized when introducing a chapter containing field data that, while his interpretations and arguments were interesting, his data were, as he felt all data to be, dull and uninteresting (Leach, 1969).[1] This view toward data is not unique. For instance, Garfinkel has pointed out how most theorists treat the swarms of features that exist in a given social setting as the "poor relatives" of the elegant properties of some formal model.[2] The data, therefore, must be presented in the quickest manner possible in order to proceed with the "more important" matters at hand, for example, the demonstration of some theory or position. If, on the other hand, we are to take our data seriously, what is the orientation of our analyses? Instead of proving, we are interested in describing. In place of locating examples from "the field" to support our models, we seek to discover members' practices as embedded in the context of their production occurrences.

In this chapter we will present a detailed account of the Kpelle video tapes. It is recommended that the tapes be considered as: (1) the intentional mediated accounts of informants, and (2) visual records of various kinds of social interactions. They are themselves *artifacts* of the settings they describe. To understand

[1]Leach states:

> I suppose that the main difficulty that every anthropologist has to face is what to do with the facts. When I read a book by one of my anthropological colleagues, I am, I must confess, frequently bored by the facts. I see no prospect of visiting either Polynesia or the Northern Territories of the Gold Coast and I cannot arouse in myself any real interest in the cultural peculiarities of either the Tikopia or the Tallensi. I read the works of Professors Firth and Fortes, not from an interest in the facts, but so as to learn something from the principles behind the facts. I take it for granted that the vast majority of those who read this book will be in a similar position with regard to the Kachins. How then should I dispose of the facts, the detailed evidence?

[2]Cf. Garfinkel (1970–1971) for discussions of "swarms" of features of a setting.

them necessitates an attention not unlike that which is necessary to appreciate the significance of a Poro mask or Snake Society (*Kali Sale*) fetish medicine. Such objects can be placed behind the thick glass cages of museums and valued for their "strange" appearance and form, or they can be given a wholly different perspective—a presentation of their modes of appearance and a description of the ways they become meaningful for members. Our task is to present procedures necessary to interpret the tapes and their content from the point of view of their producers.

In the previous chapter, we discussed some of the features of traditional Kpelle accounts. We saw how our interpretive practices needed to be revised in order to locate the subjective meaning of different Kpelle narratives. Similarly, an understanding of what the Kpelle camerapersons "were up to" in taping a given segment or using a particular camera technique requires knowledge of what a Kpelle member treats as "an event" and how different "events" are recognized as conjunctive or disjunctive or follow serially or concurrently. However, we shall begin by presenting the field methods used to introduce video to Sucromu, and a brief biography of the informants. It is hoped that that presentation will satisfy most questions about whether Kpelle filming practices resulted from procedures learned from the way the media was introduced, or from the particular idiosyncratic characteristics of those who participated in the project.

INTRODUCING VIDEO TO SUCROMU

During the summer of 1973, Beryl Bellman returned to Sucromu after an absence of almost four years. He had, however, maintained written correspondence with several literate members of the village and had informed them of his plans to continue his research. After arriving and settling into his old house with his wife and son, he spent the next few days relaxing and catching up on the news and gossip of the community. On the second day of his return, he passed out *ngamas* or gifts to his friends and various of the town elders and priests.[3] He gave one of his closest friends, the major informant of his previous research, Folpahzoi, a cassette audio tape recorder. They spent a good part of that day and most of the next walking about town recording members of Folpahzoi's family and musicians who were eager to hear themselves on tape. Bellman then described what a video tape recorder was. He explained that it worked something like the tape recorder, but that instead of simply recording the sound it produced pictures

[3]Whenever a member of the community leaves and returns it is expected that he bring back gifts for all his relatives and close friends. Several migrants claim that they would visit their homes more often if not for this custom, as the costs of giving *ngjamas* is often excessive. When one returns to the village the call *ngjama kaw,* "Where is my *ngjama?*" is part of the greeting. For persons who are somewhat distant, the visitor normally can say "I will try," which usually suffices. Nevertheless, it is crucial that those closest to the visitor receive some gift.

"quick service." The latter phrase, spoken in English, was normally applied to Polaroid pictures. The ability to have photographs developed instantaneously in the camera was, consequently, both known and highly appreciated by most members of the village. During his previous stay Bellman had used both the Polaroid and 35 mm camera. In that way he was able to give away the Polaroid shots and take a longer series with the 35 mm for his own records.

Bellman presented the videotaping project from the outset as informant directed and controlled. After explaining his plan to Folpahzoi they presented the idea to James Mulbah, Folpahzoi's younger brother. James had a high school education and taught in the village school.[4] James had never seen video before but did have some familiarity with film. He was immediately interested in seeing the camera and suggested that they discuss their research plans with the town chief and his fathers, the members of the Poro priesthood.

They first went to Chief Vallai, the clan chief and past town chief. He was, as in the previous research, supportive and agreeable to the work. They also presented this proposal to the town chief, Bakolee Volpoi.[5] This request was mostly a formality, since Bellman already had their consent to continue research and live in Sucromu from his previous field work. Both chiefs required only the sketchiest plans and readily agreed to allow the work to proceed. They then discussed this work with Mulbah Sumo Jakolii, the head Poro Zo or priest of the clan, who also agreed without much explanation.

The next day Joan Logue, a faculty member from the School of Video of California Institute of the Arts, arrived with the second portapak (camera and recording deck).[6] Bellman brought the first equipment to Sucromu but did not begin work until both cameras were in the field and he had the technical assistance of Ms. Logue. That afternoon Bellman and Logue gave their first instruction on the portapak to Folpahzoi. That and all other teaching sessions were audiotaped and photographed. The sessions went as follows: They chose an area of the house that was relatively well lighted, but not too visible from outside. This was to avoid the stares through the windows of onlookers, mostly children. The researchers first showed Folpahzoi how to thread the tape. This was done slowly but without great attention to the description since they wanted their

---

[4]The village school was built by the Peace Corps in the mid-1960s. It has classes in basic literacy to the 6th grade. At that time, those students who elect to continue take an examination. Depending on their performance on that test, they are permitted to attend high school in the market town of Zorzor.

[5]Vallai was the town chief when Bellman first visited Sucromu, and was the subject of the attempted coup palaver discussed in Chapter 3. He became the clan chief shortly after that palaver, but still maintains much power at the community level. The quarter chief of Gbanya quarter in the other moiety (Sucronsu) became acting town chief for the duration of Vallai's term. The latter, Bakolee Volpoi, is the one referred to in this chapter as the town chief.

[6]At the time of the field research, Joan Logue was a colleague of Bellman's at California Institute of the Arts, where she taught video and television studio techniques. Bellman invited her to act as technical advisor to the project and to assist in the instruction of the Kpelle informants. In the course of her stay, she also made several video tapes which she is currently editing for presentation.

informant to understand what the camera could do before bothering about setting it up or maintaining the equipment. They did however present what they called "laws of the camera." Bellman chose this way to present warnings about pointing the camera into the sun, pointing it directly down, dropping it, and getting it dirty since it corresponded well with the Kpelle concept of "laws of the medicine." The Kpelle maintain that all medicines (*sale*) have certain laws that must be followed. For example, some medicines cannot be used if that person has touched lime or pumpkin. Others no woman—or man—can approach or see. Still others have certain words that cannot be uttered in their presence. For the more important medicines which protect the town as a whole or the Sande and Poro bush schools while in session, no murder, rape, fighting, or violation of a girl before puberty is permitted. If a law is broken the violator must bring a *tee* or chicken to be sacrificed (*sala*). For the more minor medicines a *tee* will be an actual chicken or a bottle of cane juice (raw rum). The more serious the law or medicine, the greater the sacrifice demanded. Thus, for a violation such as murder the life of the violator must be given, or in some cases a cow is sacrificed. Once a law is violated the medicine is ineffectual until the correct sacrifice is made. Thus, to violate one of the "laws of the camera" connotes that it would cease to function. In every case, once the "laws" were given they were *never* violated. Consequently, the equipment remained in surprisingly good condition.[7]

After presenting the "laws of the camera" the researchers put the camera to their informant's eye and showed him how to pull the trigger turning the recording deck on. After recording a few seconds they immediately rewound the tape and played back what the informant recorded. They then instructed their informant to record once again. This time they turned the zoom ring on the video lens to demonstrate its function. They then asked the informant to play with the zoom to see how it worked. Next, they turned the f-stop ring on the lens to demonstrate differences in lighting. Once the informant discriminated correctly between the two rings, they had him turn in different positions pointing the camera to various parts of the room, each varying in amount of light. These changes required the informant to make necessary adjustments on the f-stop. Since the number size of the opening was not a necessary part of operating the camera the concept of f-stop was taught solely by the visible changes in light caused by changing positions of the camera (and later by changes in lighting due to the onset of sudden rain storms). Next, the informant was shown the focus ring on the front of the lens. He was told how to zoom up close, focus, and then zoom all the way back to get the whole field or focal length of the lens in focus. After this period of instruction the tape was rewound and the recorded portion was again shown. The tape was

---

[7]About midway through the study the high voltage went out on one of the cameras. This was not due to any fault of the informant videoists. The equipment was over three years old and had been used extensively in classes at California Institute of the Arts.

again rewound so that the deck needed rethreading. At this point the threading procedure was demonstrated in detail. After the informant could correctly thread the deck by himself (usually after two or three attempts) the researchers and the informant would do a "walkabout tape." This consisted of the informant walking about the town videotaping anything that he desired. During this period, the researchers would periodically play back portions so that the informant would see what he shot. At that time gross mistakes were corrected. We will discuss this again later, but for the moment a single example should suffice. Often the informant would look through the camera with both eyes open, thinking that the center of the field was the center of his line of vision. As a result, those shots were all far off-center depending on which eye was away from the camera. Several informants overcame this difficulty by holding a hand over one eye while shooting.

After the informants had successfully finished their walkabout tapes, they were told that they could tape anything they wished whenever they desired. At first the proposition was exciting, but subsequently most infomants had great difficulty in choosing a project that would take up an entire reel of tape (30 minutes). After having made a second tape the equipment was made available to each informant. The only qualifications were that there should be enough light and enough time left on the battery. The latter was more of a problem in the morning than in the late afternoon. Since Sucromu did not have electricity, the researchers hired a special assistant from the community to "run" the two three-hour batteries to the market town of Zorzor for recharging each evening. Every morning that assistant went to Zorzor and returned with the charged batteries. Zorzor is located approximately 10 miles from Sucromu and takes about two hours to walk. The assistant usually left at sunup and returned by 7 or 8 o'clock.

Serious palavers would often take place early in the morning or in the late evening so that witnesses could be away from their farms as little as possible. Because of this some palavers were unable to be taped, and in one case only a partial recording was made with several interruptions to charge batteries. The researchers had three half-hour batteries which they used for such emergencies. Unfortunately, the batteries only kept their charge for about fifteen minutes. Consequently, they had to be charged three times during the same palaver.

In all, seven informants were taught how to use the video portapaks. The researchers originally had hoped to have an equal number of men and women. A problem developed, however, when the first woman taught showed her tape in a viewing session in the market town. At that time, there were three informants: two men and one woman. The two men were Folpahzoi and his brother James Mulbah, the school teacher. The woman, Anna Juah, had been a student in James' class a few years before and had occasional aspirations to return to school. She had left after the third grade. The tapes shown that afternoon were their first walkabout tapes. Anna had developed a sense of framing and camera technique very quickly. James, on the other hand, had a serious problem with framing. He shot with both eyes open and consequently centered his picture from the binocular perspective. As a result, his frames were all off-center, and in some instances what he wanted to tape was not recorded. James took the critique of his tape quietly and immediately after the review session asked to do another walk-about as soon as possible. Anna, on the other hand, was very embarrassed and did not say much after the tape had finished.

The next day, James came to the house very early and went through another session of instruction. This time he made a very successful tape that will be discussed later. When James finished, the researchers went to find Anna who had requested, previous to the viewing session, to do some taping that afternoon. She was nowhere to be found. That evening she said she had to go to the farm but would tape the next day. She agreed, however, with a noticeable lack of enthusiasm.

It should be mentioned that the researchers in recruiting the informants told them they would pay a small amount of money for assistance, since working with the video equipment took at least half a day from necessary work that had to be done on the farms. They paid each informant fifty cents, or the equivalent of a day's wage for migrant labor.[8] Although criticism can be leveled at the project for introducing the pecuniary motive in making tapes, we do not believe that this was a strong factor for most of the informants. This will become more obvious shortly.

Anna, however, made her second tape mostly to fulfill obligations and to receive payment. The researchers felt that Anna's initial interest was genuine, but it declined when her first tape proved to be aesthetically more pleasing and technically more proficient than a man's. Her second tape concerned work on a rice farm. She shot a short portion showing an infant being force fed wet rice, and then some brief shots of a woman's *kuu* or cooperative work group weeding the rice farm. After approximately five minutes of taping, she announced that she had recorded enough and was ready to return to town. This was especially upsetting to the researchers, since they had walked about 45 minutes to the farm for the taping. Joan Logue suggested that she shoot some more. Anna stated that she thought she had gotten what she wanted, but if Joan desired she would be willing to tape more. Joan then walked over to where the women were weeding which required walking through a swamp area. Anna refused to follow. Instead, she stood on the far side of the swamp and used the zoom lens to get a closer shot. She taped for an additional ten minutes and said that now she was ready to return to town. After that incident she refused to do any more taping, saying that she was too busy with farm work and preparing for a forthcoming trip to Bomi Hills, a migrant labor area.

[8]Although most of the informants would have participated in the project out of interest rather than for pay, Bellman felt that they should receive some financial remuneration since they would be required to spend most of a work day in taping.

The second woman instructed was Cortoe. Cortoe was an older woman who was considered a very powerful female Zo in several secret societies. The researchers selected her because of her willingness to participate in the project but primarily because she had a very high status position in the community. That, Bellman felt, would circumvent her feeling that she was competing with men. He also hoped that it would make Anna more at ease since a powerful woman would be taping with her.

Although Cortoe was not literate, she was able to communicate in Liberian English. She had learned it in the market and migrant labor areas. As a result of her experiences she had an interest in *kwii* (nontraditional) matters. She owned a shortwave radio, and often played it in the evening, attracting several young persons to her house. In spite of her being middle-aged, she often had young lovers, who included educated men in the town and market community. Several car ot taxi drivers would stop by her house for a visit and a bowl of rice. She was as well liked as she was feared, for her medicine knowledge and secret society activities. She was reputed to belong to a *kwii* secret society that occasionally sacrificed human beings to their medicine. Several people in the town maintained that various high ranking local government officials from the district and country headquarters were affiliated with that association. However, Bellman, who had done field work in the area for approximately two years, never saw evidence of this society's activities. That did not dispel rumors regarding the organization. The threat of the society caused members of the community to avoid walking on the dirt motor road at night. Instead, they often took bush trails which added additional time to their travel. The claim of human sacrifice to medicines, however, is unsubstantiated in individual cases. It was said that the palm of the left hand, the index finger, and the forehead of a corpse were necessary ingredients for certain powerful medicines. Occasionally persons were arrested for making such medicines or for killing someone for that purpose.

This rather gruesome tangent is not meant to imply that Cortoe made such medicines or actually belonged to societies that frequently engage in human sacrifice. Rather, many members of the community feared Cortoe for her reputation of membership in such associations as well as her status in the Sande and other major societies. As a consequence of Cortoe's participation in the project, the elders in the community took a serious interest in what the researchers were doing. Later, the two head Poro priests or Zo asked to learn how to operate the portapaks, and each made walkabout tapes. Although Cortoe had an interest in the project, she had great difficulty holding the camera for an extended period of time. She made a walkabout tape in different sessions on consecutive days. When she finished it, she considered that her participation was complete, even though the researchers offered her the use of the equipment whenever she desired.

The remainder of the informants were male. Two of them, as mentioned above, were the leaders of the town's Poro society. The other three men were the most active users of the video materials and made most of the tapes.

In choosing the informants, the researchers wanted to have some control over the possible effects of literacy on the development of use of the camera. This was based on the results of Michael Cole and his associates' cross-cultural psychological research on the Kpelle (cf. Cole, Gay, Glick, & Sharp, 1971; Gay & Cole, 1967). In the light of that research Bellman attempted to find informants with differing amounts of education. As mentioned already, Anna Juah had three years of formal education in the community's school. This amounted to basic literacy and some fluency with English. Cortoe had no formal education and was able to communicate in English, but with a much more restricted vocabulary than Anna. As for the men, James Mulbah had the most education. He had attended public school in Sucromu and after passing the sixth grade examinations had gone to Zorzor, the market town, for further education. He eventually went on to Zorzor Teaching Institute (ZTI) where he was awarded a high school diploma. He then returned, at his request, to Sucromu where he taught in the same school in which he first learned to read and write. Because of his education and membership in the Poro caste of priests (*Zo*) he often functioned as the Poro society's scribe.

Folpahzoi was James Mulbah's older brother (*nia*). He had five years of formal education in the Sucromu school and a good command of English. Although he wrote in a highly restricted code he often functioned as a scribe or letter writer and interpreter for nonliterate members of the community.[9] Folpahzoi originally wanted to become a migrant–soldier, but in 1959 he suffered an unfortunate accident. He had been cutting palm nuts from a palm tree when a snake attacked him. He warded off the attack by knocking the snake to the ground, but the snake then, reportedly, came up the tree after him and entered his pant leg. Folpah threw out his foot, lost his balance, and fell out of the tree, causing him to break his back. It was later divined through the *faa sale,* the oracle of the Gbo Gbling secret society, that the snake was the physical manifestation of a water woman (*nyai nenu*) dream spirit (see Bellman, 1975b, for a detailed discussion). It was divined that he had a sexual relationship with the spirit and that she was angered because Folpah had too many lovers in the waking state.

Folpah eventually was able to walk again, but with a very noticeable limp, and his interest in *kwii* ideas was not dampened. He became an apprentice tailor and saved enough money to purchase a manual sewing machine. At the time of the research he was one of three such tailors in Sucromu. His ability to thread

---

[9]The use of a mediated communication code is not new among the Kpelle. Traditionally, they had a system of drum syllables that operated as a telegraphing device between villages. Several years ago, when various persons in communities became somewhat literate, a system of scribes was created. This is the most prevalent mode of mediated communication that exists in this area. It is, however, very restricted, as it requires the scribe to translate spoken Kpelle into written English. Since most scribes possess at most only a few years of schooling, the messages are highly abbreviated. It then necessitates another scribe in the recipient's town to translate the message back into Kpelle. As a result, messages are often confused or very formal in nature.

sewing machines obviously assisted him in learning on the first demonstration how to thread the video tape deck without error.

Folpah was the first informant instructed in the use of the portapaks, for several reasons. First, he was one of Bellman's closest friends and informants. Second, he was considered by all men in the community to be "the young men's chief" because of his ability to adjudicate palavers and his respected position with the elders. Palavers were often taken to Folpah rather than an elder in the hope that it could be tried in a less costly fashion. Folpah also had the ability to read and write English, albeit in a highly restricted manner. Thus, he was able to read contracts and draw up agreements between parties in a dispute. Finally, Folpah was a high ranking member of the Poro priesthood. He held the number five position as ranked by those who take new initiates into the bush during the *ngamu* or devil ritual, and acted as a tester for malevolent medicines the town wanted to use against enemies in other communities. The *koi sale* (war medicine) would first be tried on Folpah. If he remained standing another medicine would be given since the prospective victim was said to have an anecdote for the one tried. When Folpah fell to the ground in a convulsion the medicine was believed effective. He also acted as the Poro's scribe and occasional clerk to the Zo's court. As a result of his position of respect and power in the community and his personal interest in *kwii* (modern) matters, he was an ideal choice for first informant.

Folpah's first tape is of particular interest since it affected how video was interpreted by others in the community. It also served as a basis for instructing other informants. After Folpah learned how to operate the VTR, he walked about town with Bellman and Logue to record "anything that he felt was interesting." The concept of "walking about town" is a traditional one. "Walking about" is a favorite activity in the late afternoon and early evening, or when visiting a different town. The walk, however, is not random. The warning is often given that one must be very careful which quarters to enter, as it is very easy for someone to "set a medicine" or poison him while walking past the medicine maker's house. The walk is also structured by the order of persons the walker (or walkers) greets. For example, a man will greet his various wives, their families, his publicly acknowledged girl friends, his secret or intended girl friends, and other men with whom the walker has various kinds of business (ranging from farm work to secret society activity) in that order.

The walkabout is also used as a highly structured ritual for the various secret societies. After a society has met inside the medicine house (*sale pele*) or fence (*korong*) they publicly walk through the town stopping at various homes to greet those inside. When they arrive at a house the people inside are obliged to give a small amount of cane juice (or money to purchase a small bottle) to the membership. This procedure is also followed in the procession of the *ngamu* and *balasilangamu* devils of the Poro society. In addition to their formal performance and accomplishment of the specific reason for the ritual the devils walk about town greeting various powerful personages in the community. The order of the persons greeted and the path the respective devil takes through town provide clues to the societal members as to the reason for the ritual and the status structure for that particular *meni*. When the devil (*ngamu*) leaves the Poro temple or fence he is preceded by a member called "the holder of the stick" (*ngamu sia tua nuu*). The latter walks the path that the *ngamu* will follow and stops at all houses where the *ngamu* will greet those inside. When the *ngamu* arrives at the house he speaks a secret language which is interpreted by the "speaker for the devil" (*pene woo*).[10] The importance of the societally structured walkabout will be a major feature in our analysis of a Sande ritual video taped by Folpah's younger brother, James Mulbah.

The casual walkabout also has its own formal structure. That structure is not always the same for different walks. Rather, the order of houses visited and persons greeted reflects the particular order of reality or *meni* that provides the organizational grounding or meaning context for the walk itself. Thus, the order shifts from one *meni* to another. A member's recognition of the ordering of a walkabout provides cues for interpreting which *meni* obtains at that time. The analysis of the ordering of Folpah's walkabout video tape, consequently, furnishes data concerning the structure of the *meni* he was participating in. That *meni* in a large part concerned the introduction and acceptance of the new *kwii* (or concept) into the community.

The introduction of the new technology created a particular kind of *meni*:[11] making a video tape. In many instances, certain departures from expected behaviors and acceptances of "strange" positions to participants in an interaction were tolerated for the camerapersons while recording some event. This is not to say that the position of the cameraperson was the same no matter who was taping. It will be shown later how an organizational *meni* and the cameraperson's speaking prerogative within it is reflected in the format of tapes.

Folpah's walkabout tapes: Folpah began his walkabout tape in Yamii quarter where Bellman's house was located. He immediately went to his subquarter, *Balamii*, within *Yamii*. *Balamii* is part of the *Yamii* compound where the Poro priests (from Zoman quarter) live avunculocally as the caretakers of the Poro temple or fence. He visited his house and taped the open area separating it from the houses of his fathers. He then went around behind his quarter to the central area of Yamii, where one of his favorite wives was living. He taped women beating rice and children playing. He then walked past the house of Kaboku, the quarter chief of Yamii quarter, and into the town chief's compound, *Gbanya koli*. He stopped at the town chief's palaver hut to show him through the camera's eyepiece what he had just shot.

[10]This is discussed in depth in Bellman (1974a).

[11]This will be discussed in Chapter 6 when the filmmaking of informants is compared with that of American camerapersons. A more general overview will be given in Chapter 7.

As he was walking through the quarters, about twenty young boys surrounded him. When Folpah stopped and replayed what he had just taped, several of them attempted to jump into view of the camera and mug. The children were quite exicted. Often while taping Folpah had to shout at the children to move out of the way.[12] When he reached the town chief's palaver hut, the children seemed to multiply twofold. When he tried to show the chief what he had recorded, the children surrounded the chief and tried to peer into the eyepiece with him. The chief shouted at the children to move to no avail. Finally, out of desperation he took his umbrella and began to beat several of them. The children moved back, laughing as they fended off the blows. As soon as the chief resumed his position at the camera, the children approached him again. At that the chief furiously turned around and once again began to strike out at the children, hitting their shoulders and upper arms as they guarded their heads. This procedure went on for several minutes. Somehow the chief did see several minutes of the tape and expressed how delighted he was. When Folpah left the children followed.

It may seem strange that a chief was unable to order small children from his hut, or at least away from the camera. In Chapter 3 we discussed how Sucromu has both a secular and sacred ruling structure. Each in turn is organized by an indefinite number of *meni* or orders of social reality. The chief and the other members of the secular ruling structure adjudicate mundane palavers and have no formal authoritative voice. When community work is needed, whether it be to clean a road, brush some forest, or collect taxes, the *ngamu* or sacred ruling structure must make the announcement. The chief's ability to order people about is, therefore, a feature of the specific situation in which he is a participant. His speaking prerogative reflected his position in the *meni* that served as the grounding for the interaction. Since the chief viewed the video tape as an instrument of *kwii* technology, introduced by *kwii* people, the organizational *meni* was *kwii meni*. The children, because of their attendance at the Sucromu public school, had rights within that *meni*. The chief, who was nonliterate, had few, if any (cf. Bellman, 1975b).[13] Folpah had authority in *kwii meni* and was successful in ordering the children from in front of the camera. Throughout his first walkabout, however, he was unable to avoid their presence. Later in other tapes he was able to tell the children to leave. They obeyed but in some cases reluctantly.

The importance of *meni* and the ability to operate freely with the camera without the intrusion of the children is demonstrated in a walkabout tape Folpah

---

[12]When serious taping took place, the children were warned to move aside. Ritual language was employed for this purpose. The person warning the children had to have authority in that *meni*.

[13]There, a case is described of a very powerful Zo of the Snake Society who was tossed out of a *kwii* party by children attending the village school. The students claimed that the Zo was too loud and abusive. They physically carried the elder from the house and mocked his angry abuses and threats, saying that he "knows nothing about *kwii meni*." In a similar manner, the chief lacked authority to chase the *kwii* or school children from the camera. The latter was their purview and the chief was only a spectator to it.

made during the July 26th (Independence Day) celebrations. He took the camera to the school yard outside of town to record the school children playing soccer. The children surrounded him as he attempted to tape, often jumping in front of the camera and mugging in a variety of poses. After the game, Folpah took the camera to the entrance of the town and taped the children returning home. He remained a few more moments after the children were well into the town to record some of the people sitting about the area. Occasionally, a boy would turn toward the camera, and Folpah would pan away from him. After taping awhile in that location, Folpah walked back toward the center of town. On the way he came across some Sande dancers. He stood in one position and taped them. After a few minutes a boy jumped in front of the camera. At that Folpah shouted very sharply for him to move from there.[14] The startled boy moved immediately and left the area.

Folpah's second tape was to be "anything that he considered interesting enough to make an entire tape." The instruction was given so that he would have to plan out a tape rather than record what he saw randomly as he walked about the town. This proved to be a very difficult task. At first he said he was not sure what he felt would make an interesting tape. Bellman tried not to coax him into recording specific events but suggested that he might want to tape various people working in or about the town. Folpah finally settled on tapping a palm tree.

Tapping a palm tree is the process of obtaining sap or palm wine from either the piasavva or oil palm. Since the latter trees are often over 30 feet tall, tapping them is very risky. Besides, any mistake could kill the tree and thus reduce a source of palm oil. The piasavva palm tree is normally about 12 feet tall and produces the wine during only one period in its life. If the tree is tapped prematurely the wine will be too sweet, and drinking large quantities of it can cause dysentery. On the other hand, if the tree is tapped late the wine will be very yeasty and bitter. Consequently, knowledge of when and how to tap a tree is considered almost an art.

Folpah chose a young boy named Labulah as the subject of his taping. The boy was the son of his mother's brother (*ngala*) and was a general helper around his house. Labulah had successfully tapped several trees in the past and was eager to try again. Folpah made his choice also because he was available throughout the day and would go to the forest to find a tree at Folpah's own convenience rather than his own. Labulah chose a tree in a marshy area about twenty minutes walk from the town. Two other boys accompanied Folpah to help carry the equipment. Besides Bellman and Logue, one of Bellman's students, Harold Miller, went with the group. Miller was doing ethnographic research in Kpaiyea, a nearby Kpelle community, and had come to Sucromu for a consultation. Miller brought along a super 8 mm camera and also taped the tapping session.

---

[14]The instruction "*ka lii belei mu*" or "go into the house" is similar to the instruction given to nonmembers of the Poro society when the devil is about to walk through the village.

When the group reached the tree, Folpah began immediately to set up his equipment. He chose a position directly under Labulah. Logue stood to one side of him and Miller the other. It was obvious to Logue that a side position was a better angle for the shooting since Labulah's arm movements were more visible. She suggested first through Bellman and then directly that Folpah ought to change his position. Folpah said that he had the best position and did not want to move. He had positioned himself on his knees and shot directly under Labulah using his zoom lens now and then to record various movements on the tree.

Labulah located the center stalk of bamboo and bored a small hole into it. He then set a small bowl under the hole to catch the seeping wine. Palm wine comes directly from the tree, already fermented. It is usually a bit sweet at first, but after sitting for an hour or so it becomes more yeasty. If the wine is very sweet it is referred to as *nenu kililaw* (women's palm wine) and if too strong it is referred to as *surong kililaw* (men's palm wine). The trick is to make it come out somewhere in between. When the tree is flowing at its peak it yields about two gallons of wine a day. It must be cleaned twice a day or else the tree will spoil (all the wine will be *surong kpo*—strong man). In order to make the wine the correct strength a little is left in the cup after the cleaning. This becomes *surong kpo* wine which, when mixed with the new wine (*nenu*), produces the desired strength.

Labulah only started the tree and said that it would take several days before it would yield a drinkable beverage. Folpah said that he would return to finish the tape when the wine was ready. He taped approximately seven minutes in that session. Unfortunately the tree died. Labulah had cut into the tree incorrectly. As a result several weeks later Folpah decided to videotape someone else taking wine from his tree. He put that tape on the same reel as Labulah's attempt. Thus, he did attempt to follow through with a tape but was unable to do so because of the subject matter.

The second tape of palm wine tapping contained many of the features of the first. Folpah recruited several young men in their late teens to accompany him on the project. He chose to tape a close friend, Mulbah Sumo, who had a reputation for making excellent palm wine. Mulbah's farm was about 30 minutes walk into the forest. His tree was on the far end of a patch of sugar cane that Mulbah was growing to distill into cane juice.

Once at the location, Mulbah pointed out the tree that he was going to tap. Folpah positioned himself about fifty yards away near the crest of a small hill. He set the recording deck down next to him and attached the camera. Then, he signaled for Mulbah to begin. Although his position was different from the Labulah tape, he insisted on staying in a single location immediately in front of the tree. Because he was at a distance from the tree he was unable to record the specific maneuvers Mulbah performed on the tree. Instead, the tape shows Mulbah climbing the tree and zoom-in shots of him working on it. As Mulbah was working, Bellman walked around the tree, testing various shooting angles with his 35 mm camera. He then suggested to Folpah that other angles would be possible. Folpah, however, insisted that his position was the best for getting what he wanted.

After Mulbah climbed down from the tree, Folpah put the equipment away. While doing so he announced to Bellman that as soon as they finished they would go to the *gele* (rice kitchen) to drink the wine. Bellman asked if he wanted to tape the drinking of the wine, but Folpah replied that the tape was complete, and that the drinking was a separate activity from the tapping and was not of particular interest.

The two tapes demonstrate Folpah's use of position in regard to an activity. Instead of dollying with the camera he insisted on maintaining one position. To show particular or significant events within the event he used zoom (to Labulah's hands when cutting the tree and to Mulbah's backside and arms when he collected the wine). We will see shortly how shifts in positions mark separate events, whereas zoom and pan segment a single event into constitutive units.

After Folpah completed the Labulah portion of his palm wine tape, he said he wanted to tape the blacksmith making a machete. Folpah chose the blacksmith shop of Sucronsu moiety. Each of the *taa,* Sucronsu and Twasamu, has its own blacksmith shop. The blacksmith has one of the few specialized occupations in the community. He trains under another blacksmith for several years and assists the head blacksmith on small jobs. He is one of the major priests in the Poro society and is responsible for casting and carving many of the fetish medicines. He is also one of the major leaders of the Mina and Moling secret societies. In addition he has his own medicine practice by making various *mina* (horn protection) medicines to protect unborn children from members of their patrilineage who act as malevolent dream spirits known as *wulu nuu* (stick people) that kill them for special sacrifices.

The blacksmith's day is usually spent either making machetes, hoes, or rice harvesting knives, depending on the season. Folpah recorded the making of a bush machete. This is one of two kinds. The other is for cutting trees (*wulu gbexe*) and is larger, with iron pegs holding the handle, whereas the bush machete (*noi gbexe*) fits into a carved handle. When either is made the owner or client supplies the blacksmith and any friends in attendance with cane juice to drink and the afternoon meal. He also pays the smith fifty cents for the day's work. Since there is good food and drink at the shop, it is an active place and is frequented throughout the day by friends of the client, who keep him company and tell about the latest gossip of the town.

Folpah approached the shop and taped from a standing position outside. After a few minutes he asked Bellman, who was accompanying him, if he thought he should go inside and tape some more. Bellman agreed, and Folpah sat on a bench in front of the bellows, placing the recording deck next to him. He taped for approximately five minutes and then asked the blacksmith whose machete he was making. The question was for the record since it was known by everyone in the shop (including Folpah and Bellman) that the machete belonged to Koboku,

Folpah's *ngala* (mother's brother). The blacksmith replied that the machete belonged to Kaboku and held it up for Folpah, who zoomed in on it. He then placed the half-finished object back into the bellows' fire. Folpah followed with a horizontal pan. He used the pan throughout the tape, keeping the machete in the center of his visual field. Whenever someone new entered the blacksmith's *gele* (kitchen) he used vertical pan up and horizontal over to the new center of activity. He never used a full zoom throughout the tape. Instead he always kept the object or person focused on at least within the immediate context of the work on the machete.

Folpah did not complete the tape that afternoon. Instead he followed Kaboku when he left the kitchen to attend a palaver in the clan chief's court. There he finished the tape on the deck and two-thirds of another.

The palaver concerned a confession over *kafu* medicine. A man from Yamii quarter had taken some rice from the *gele* of an elder in the quarter. The elder, after learning that some of his rice was missing, had Mulbahzua, Folpah's father, place a special medicine at the kitchen to catch (*zong*) the culprit. The next day the man confessed to Kaboku. They then called a hearing at the clan chief's court where he swore over the medicine that he had taken the rice.

Folpah arrived immediately after the swearing over the medicine. He was disappointed since he said he wanted very much to record the actual swearing over the *kafu*. However, he was able to record the events immediately following that portion of the palaver and stayed until the case was completed. This was one of three palaver tapes made by Folpah. We will discuss them shortly when we discuss the relation of format structure to orders of social reality or *meni*.

Briefly, the two other palavers concerned a fight that had taken place during the July 26th celebration, and a dispute over monies owed Mulbah Koplah, the Snake Society Zo, after he had cured a woman from a serious snake bite. Each of the three palaver tapes contained the same use of cademic markers but differed significantly in their order of appearance and placement. The last major tape Folpah made was a continuation of his machete tape. He decided that he wanted to tape the blacksmith making a different kind of machete. This tape was similar to the first in its use of panning and constricted use of zoom techniques.

JAMES MULBAH: THE TEACHER

The second person to learn the use of videotaping was James Mulbah. James had attended the Sucromu school as a young boy and then went on to Zorzor, where he eventually was awarded a high school diploma. He then returned to Sucromu to teach in the public school. As a person concerned with *kwii* matters James was eager to learn about the use of video recording. He had never seen television before, but did have some exposure to motion pictures both in high school and during his occasional visits to Monrovia, the capital city.

It is curious that, although he was the best educated of Bellman's informants, he had the most difficulty initially in learning to record. His first walkabout tape was out of focus and demonstrated his difficulty with centering the field. When he saw his tape during a viewing session he immediately asked to have another try. The next day he did his second walkabout. This tape was significantly different from the first. The first few shots did show some difficulty in holding the camera steady, but all takes were well centered and in focus. It was obvious that James thought about what he wanted to record before shooting. In the walkabout he went to the river bank outside of town to film the wives of his friend, Walawulu, washing clothes. In that segment he selected the important women and used pan to follow their actions. We will discuss this in greater detail shortly when we analyze the relationship of camera techniques to the events recorded.

The other significant portion of the tape was at its conclusion. He taped a short documentary on the well-baby clinic outside of town. He began this segment by walking up to the clinic, stopping, and narrating into the camera, saying: "This is the well-baby clinic of Sucromu, built by Cross Roaders in 1964."[15] He then turned the camera off and entered the building. He turned the camera on to record two midwives dispensing medicines in the lobby. He then turned the camera off and entered the clinic supervisor's room. The supervisor functions as the physician and organizer of clinic activities. He is a Loma man from a community approximately 15 miles from Sucromu, trained at the Curen mission hospital in Zorzor.

James entered the room and set down his equipment. The supervisor asked a young mother and her six-month-old baby to enter. The supervisor put the child on a scale. James shot the child sitting on the scale and zoomed in again, keeping the child directly in front of a sign showing the correct and incorrect way to feed an infant. The supervisor put a thermometer in the child's mouth, waited a few seconds, and took it out to read. He then gave the child back to the mother and pointed for her to sit down at his table. Next he took her blood pressure and temperature. Then, he sat across the table from the woman and asked her questions about the child's health. When the interview was nearly complete, James ran out of tape.

The significance of the last segment is in James' obvious planning and setting up of shots. He viewed this segment as a documentary feature as evidenced by his use of narration and construction of events for taping. Both James and Folpah, therefore, perceived the camera as a communicative device for nonmembers. They used it analogously to their role as informants for their community. Those segments of tape can be understood as similar to their verbal explanations

---

[15]The well-baby clinic was built in 1965 but did not begin operation until after 1970. It is run by the supervisor who is responsible to the mission hospital in Zorzor. The clinic provides health care advice and simple medicines such as vitamins and cold medications.

to a nonmember. This will be important for our discussion of the Sande dance ritual taped by James a few weeks after his second walkabout tape.

The Sande dance tape was the third tape James made. He specifically requested to tape the event early in the morning of July 26th. It is important to note that his tape contained many features observed in the two portions of his second walkabout, for example, the following of central action and personages and the use of informant narration.

THE NON-ENGLISH-SPEAKING INFORMANTS

The last three persons instructed differed from the first four in that they did not speak English and had no formal education. The first was Veselee, the drummer. Veselee had come from Gbansu, a sister town of Sucromu, in Guinea, several years before, and was living avunculocally in Yamii quarter.[16] As a drummer he belonged to several different *kuu* or cooperative work groups. His reputation was widespread through the clan and he was always in demand as a musician, especially for farm work. Veselee had been a friend of Bellman's since his first field work in Sucromu. At that time Bellman had joined several *kuu* to make a subsistence upland rice farm.[17] Veselee had been the drummer. Bellman especially wanted to teach Veselee since as a musician he manifested strong aesthetic abilities. He had accompanied Folpah during some of his taping, and was in attendance when James videotaped the Sande ritual.

His instruction differed from that of the previous informants in that he was taught by Folpah rather than Bellman and Logue. Bellman was in attendance during that session to answer any questions Folpah might have. Folpah instructed him without any trouble, and went with him on his first walkabout. That tape was made primarily in Yamii quarter and consisted mostly of women beating rice, girls braiding hair, and elders sitting about the compound.

Veselee's next taping session recorded the thatching of a *gele* (kitchen) on a friend's sugar cane farm. The cane remains in a *gele* until it is ready for squeez-

---

[16]Gbansu in Guinea is considered to be almost a sister town to Sucromu. They share many of the same quarters and thus many persons in both villages consider themselves to be of the same family. Often farm workers (*kuu* members) go to Gbansu to assist them in brushing the forest or cutting the trees. Gbansu is considered to be mother's brother to Sucromu.

[17]A farm *kuu* is a cooperative work society that is mostly, but not exclusively, quarter based. It is formed by men to brush the forest and later to cut the trees. The former kind of *kuu* has approximately 20 members. The *kuu* goes to each person's farm once. Thus, each member has 20 people to work on his farm for one day. The *kuu* members are divided into three categories. Promotion is a highly ritualized affair accompanied with much ceremony. The women also have *kuu* for planting the rice, weeding the fields, and harvesting. They also have three categories of members. It is curious to note that the Loma do not practice *kuu*. Thus, the next village from Sucromu, that is, Loma, has a different system for farm work.

ing. The juice is then stored in it for several weeks until appropriately fermented, after which it is distilled into cane juice or raw rum.

Veselee made three tapes of the thatching. The first showed most of the thatching process including conversations of the workers, close-ups of tying techniques, and the palm wine and cane juice break. The second tape was unsuccessful because Veselee, in his haste to record one of the workers cutting thatch from a tall palm tree, threaded the deck incorrectly. He positioned himself directly underneath the tree and taped on his back. The third tape showed additional scenes of the men working, the completion of the project, and the workers eating a large meal prepared by the wife of the farm's owner.

Around the last week of the project Folpah's father, Mulbahzua, one of the major Zo of the Poro society, asked if he could make a videotape. Both James and Folpah showed him how to operate the machine. He made one walkabout tape. The next day his brother, Mulbah Sumo Jakolii, who was the paramount chief of all Zo in the clan, decided that he also wanted to make a tape. He made two walkabout tapes in only one session. This was because in the middle of the first tape the Iron Society called Bellman to his house. Mulbah Sumo and Bellman went to see what they wanted. The society presented Bellman with a medicine to publicly announce his promotion in the secret society.[18] They then performed and danced with the medicine. One of Bellman's students danced to the music upon being prodded by several of the members. Folpah, who also was a member of the society, took the camera and taped most of the performance. When finished he gave the camera back to Mulbah Sumo who then continued his walkabout.

The informants who participated in the project and several of the people who were subjects of the tapes went to the Curren Hospital in Zorzor to view them on the weekends.[19] Although these sessions were audiotaped and in the final screening filmed with a Super 8 mm camera, talk was rare except for an occasional exclamation and laughter. An instance of this happened during the showing of Folpah's palm wine tapping tape. At the conclusion of the first segment, the audience roared with laughter when they observed at the descent of Labulah from the palm tree that he was a young boy. Most in attendance had thought that he was an old man. This is noteworthy since there were several shots of the young man climbing the tree and of his body while tapping. The audience assumed, however, that the tapper was an elder because he was Folpah's intentionally chosen subject. In the showing of the walkabout, most of the conversation

---

[18]In the societies, various persons are responsible for certain of the medicines. That task denotes that one is a part of the societal leadership. While in the field conducting the present study, Bellman was promoted and given a medicine. He joined the society during his first field study in 1967.

[19]Curren Hospital in Zorzor is both a hospital and school for nurses and supervisors of well-baby clinics. It is highly thought of by all villages in the area. Much of that is due to the excellent work of Dr. Paul Mertons and his staff.

concerned the correct identification of personages recorded. This also occurred during several segments of the Sande dance tape.

THE INTENTIONAL STRUCTURE OF CAMERA TECHNIQUES

The structure of the various walkabout tapes provides a cognitive mapping of Sucromu. The structure of those maps is not necessarily the same as the map emerging during a casual walkabout without the video equipment. The latter structure, nevertheless, is a constitutive property of the former. That is, the normal walking paths, houses approached, and personages greeted are relevant features to each videoist as he taped his community. Hence, in Folpahzoi's tape he first greeted the clan chief and then the town chief to demonstrate his introduction of the new technology. He then proceeded on a path showing each of the quarters in their relative order of importance from his perspective, that is, as an avunculocal resident of Yamii quarter from Zoman quarter in Sucronsu *taa*.

Not only does the event structure of the tape reflect cognitive mapping, but the individual shots are ordered by various cademic markers. This is exemplified by a segment of Folpahzoi's walkabout in which he presented *Banamii koli,* his patrilineage's avunculocal residence compound. The segment begins with a dolly into the area from the blacksmith shop. Several children surrounded him as he shot the front of his house. He cradled the camera in his arm, leaving it on "record," and in Kpelle loudly ordered the children from the front of five houses in the area. He then picked up the camera and proceeded to present his quarter. The following is a transcript of that segment:

Cademic Markers	Narrative
Horizontal short pans showing various people (mostly children) who were standing to the left of Folpahzoi to watch what he was doing.	(in Kpelle) I want you all to move from there. I am going to make a photograph of my houses and the houses of my fathers (*nangi*). If you want to act foolish you go inside of the houses. You there move over to the side. I want everybody to be quiet when I am making the photograph.
Fast horizontal movement, followed by a steady shot of a house.	
Shot of house.	(in English) This is my quarter. It is called Banamii quarter. That is my house.
Slow horizontal pan to the left, camera swoops low, raises and focuses on a next house.	That is the house of my brother. His name is Flumo Tokpah.
Slow horizontal pan to the left, camera stops and focuses on next house.	This is the house of my father Kokulah.

Cademic Markers	*Narrative*
Slow horizontal pan to left, camera stops and focuses on house.	And this is the house of my father Mulbahzua.
Fast horizontal pan to right, camera drops low moving across ground, swoops up in midst of pan, camera moves quickly across two houses and focuses on a house that was immediately to the right of the previous house focused on.	
Focus on house.	This is the house of my father's brother, the blacksmith Yakpazua.
Camera pans to right slightly and focuses on a man sitting in front of the house.	That is Yakpazua the blacksmith of Sucronsu. He is the head blacksmith of the town.
Camera pans horizontally to the left, moves quickly past a small thatch hut and focuses on a house next to it.	This is the house of my uncle Tokpahlongwolo. He is the uncle for all of us living here in Yamii quarter.
Camera pans left back to Folpah's house.	That is my quarter. I am very happy to be able to take pictures of the houses for my family.
Camera off, marking the end of segment.	

In the above segment Folpahzoi intentionally used camera techniques to show the houses of his quarter. It is significant that after showing Mulbahzua's house he panned back and all the way around in order to show a house that was immediately adjacent to it. This strongly suggests that the first continuous series of shots (his house, and that of his brother, his father Kokulah, and his father Mulbahzua) tied together members of the same group. According to Kpelle kinship the three men, Mulbahzua, Kokulah, and Yakpazua, are all *sabolo* or brothers to one another and hence *nangi* or fathers to Folpahzoi.[20] Mulbahzua and Kokulah, however, are closer to Folpahzoi than Yakpazua in their kinship tie, since they are twins. In many domains of social interaction they are considered to be the same individual. However, they formally maintain separate identities by speaking different languages. Since Sucromu is the last Kpelle town bordering Loma country all persons in the community are fluent in both Kpelle and Loma. Mulbahzua speaks only Kpelle, while his brother Kokulah talks only in Loma (even when Kpelle is spoken to him he replies in Loma).

Mulbahzua is Folpahzoi's biological father. Since Mulbahzua and Kokulah are twins, Folpahzoi treats the latter with much the same deference as the former.

---

[20]A short study on the Fala Kpelle kinship system is presented in Bellman (1975b).

When, therefore, Folpah differentiated between members in his living compound he used the technique of tilt embedded in horizontal pan. He employed this technique in other tapes also to segment events within an ongoing interaction. He turned the camera off and on only at the conclusion of an event or to change physical location within the same interactional setting. This cademic marker has the same function in all of the informant's tapes. We will discuss it again in the context of our analysis of the Sande dance ritual tape made by James Mulbah.

Horizontal pan was used as a following device by each informant early in his respective walkabout tapes. This is exemplified in James Mulbah's usage of very subtle horizontal left and right pans to follow central personages in a segment showing the wives of his friend, Walawulu, washing clothes at a stream outside of town. In the segment he focused primarily on two women, Lopu and Kepe, the head wife and second wife, respectively, of Walawulu. He began by making a horizontal right and left pan of the area, and then placed Kepe in the center of his visual field. He then moved the camera with a slight horizontal left pan to center on Lopu beating a lappa (cloth) against a rock. He then quickly returned to Kepe, and back to Lopu. After a few moments Lopu walked to the far left of the visual field. James followed her movement, keeping her in center field until she passed from the area behind some trees. He then used a right horizontal pan back to Kepe and focused on her washing for about 15 seconds. He then panned back (left horizontal) to the area where Lopu disappeared. She had not returned so he panned back to Kepe. He then immediately panned left again and caught Lopu as she returned to the setting. He followed her movement until she reached Kepe.

Throughout the above segment James never used zoom. This is not evidence of his lack of knowledge of that technique. In a second portion of that tape, he made extensive use of it to show his friend Wolobah drinking some palm wine that he had purchased earlier in the walkabout. In that segment, James zoomed in on the upper part of Wulubah and conversed with him in a joking manner. The dialogue was as follows:

Cademic Markers	*Narrative*
Off/on, middle zoom shot of Wolobah showing upper torso and head.	(in English) JAMES: Have some palm wine. WULUBAH: don't mind if I do. JAMES: Is it sweet? WULUBAH: It is very sweet. JAMES: Save some for me. WULUBAH: I will try.

Immediately after the above "skit" James turned the camera off, zoomed out, and called to Lopu asking if she wanted to have some wine. Lopu walked over to Wolobah, and James taped her receiving the wine and drinking from the zoom-out position.

Horizontal panning was used to follow action, whereas zoom posited particular acts of single individuals, except when zoom took the place of dolly. This happened in the Sande (women's society) dance tape to be discussed shortly. In that segment the videoist, James Mulbah, was unable to walk in close to the action since, as a male, he was forbidden to come too close to Sande medicines.

The women dancers approached some of the leaders of the Sande and the number one Zo of the Poro. James held his position and zoomed in (out of focus) to show the action. For most of that tape, James used either horizontal pans or turned the camera and changed physical location or position. When he used zoom it was never in the above cited instance, except full zoom, but rather highly restricted and at most only half.

Vertical panning had a different use. It was used to study a single individual in the course of an action without positing in any particular order the elements which composed it. This marker may be opposed to the use of close-in zoom to focus on the activities of an actor. A good example of the use of vertical pan occurred in Anna Juah's walkabout tape. In one segment, Anna recorded an elderly woman taking the rice kernels off stalks of rice with her feet. Anna focused on the woman's whole body, tilted the camera down so that the lower part of her body was in center field, and then tilted up to the first position. This can be contrasted to the use of zoom when the subject changed behavior in the course of an activity. In Folpahzoi's first palm wine tapping tape, as mentioned earlier, Folpah stood immediately under Labulah and taped from a single position. When Labulah cut into the tree Folpah zoomed in and held the close shot until the action was complete. He then zoomed out to the previous position. His use of zoom marked the action into significant components, whereas Anna's use of vertical pan studied an action in the course of its production without attention to any of its composing units. This comparison will become a topic in our later discussion of Folpahzoi's three palaver tapes. Briefly, Folpah used vertical pan in these tapes in the same manner as Anna, to refer to parts of an activity without any sense of the placement of the object or focusing on the event as it was produced. Folpah vertically panned a speaking subject without any explicit reference to the content of the speach. This is not to say that those pans were randomly produced. As we will discuss shortly, their appearance during the course of an interaction was structured by openings or slots in dialogues when wandering of a listener's attention was permissible. On the other hand, when correct listener responses were called for by a speaker in the course of a narrative the videoist used either fast direct horizontal pans or partial zooms.

The use of off/on segmented an event into constitutive meaningful elements or provided the opportunity for the videoist to change physical location. Both occurred at the conclusion of some set of activities and before the beginning of other acts. Turning the camera off and on, consequently, marks a tape into meaningful segments from the informant's perspective. For example, in a segment of a tape made by Anna Juah showing women working on a rice farm she recorded two women force feeding an infant some wet rice. Anna taped the feeding, and then turned the camera off when the infant's mother stopped to turn around and get a cup of water for the child to drink. She turned the camera on again as the mother was returning to the child and recorded him drinking while his mother and another woman held his head back. When the child finished Anna turned the camera off. She turned it on again when she was outside the rice kitchen and recorded several women weeding the farm. After taping for several minutes, she turned the camera off and walked to a new position much closer to the farm workers. She then turned the camera on and taped from that location. At no time did she walk with the camera (dolly) to a new location.

This technique of turning the camera off to switch positions is observable in many of the other informant tapes. We will discuss its operation again as we analyze the Sande dance ritual taped by James Mulbah. In that tape the various cademic markers we have described above operate and segment the ritual into constitutive and, from an informant's perspective, meaningful parts. In the appendix to this chapter is a transcript of that tape. The reader is asked to refer to it and then attend to the following discussion of its segments. In that presentation we will compare the markers that appear in it to tape recordings of other events belonging to different organizational *meni*. We will then discuss various of its segments and compare the markers that appear in it to tape recordings of other events belong to different organizational *meni*.

THE SANDE DANCE TAPE

The ritual presented below was performed by the Zo or priestesses of the Sande for the members of the Poro Zo or priesthood (see Fig. 6). Throughout Liberia, July 26 is celebrated with various traditional musical and dance performances, large feasts, drinking, and giving of gifts. Sucromu used this occasion to celebrate an additional event—the election of Mulbah Sumo Jakolii as the Paramount Chief of all Zo in the Vavala clan. As a result both the Sande and the Poro wanted to publicly celebrate the event. The members of the dancing devil society or *Ngamunea* (ngamu's wife's society) began preparations for their devil to appear. The members of the Sande dance society, however, began before the men could get together. As a result the dancing devil did not appear since both societies cannot perform at the same time.

The women began by dancing inside of the Sande fence near the center of Sucromu. After performing special rituals inside their medicine house, they began their procession and performance about the town. The first quarter they went to was the Balamii sector of Yamii koli, where the Poro priests reside who are living avunculocally with their mother's brothers in Yamii.

When the women arrived at the quarter, James Mulbah immediately went to Bellman's house in the other sector of Yamii to get the video deck and camera. He set up the equipment at Bellman's house and walked to his sector. On the way he asked one of his friends, Flumo Tokpah, to carry the tape deck while he operated the camera. At various times throughout the ritual James and Flumo commented on significant or interesting events that took place during the performance.

FIG. 6   The Sande dancers perform for the Zo of the Poro Society. This ritual was videotaped by James Mulbah, the schoolteacher. (Photo by H. Miller)

When James arrived on the scene with the recording equipment he went to the head woman Zo of the dance society and presented her with a dollar as *kola* or thanks for the performance.[21] He explained that he wanted to record the ritual and obtained the woman's permission. When she agreed, James set up his camera in front of the muscians and two major Sande dancers. Figure 7 shows the area of the performance and some of the positions that James took throughout the performance.

When the Sande dancers left the compound they went to the second sector of Yamii, *Kamu koli*. James continued to videotape for another ten minutes until the tape finally ran out. He then handed the VTR to Bellman and Logue and left for the public school where he was to referee a soccer match. The Sande women danced in the area for another ten minutes and then walked through the town in a formal procession. They stopped at the homes of various important personages in

[21]Kola nuts are given as tribute for exceptional performances. Often money is given in its place but such gifts are still referred to as a kola presentation.

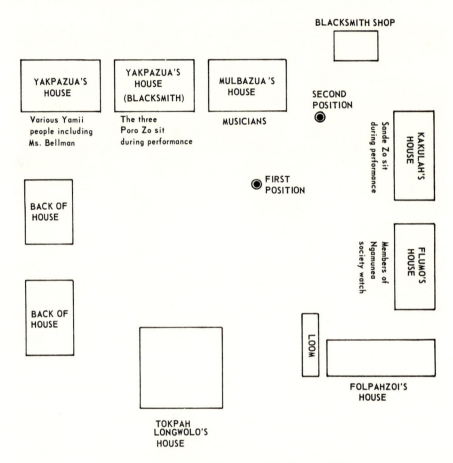

FIG. 7   Yamii Koli, site of the Sande dance ceremony.

the Sande society and to greet the town chief, clan chief, and the several quarter chiefs and headmen in the community.

The transcript lists many of the cademic markers we characterized briefly in the discussions about the walkabout tapes. Their appearances mark the ritual event into a variety of different segments. The recognizable segments are as follows:

1.   000 to 031.   The Sande dancers began their performance. The camera studied their movements, the special medicine belts around their waists, and various shots showing the interaction between the two main dancers and the first two dance elders.

2.   033–114.   The male Zo of the Poro society entered the compound area and took seats on a bench in front of one of the Zo's houses. The camera focused

on the first two Zo and followed their movement to their seats. The camera then panned back to look for the third Zo, Mulbah Sumo Jakolii. Seeing that he was not yet in the area, the camera panned slightly to the left and focused on the two main Sande dancers until he arrived. When the Zo entered, the Sande dancers moved in close to him in a crouched position. The camera followed the dancers with a full zoom. The women greeted Mulbah, and moved back. The camera zoomed out. The women continued their dance, with the camera showing the interaction between the dancers and the dance elders.

3. 114–130.   The dancers and elders danced to Bellman's wife and greeted her. The camera followed their movement to Marylyn Bellman and then back to the area of the musicians. Mulbah Sumo Jakolii's wife walked up to one of the dance elders with coins as tribute. She handed the money. Camera turned off.

4. 130–161.   The camera was placed in a new position and turned on. The camera studied the musicians, first focusing on the head musician and then panning to the right to show all. The camera then panned to the dancers and with a series of right and left horizontal pans showed the interaction between dance elders and dancers. The camera then zoomed in midway to study the dancers and continued to pan back and forth between them and the elders.

5. 161–222.   James turned the camera off and changed position. He stood directly behind the dancers and turned the camera on, focusing on their backs. The music slowed to a single beat and the dance elders came up one at a time to wipe the forehead of the dancers and the head musicians as tribute for their performance. Each dance elder wiped the forehead of a specific person.

6. 222–245.   James turned the camera off and changed position by moving over to the side of his previous location. Mulbah Sumo Jakolii danced with the Sande elders. James zoomed in and out and then used small pans as follow shots to cover Mulbah's movement. James and his assistant announced into the camera what was occurring. When the music stopped, Mulbah walked over to the bench where his two brothers and the other Zo of the Poro, were sitting. The camera followed his movement.

7. 245–262.   James turned the camera off and changed position to the immediate side of the musicians. He studied the musicians for a brief period until an elder woman from the quarter walked in front of him with two little girls. The girls were her granddaughters who had recently arrived from the capital. They would join the Sande during the next initiation period and eventually become Zo in the hierarchy. This was their first formal introduction to the society.

8. 262–290.   After the woman and her granddaughters left the area, various elder women from the quarter danced before the musicians. The camera studied certain of the women as they performed and left the area of dancing.

9. 290–355.   James turned the camera off and changed position to in front of the musicians. When he turned the deck on again Mulbah Sumo was again performing with some of the Zo women. The camera followed their movements with pans and mid-zooms in and out. After a few moments James announced into

the camera what was taking place. His assistant made a similar statement after James finished. The camera stayed on the action for several moments and then panned over to the nonperforming Zo women sitting on benches to the right of the camera, and then back to the dancers. The music stopped and Mulbah walked over to his bench, while the camera followed his movement with a follow horizontal pan. The camera then panned back to the dancers and elders interacting, and panned to the elders on the right of the musicians keeping the main dancers still in view.

10. 335–359.   James turned the camera off, zoomed in to a middle position, centered the field on the musicians, and turned the camera back on. He shot the musicians full front, panned to the first musician, and then panned the line. He then zoomed out and panned to the left to the dancers. He followed the dancers, keeping the musicians in the back of the field.

11. 359–368.   Camera panned to the right where the Zo women were sitting. James focused on the two little girls who were introduced to the Sande earlier by their grandmother. He zoomed in middle length to study them, and then panned back to the dancers. When the camera was on them he zoomed all the way back out.

12. 368–396.   The segment began with a shot of dancers in front of musicians. Suddenly an elder woman jumped in front of the musicians and danced in a kind of possessed rhythm. The camera stayed on her for several moments. As he was taping, James laughed at what was occurring. After a few more moments, the two main dancers performed in front of the camera and moved to the left of the area. James followed them, with a left horizontal pan. The dancers instructed the musicians to stop playing. They stopped and the woman came out of her trance. The camera panned over to her and then immediately back to the dancers. The dancers continued to move to the left of the area. The camera followed their movements. They came before another elder from the quarter who gave them coins as tribute. The dancers and elders (including the possessed woman) came before the elder. When they had finished, the dancers and elders moved back to the area in front of the musicians. The camera followed their movement.

13. 396–415.   Shot of the two main dancers interacting with the dance elders. The elders separated them from the Zo members of the Sande who were sitting on the right of the camera. The camera panned back and forth between the dancers and the Zo women.

14. 415–436.   The camera made a long right horizontal pan all the way around to record the male members of the *ngamunea* or men's dancing society who were at the far end of the performance area. The men greeted one another. James then panned, following the same line of movement as he used to get to that position, back to the main Sande dancers. The camera stayed on the dancers and elders for a few seconds and then panned to the three Poro Zo sitting on the bench to the left of the performance. The camera then panned back to the dancers.

15.   436–451.   James panned to his left to record Bellman taking his photograph. As soon as Bellman finished, James panned back to the dancers.

16.   451–453.   The dancers moved up to James in a crouched position. He tilted the camera down in a vertical movement. The women asked him for a kola tribute. He told them that he would give it to them later after he finished taping. The women then moved away from him. He followed their movement with an upward (vertical) pan.

17.   453–478.   Horizontal pans between elders and main Sande dancers performing in front of the musicians. Mulbahzua, the first Poro Zo to come into the area, got up and went into his house. His wife came out and handed the Sande dancers a coin tribute.

18.   478–487.   Shot of elders and dancers. The assistant cameraman announced that they were about to move to a new area. An elder came in front of the camera. The tape broke.

Each of these eighteen segments is marked by changes in cademic markers. Within each of the segments, there are also events locatable through the different uses of cademic markers. Each of those segments or subevents permits an analysis of the larger event sequence. The fact that James was recording with the idealized notion of what comes next in mind is exemplified particularly in segment 11 in which the elder woman introduced her granddaughters to the members of the Sande society. The segment began with James having turned the camera off while he changed positions to a location directly behind the area where the elder woman would make her appearance. He then taped a few seconds of the musicians until the woman appeared. Next he recorded her introduction, and after it was finished, zoomed out and panned to the dancers, which initiated a new segment. Then James "knew" that the interaction was about to occur when he moved next to the musicians. The new location provided a vantage point from which he could record close up without having to move into the area of the dancers. The latter would have been an impossibility for any man except Mulbah Sumo Jakolii since to approach too close to the medicines worn by the Zo dancers could result in a man's contracting elephantiasis of the scrotum.

The use of cademic markers during the course of a segment was also structured by the cameraman's situated formulation about what was going on. This can be seen in segment 12 in which an elder woman from Yamii quarter intruded into the ritual, danced before the musicians in a trance-like position, was brought out of her trance state, given kola tribute by another elder from the compound, and directed from the performance area by the dance elders. What is particularly significant about that segment is James' choice of what to shoot, when to pan, and who to focus on during the interaction.

The segment began after the main Sande dancers had formally completed a series of dances that had opened up the ritual to quarter-specific activities. The latter started with the celebration of Mulbah Sumo Jakolii's becoming the paramount chief of all Zo in the Vavala clan. Shortly after his performance, the elder women introduced her granddaughters to the Sande. Then, a number of elder women from the quarter performed before the dancers. The "possessed woman" first performed shortly after the granddaughter-introduction segment. She danced in a trance-like fashion for a brief period, and stopped when the musicians ceased playing. A short while later another elder woman started to perform before the dancers and the woman in question jumped in front of her and began her trance-like dance once again. The first woman held out her arms and then stood back to watch her perform. The two other women in the Sande then came up to her and wiped her forehead as tribute to her performance. The wiping of foreheads is similar to applause. The first woman wiped the old woman's head and then the head of the musician signifying the intensity of both of their mutual performances. Then, the wife of Mulbah Sumo Jakolii came up and wiped the woman's head and then her own with a scarf. This signified that she thanked her in the role of the personage for whom the ritual was being performed. At that the segment should have finished. The two Sande dancers moved in front of the camera and James followed their movements (as the central phenomenon) away from the old woman and the musicians. The old woman did not respond to her cue to finish so the first dancer instructed the musicians to stop playing. The musicians, seemingly enjoying the woman's trance-like dance to their music, did not attend to the dancer's instructions. Then one of the Zo elders walked up to the musicians and signaled for them to stop. James panned to shoot her instructions. As soon as the musicians finished playing, James panned back to the two main dancers. The dancers then moved to the far left to the area to accept tribute from another elder from the quarter. The dance elders moved behind them. James followed the dancers with slight left horizontal pans. He kept both of them in central field while including the elder woman and later the dance elders when they arrived at the spot where the elder woman was standing. When they all reached the elder, James stopped panning and focused on the action with a long shot. He maintained that shot throughout the elder's giving of tribute. When she finished, the dancers and dance elders moved to the right of the field and instructed the previously possessed old woman to move away from the area. The camera followed the dancers and elders with a slow right horizontal follow shot. The elders pointed back to the previously possessed woman to leave the area. James kept the camera focused on the dance elders until the old woman was well out of the area. He then turned the camera off and changed positions to begin a new segment.

James' use of the camera kept the important personages always in focus, even though other activities (i.e., the possessed woman's extended dance, her refusal to stop, and her reluctance to leave the performance area after receiving tribute) surrounded him. This is not to say that those "other activities" were not of interest to him. As seen by his laughter during the possessed's dance he was interested, but used his camera to follow the participants according to their importance in the event and their relative status (speaking prerogative) positions. Hence, the dancers were able to direct the camera away from the possessed woman and musicians even though the latter were the central problem of the event. James kept the camera on the dancers until a dance elder (with a higher speaking or status prerogative) walked up to the musicians and ordered them to stop. It is significant that the musicians did not respond to the orders of the dancers, but rather stopped only after being instructed to do so by an elder. The relative positions of the various personages to each other are observable not only by the order of whom James followed with his camera, but also in the giving of tribute ritual by the other elders of Yamii quarter. In that episode the proxemic arrangement of actors and the order of passing of kola among the women communicated the status or speaking prerogative structure relevant in that setting.

The elder woman gave her kola tribute to the members of the dance society. Before giving the money, the members of the society arranged themselves about the elder in a specific manner. That arrangement of arms and elbows, depth of crouch, distance between persons, and the like reflected the relative status of the persons in the setting, in the same way as the physical arrangement of persons inside a medicine hut reflected the structure of a secret society.

When the two dancers crouched before the elder giving tribute, the previously possessed woman hurriedly ran in between the dance elders and took a position next to them (the first position). The dance elders moved in in a half-standing posture before the dancers. Then the head dance elder (elder number two) moved up to the group. The latter elder then tapped the head of the previously possessed woman, signifying for her to turn in the appropriate direction (she had been facing the elder giving tribute). The elder then reached into her lappa and took out some coins. Dance elder number two immediately reached out her hand and placed it between the elder's hand with the coins inside and the previously possessed woman. She then guided the elder's hand to the first of the two dancers. This choice was not a random one. Each of the dance elders had a special relationship either to one of the dancers or to the musicians. This is evidenced in the segment of the ritual (segment 5) in which two of the dance elders each wiped the heads of a different dancer, and a third elder wiped the head of the main or head musician. When, in the giving of tribute episode, the second dance elder guided the hand of the elder woman from Yamii quarter, she directed the tribute to the hand of the dancer's whose head she had wiped in segment 5. That dancer in turn gave the money to the second dancer and the group began to rise. The previously possessed woman then moved up to the dancer with her hand outstretched. The dancer made a move away from her, back-stepped, and handed her the money. This signified that the old woman was accepted in the interaction as one of the "dancers," but was then immediately told that she could no longer participate. Hence, the members of the Sande dance society recognized the woman's demand to be recognized as a Sande main dancer. She made this demand observable by assuming a low crouched position next to the two main dancers between the tribute-giving elder and the other dance elders. After giving the woman her recognition the members terminated her participation in the ritual and directed her from the dance area.

The order of persons involved in the tribute-giving episode reflected the order of persons that James Mulbah followed with his camera. That is, first James recorded the dancers and musicians, then the old woman intruding into another elder's dance. He focused on her performance until the two main dancers, who held a greater status (speaking) prerogative in Sande dance ritual *meni* (order of social reality) than the old woman, passed before the camera. James followed their movements and kept the camera on them while they ordered the musicians to stop playing. When a dance elder finally had to intrude and order the musicians to stop, James panned (right horizontal) over to her. Her position in the Sande dance *meni* was higher than that of the main dancers since she had been a dancer years earlier and now was a major Zo and dance instructor in the society. When she finished giving her instructions James returned (left horizontal pan) to the dancers and followed them to the Yamii elder woman who was giving tribute. Hence, the structure of the interactional relationship between dancers and Sande members from Yamii quarter (and among dancers and dance elders) was reflected both in James' choice of whom to record and follow with his camera, and in the tribute-giving episode. That is, the cademic structure (format of the tape) reveals in a large part the intentional structure of the interactional occasion or content of the tape.

ORDERS OF REALITY AND FORMAT STRUCTURE

Thus far we have shown how the appearance of cademic markers permits an analysis of an event sequence. The argument to follow will demonstrate how the use of camera techniques and when they occur are affected by the particular order of reality or *meni* that provides the organizational grounding for the recorded events. This is evidenced in the format structure of three different palaver tapes made by Folpahzoi. Since each palaver belonged to a separate *meni,* Folpah's position (or speaking prerogative) in each recorded event differed, as did his particular project in making the tape.

The first palaver occurred in the afternoon while Folpah was making the tape of the blacksmith from Sucronsu moiety making a bush machete. After he had taped some 15 minutes, the client left the blacksmith's kitchen. Folpah continued to record for another few moments and then asked Bellman if he wanted to go to hear the palaver at the clan chief's court, where the blacksmith's client had just gone.

On the way to the court-kitchen (palaver hut) Folpah told Bellman what he knew about the case. Two evenings before, a man from Gbanya quarter had walked about town shouting loudly that someone had stolen some rice from his rice *gele* (kitchen). The next morning he went to Folpah's father, Mulbahzua, for a special medicine.[22] After it was prepared, a man from Yamii quarter confessed to stealing the rice to Kaboku, the quarter chief (and the man who had ordered the machete). Folpah said that the matter being heard before the clan chief was the man's confession before the medicine and his payment in money for the "wrong" he committed.

By the time Folpah arrived at the clan chief's palaver hut and set up the video equipment, the accused had finished making his statement before the medicine. The court was very crowded, but the central talk was recorded on tape. The first several minutes of the taped palaver took place inside the hut. Then, everyone went outside to distribute a $15 fine that the accused had been required to pay. After about 10 minutes of recording various conversations outside the palaver hut and showing the distribution of the money, it began to rain. Everyone then either left for their own homes or went inside the palaver hut to wait for it to finish. Folpah recorded inside for another five minutes until the tape on the recording deck was finished.

Although the tape made outside the hut shows various arrangements of people around the clan chief, most of the talk is indecipherable since many people were speaking loudly at the same time. Folpah had to maneuver himself into position but was often blocked by people attending the meeting. Several had come from the neighboring town of Gbangway because the accused was living avunculo-cally in Sucromu and his actual patrilocal compound was in that town. Hence, Folpah had to wait for various people to move in order to obtain the shots he desired. He did not have the status prerogative within that *meni* to always position himself in the location best for recording what he wanted to take. As a result the tape is very uneven containing segments of varying lengths interrupted by persons coming in front of the camera or moving away from it.

The tape made inside the palaver hut also reflects Folpah's position within the *meni*. Folpah fluctuated between following the conversations and central action of the confession sequence and doing a study of the medicine and various person-ages in attendance without direct relation to the content of the ongoing dialogue.

In the segment presented in the Appendix Folpah did follow the dialogue at significant junctures in the event, but spent most of his time taping the medicine sitting on the floor with various people who were not speakers, on the right side of the palaver hut. This structure can be contrasted to Folpah's videotape of a palaver in which his fathers, Mulbahzua and Mulbah Sumo Jakolii, heard a case as part of Poro business or *meni*. Folpah was the number five member of the Poro

---

[22]Medicines are set to catch persons who steal. If the thief does not confess, he will die. In the palaver considered here, the man who confessed recognized this and confessed even though he felt justified in taking the rice.

and sat next to his fathers in front of the Zo's house. In the tape Folpah attended more to the content of the interactions, but in one segment he did pan the area showing the various persons in attendance.

The palaver occurred early in the morning. It concerned three men who had gotten into a fist fight during the July 26 celebrations. Since fighting is a violation of the laws of the Poro medicine (i.e., only the *ngamu* or devil can permit fighting) the matter was heard before members of the sacred ruling structure, that is, the Poro priesthood. In the Appendix to this chapter is a transcript of a portion of that palaver.

In this tape, Folpah followed the course of action much more closely than in the previous palaver. At various points he panned over to individuals who were being discussed by the witness, and on different occasions panned to specific personages to obtain their responses to what was just said. This is particularly evident when Mulbah Sumo Jakolii intruded into the dyadic interchange between the first witness and one of the accused. Mulbah introduced a parable: "the devil cannot chase the owl" which ended the interaction, viz., the accused asking questions of the witness. The witness immediately entered into a joking sequence which terminated in his leaving the witness area and taking a seat next to the schoolmaster, James Flumo.[23] When Mulbah Sumo Jakolii intruded, the camera was on the witness. Folpah immediately panned to Mulbah Sumo and then back to the witness. It should be noted that when Mulbah contributed his parable he communicated that the two interactants would not be able to resolve their dispute. The devil or *ngamu* of the Poro society is said to be virtually powerless against *wulu nuu* (literally, stick people) who are the dream spirits of living persons that commit spirit (or soul) assassination on their victims. Such is the reason for the *Mina* or "horn" secret society which has medicines to catch (*zong*) such individuals. Owls are known to be directly associated with these kinds of spirits, and are present whenever they are active in the community.

When Mulbah Sumo introduced the parable he assumed the speaking position to be taken by the accused. The witness, then, had the next floor privilege or right to respond. In doing so he ended the interchange.

Another instance of Folpahzoi's direct following with his camera of the course of action was his directing the camera to the Zo in front of Kokulah's house after the first witness swore that he was not lying before the medicine. The group laughed at the act, and Folpah panned immediately to pick up their response. The witness, in turn, responded to their laughter by repeating his oath.[24] Note in the transcript that during instances of side comments off-camera (Folpah did not direct the camera to the side activity) the speaker did not directly respond to

---

[23] James Flumo is the principal of the Sucromu village school. Although his education is limited, he is the first teacher in Sucromu from the town itself. As a result, he is considered the major person responsible for *kwii* matters in the community. He was, consequently, responsible for the supervisor of the clinic who was one of the defendants in the palaver.

[24] The witness thereby regained the floor and reasserted his centrality in the interaction.

them. This suggests that Folpah discriminated between relevant and tangential side comments concomitant with the speaker's decision about them as they occurred.

However, Folpah's tape was not always a direct following of the conversational activity. When he began his tape, he first studied the witness and then the medicine he was standing over. Then, while the witness was in the midst of his account, Folpah panned over the area to study all persons who were attending the palaver. That pan is particularly significant. He began by panning the Zo who were adjudicating the matter, then moved to the various Zo in attendance sitting in front of Kokulah's house. He next moved the camera to show the town chief, the quarter chief, and two of the disputants. Then he panned to a group on the other side of the area which consisted of various young men from the community who were friends with certain of the three defendants. He then panned to an elder walking into the area. He lifted his camera slightly to get a full shot of him, and then panned to a group of men sitting immediately to the right of the adjudicating Zo. He focused for a long pause on James Flumo, the schoolmaster, who was with that group. Since one of the accused was a Loma man from another community, he had to have someone in town who was responsible for him. Such a person is known as the *namu weia* or "owner of the stranger" (also called "stranger father"). The accused was living in Sucromu as a medical dresser (first-aid technician) and supervisor of the "well-baby clinic." Because of his familiarity with European matters, James Flumo, as the schoolmaster, acted as his stranger father.[25]

After holding the camera on James Flumo for a short pause, Folpahzoi tilted the camera down and panned across the ground back to the witness. This pan contained the same combination of down tilt, fast pan, and tilt up as did the last pan in Folpah's walkabout tape of his patrilocal quarter. In both instances he used the same cademe tilt down, fast horizontal pan, and tilt up to segment a display into constitutive units. When Folpah used the pan/tilt cademic marker in the second palaver tape, he differentiated two separate scenes: the pan of those listening to the matter and the matter itself. Folpah's attention to the matter being discussed and his use of camera technique to follow the course of action was a property of his speaking rights within the *meni* that provided the basis of the interaction.

In the last palaver Folpah taped, he recorded a dispute while at the same time acting as its principle adjudicator. Folpah had been recording a second tape on the Sucronsu blacksmith making a machete. After making half a tape, he left the blacksmith's *gele* to return the equipment to Bellman's house. On the way, his good friend Gbanya, from the neighboring town of Kpaiyea, asked him to hear a

---

[25]The supervisor or dresser (first-aid worker) was from a Loma community about 10 miles from Sucromu. He had about four years of schooling and was trained in Curen Hospital for his position in Sucromu.

palaver between his apprentice tailor and the Zo of the Snake Society. Folpah agreed and immediately followed Gbanya into a cane-juice bar near the center of town. The disputants were there waiting for him. Folpah sat down and announced that he wanted to take a picture of the proceedings.

In this case Folpahzoi was directly involved both with its recording and adjudication. However, his position within the *meni* was more than simply its adjudicator. To understand the outcome of the case, the intentional meanings of the dialogue, Folpah's attention with the camera to details of conversation, and his studies of individuals in the room, an explication of that *meni*'s structure is necessary.

At first glance, the palaver appears to be a relatively mundane argument regarding payments of money to a Zo for a cure. The debate was whether the Snake Zo had to wait for his money or be paid immediately. Mulbah Sumo argued that his lover, the person who was cured by the Zo, should be present when he paid for her treatment. Mulbah Kolpah, on the other hand, wanted his money immediately. The palaver, actually, was much more complicated to understand at first when the relationships of the central participants to each other are considered.

Mulbah Sumo and Gbanya are brothers. Gbanya lives in the neighboring town of Kpaiyea in avunculocal residence with his mother's brothers. Mulbah Sumo lives with his father, the town chief of Sucromu, in Gbanya quarter. Mulbah is an apprentice tailor under Folpahzoi and spends almost every day working around Folpah's house assisting in various jobs.[26] Folpahzoi is *maling* or sister's son to Mulbah Kolpah, the Zo. Since Folpah is a Poro Zo, he is living avunculocally in Yamii quarter under the authority of his mother's brothers. Mulbah Koplah is an elder of *Yamii* and is the leader of the Snake Society, which is located in that compound. Thus, Folpah must on various occasions act with deference to Mulbah as his mother's brother and is officially under his authority. Finally, Folpah and Gbanya are very close friends. Gbanya acts as Folpah's "stranger father" or *namu weia* (owner of the stranger) when he visits Kpaiyea. This is especially important because Folpah recently paid dowry for his fifth wife from the compound where Gbanya lives in avunculocal residence. Because he took a wife from that quarter he is expected to watch out for the interests of its members. The other persons attending the palaver were elders of Yamii quarter and, consequently, mother's brothers (*ngala*) to Folpah and brothers (*sabolo*) to Mulbah. In addition to those present the woman in question, Mulbah Sumo's girlfriend, was a resident of Zoman quarter. She was, consequently, an extended sister (*sabolo*) to Folpahzoi. As a result he also had her interests and those of her family to consider while making his judgment.

---

[26]The concept of apprenticeship extends from the relationship between a Zo and his students to the learning of *kwii* trades. Mulbah Sumo was learning how to become a tailor from Folpahzoi. He was consequently under his authority in the most mundane matters of daily life.

At one level, the palaver was not about Mulbah Sumo's refusal to pay Mulbah Kolpah. Rather, Mulbah Sumo wanted his girlfriend's parents to be aware that he was giving the 60¢ to Mulbah Kolpah on her behalf. Such an act would then be taken as a kind of marriage or dowry payment. If, in the future, Mulbah and the woman should break off their relationship, he could demand to be repaid. By raising the matter as a formal palaver Mulbah Sumo assured that his payment was accepted in that way. Note that Mulbah was willing to pay the Snake Zo a chicken (worth approximately $1.50) as "cold water" until the woman returned from the hospital in Kpaiyea.[27] The palaver was, consequently, a public performance to formalize a dowry relationship. The result was that Mulbah Sumo paid his debt to the Snake Zo, but in the presence of the girl's family.

Folpah's recording of the matter followed the various conversational interactions much more closely than in the previously described palavers. He maintained camera contact on either the speaker or person referred to in a narrative. He would often turn the camera to catch a response of a listener and then pan back to the speaker. Only at one point did he roam with the camera to do a study of others in the room and the bar itself. This occurred from 962 to about 970 on the tape. In that segment, Flumo had just finished speaking and the camera was panning back to Gbanya, who took the floor next. When Gbanya recited a parable to Mulbah Sumo, Folpah continued his pan and focused on the owner of the bar. He then lifted the camera to show the bottles of rum on the shelf and writing above the door to the back room, and then tilted the camera back down to both Mulbah Sumo and Gbanya. After that segment Folpah took the floor and thereafter was active in his role as adjudicator.

The use of parable in the conversation operated as a similar device to Mulbah Sumo Jakolii's use of parable in the previous case we presented. They both terminated their respective interactions and called for interpretations. In the first case, Mulbah Sumo Jakolii intruded into a dyadic interchange and established a new order of floor privileges. The witness no longer had to address himself to the accused, but instead ended the interaction by engaging in a joking dialogue with the adjudicating Zo. In the Snake Zo case Gbanya assumed a normal floor privilege by asking Mulbah Sumo "I want to ask you." Mulbah Sumo answered with "ask me." Gbanya then presented the parable "Did you put a rock in the mud to hit Folpah with it?" According to normal speaker turn-taking rules, the person who is asked a question usually has the floor immediately following the asker. The asker has the next response prerogative. This has been expressed by Sacks and others as having an ABA structure (cf. Sacks *et al.*, 1974; Schegloff, 1968).[28] In the palaver example, the interchange between Mulbah Sumo and

---

[27]The presentation of "cold water" is given after palavers to smooth over any bad feelings. It is normally a bottle of cane juice but in some cases may be a gourd of palm wine.

[28]Sacks et al. (1976) describe speaking rights in conversation as having an ABA structure. That is, after a speaker is responded to, he has the right to the floor in response. In cases of simultaneous talk, the first speaker will be able to maintain the floor as a consequence of this rule.

Gbanya began with this structure but changed as soon as Gbanya presented the parable. At that point various of those in the room presented similar parables establishing their membership as adjudicators. Immediately after Mulbah finished, Tokpah, Mulbah Koplah's older brother, presented a second parable, "You want to fix the matter just to please one person?" Mulbah Koplah responded with an "agreeing" laughter. Tokpah then followed with another parable, "You don't know what is in the next person's mind. If you knew, you could judge the palaver." Mulbah Sumo finally took the floor by responding "He is doing it." Gbanya intruded by asking Folpah to end the matter. Folpah presented the correct listener response, "uh." Gbanya then continued by asking Mulbah Sumo "I want to tell you a different thing." Mulbah Sumo refused by responding "I don't want to hear anything else. . . ." The presentation of parables continued for several more moments until Folpah finally (007) asked for Mulbah Sumo's girlfriend's parents to come.

When the parable episode began Folpah used the opportunity to pan to the owner of the bar and study the room. When the parable interchange finally assumed normal speaking order sequence, Folpah once again used the camera to follow the flow of conversation. When Gbanya first presented his parable, he shifted the palaver to an ending sequence of talk. This is not unusual in Kpelle palavers. Often when witnesses are finished, the adjudicators of a dispute engage in parable talk until the matter is resolved. We assert, therefore, that when Folpah panned to the owner of the bar he recognized this juncture in the palaver hearing. The use of left horizontal pan, followed by a vertical up pan (to study the room) marked this point.

SOME CONCLUDING REMARKS

In the above discussion we have given only brief attention to Kpelle palaver structure and the multitude of phenomena that comprise it. The purpose of this chapter was rather to demonstrate the relationship of the camerapersons' attention as witnessed by his use of cademic markers to the content of each videotape, and second, to show how the format structure of a tape is both reflexive to and affected by the particular *meni* or order of reality involved. The structure of cademic markers permits us an entry into a member's intentional perception of that interaction. Obviously, the palavers, rituals, and events occurring on the tapes require much more detailed attention.

APPENDIX: KPELLE VIDEOTAPES

This appendix contains transcripts of the following segments analyzed in Chapter 4:

1. The Sande Dance Tape.
2. The Rice Stealing Palaver.
3. The July 26th Fighting Palaver.
4. The Snake Zo Palaver.

1. The Sande Dance Tape

Cademic Markers	Event	Narrative (Cameraman and Assistants)
000 Camera close to subjects. Medium shot.	Two major dancers facing one another while dancing. Dance includes several turns, and low waist movements.	
004 Mid zoom in.	Elder of dance society moves close to the two dancers. Hereafter this elder will be referred to as dance elder #1.	
007 Vertical pan, camera dips low.	Focus on the *tuang* or special medicine belt worn on one of the dancers.	
011 Zoom out, camera lifts.	Two dancers in center field.	*Discussion in Kpelle between James* (A) *and assistant* (B): B: Can you see it? A: I see it. B: You see it. A: I see it. B: Is it in the camera? A: Uh huh, it is in the camera.
019 Camera zooms in short, then very quickly back out (full).	Dancers turning about while performing.	
023 Camera pans right following dancers' movements.	Two dancers in center field.	
024 Camera picks up elder #2. Holds position for 4 sec.	Dance elder #2 in field. Dance elder moves arms with music, standing to the side of the dancers.	
025 Quick horizontal pan to the left.	Two dancers in center field, dance elder #2 off field.	

Cademic Markers	*Event*	*Narrative*
Camera stays in this position for about 10 sec.		
028 Right horizontal pan.	Dance elder #3 standing in front of musicians.	
031 Left horizontal pan.	Two dancers and dance elder #1 in center field.	
033 Camera in full out position.	The two dancers perform. In background Mulbahzua, the #2 Zo of Poro society, enters and walks past the Sande Zo elders sitting in front of Kokula's house.	*Discussion in Kpelle:* B: You see him? A: Yes.
035 Camera lifts slightly, follows Mulbah's walk.	Dancers performing with Mulbah entering in background.	*in English:* B: That is Mr. Mulbah. A: My father Zua. B: The other one coming.
038 Right horizontal pan.	Camera picks up Kokulah entering visual field.	
Camera follows with left horizontal pan.	Camera follows Kokulah to benches in front of Yakpazua's house.	
042 Camera quickly makes a right horizontal pan.	Dancers slightly off center (looking for third Zo).	
043 Slight left horizontal pan.	Dancers in center field. Dance with slow steps and turnabouts.	*in English:* B: Very nice!
052 Camera in full out position.	Music slows to single beat. Dancers rise up slightly.	
	Music begins again, dancers lower bodies and start dancing.	*in English:* A: Now you have a look at it.
053 Off/on to close up (zoom in while camera off).	Two dancers moving with arms extended.	
055 Camera zooms back to full position.	Dancers move forward crouched toward area of Sande Zo. Sande dance elders #1 and #2 on each side of them. All move forward in low crouch (dancers lower than elders), Mulbah Sumo, the third Zo, enters field.	
063 Full in zoom, shot out of focus.	Dancers and dance elders crouched low before Mulbah Sumo and women Zo.	
064 Zoom back.	Mulbah Sumo in focus before women Zo. He walks past them.	

Cademic Markers	*Event*	*Narrative*
065 Camera pans right, drops down to ground raises.	Dancers walking with Mulbah Sumo Jakolii. He greets the Sande Zo.	
068 Camera follows dancers.	Two dancers with Mulbah in background.	
075 Camera in full back position.	Two dancers surrounded by dance elders #1 and #2. Music slows to single beat, dancers raise. Dancers look to #2 elder, music begins.	
080 Camera lowers (dips) in vertical downward pan.	Lower back of one of the dancers.	
082 Right horizontal upward pan.	Other dancer in center field.	
083 Left horizontal pan.	Camera back to first dancer, music slows to single beat.	
090 Right horizontal pan (slight movement).	Both dancers in center field. Dance elders #1 and #2 move to the sides of the dancers.	Talk not decipherable between A and B.
100 Short dolly (a few small steps toward dancers). Stop and shoot.	Both dancers perform in center field.	
110 Camera in full out position.	The dancers and three dance elders line up facing the Sande Zo.	*talk in Kpelle:* A: I want to get it clear.
112 Camera in full position.	Dance elder #4 points downward to legs of other dancers standing in line.	
114 Camera follows with left horizontal pan.	Group moves over to area where Bellman's wife was sitting with group of Kpelle friends.	*in Kpelle:* A: They want some cents given to them.
120 Right horizontal pan.	Camera follows dance elder #2 as she walks toward the musicians. Yangaw, Mulbah Sumo's head wife, enters into field.	
123 Left horizontal pan following Yangaw.	Yangaw walks to dance elder #2 who is now joined by the two dancers. She reaches out her hand giving them *kola* (some coins).	
130 Off/on. New location in front of musicians.	Shot of musicians playing. Small girl with bleach bottle *sawsaw* (shaker musical instrument) walks past line of musicians.	

Cademic Markers	*Event*	*Narrative*
135 Left horizontal pan, stop, left horizontal pan.	Camera pans to dance elder #2 then to dancers.	
141 Right horizontal pan, left horizontal pan, right horizontal pan, left horizontal pan, left horizontal pan, right horizontal pan, left horizontal pan.	Pan to fourth dance elder, pan back to the first dancer, back to elder, back to dancer, pan to second dancer, and then back to first dancer.	
153 Short zoom in.	Focus on first dancer.	
158 Mid zoom in.	Close-up of both dancers.	
159 Camera tilts up slightly.	Second dance elder walks in between camera and dancers.	
Left horizontal pan.	Dancers in center field.	
Right horizontal pan.	Pan to second dance elder.	
Left horizontal pan.	Pan back to dancers.	
161 Off/on. Camera in full out position.	Focus on back of both dancers, music slows to single beat.	
167 Small left horizontal pan.	Second dance elder wipes forehead of first dancer.	(talk not decipherable)
178 Right horizontal pan.	Both dancers in center field.	
Camera in full out position.	First dance elder wipes forehead of second dancer. Third dance elder moves up quickly to the first musician and wipes her forehead.	
188 Right horizontal pan, slow movement.	Camera follows first dancer to right.	
190 Left horizontal pan slight movement.	Both dancers in field.	
202 Right horizontal pan (long pan).	Pan to first dance elder stand to side.	
204 Left horizontal pan, camera holds position (full).	Pan back to dancers. The first dancer moves slightly before the other. Second dancer seems to be taking her movement cues from her.	

Cademic Markers	Event	Narrative
222 Off/on, to mid zoom in, new position taken slightly to the left of previous location.	Several Sande Zo dancing behind Mulbah Sumo. All are in front of the musicians.	*in Kpelle:* B: He is dancing with the women now.
228 Short quick zoom in, then zoom all the way out.	Long shot of the dancing behind Mulbah Sumo Jakolii.	*in English:* A: That is the Kpelle Zo, the man who is dancing in the background. B: That is Mr. Mulbah. A: Yeh. Mr. Jakolii. B: Jakolii.
235 Camera holds full position, small left horizontal pan.	Music goes to one beat, dancers stop. Mulbah goes over to bench where he was sitting previously (next to Mulbahzua and Kokulah).	
240 Camera holds position, then short right horizontal pan to center picture.	An old woman runs in front of musicians and dances with outstretched arms in a flowing possessed dance.	B: laughs (hahaha).
242 Small right horizontal pan, then small left horizontal pan back to previous position.	Dancing woman stops before the first musician, pan to first dance elder, and then pan back to the woman.	*in Kpelle:* B: See her there.
245 Off/on. Change of position. Camera beside musicians, facing the dancers.	Side view of musicians playing with dancers in front of them.	
247 Right horizontal pan.	Shot moves in on musicians until the dancers are off-field.	
249 Left horizontal pan.	Camera pans to an elder woman Zo from Yamii quarter who is holding two young girls by the hands (her granddaughters—dada). She moves arms and dances with constrained movements to the music.	*in English:* B: Is that them? A: Yeah. *in Kpelle:* A: That is her people.
252 Right horizontal pan.	Woman leads children back to house where Zo women are sitting. Camera follows her back.	
262 Left horizontal pan.	Shot of another woman Zo from Yamii quarter dancing before the musicians. The two main dancers dance behind her. Woman finishes. She walks to the dan-	

Cademic Markers	*Event*	*Narrative*
	cers behind her, greets them by touching hands, and walks off-camera. Camera now on both dancers and the second dance elder.	
268 Left horizontal pan.	Camera then follows the woman who was dancing, continues panning past her to the Zo women sitting in front of Kokulah's house.	
269 Right horizontal pan, short left horizontal pan.	Camera moves to the two dancers, goes a little past them, moves back to get them in center of visual field.	
288 Camera holds long shot.	The two dancers performing in unison.	*in Kpelle:* A: It is in their hands. B: It is. A: Yeah.
290 Off/on. Change of location, back in front of the musicians. Long or full shot.	Mulbah Sumo Jakolii is dancing by himself in front of the musicians. The second dance elder dances between camera and Mulbah with a medicine bundle balanced on top of her head.	*in English:* A: That is very nice.
299 Middle zoom, left horizontal pan.	Zoom and pan to both dancers.	
300 Small right horizontal pan. Holds for 5 sec.	Shot includes second dance elder approaching the two dancers.	
302 Right horizontal pan.	Camera pans to Mulbah Sumo and several Zo of the Sande dancing behind him. All in front of musicians.	
305 Camera holds above shot.	Mulbah and women dance.	*in English:* A: In the background is Mulbah Sumo Jakolii, the head of the Zo in the clan. And following him is the . . . uh . . . members of the Sande Society. The women now . . .
307 Right horizontal pan.	Pan to Zo women sitting in front of Kokulah's house.	and under the eaves of the thatch roof are the members of the Sande Society in Sucromu.

Cademic Markers	*Event*	*Narrative*
311 Left horizontal pan, hold, left horizontal pan.	Pan back to Mulbah Sumo and the Sande Zo dancers. Then another pan to both main dancers, performing next to the second dance elder. All move together.	*in English:* B: They are the Sande Zo with the Poro Zo.
314 Right horizontal pan.	Camera follows the dancers to the right of the musicians. The music reduces to a single beat. The performers stop dancing.	
318 Right horizontal pan.	Pan both dancers performing with the three dance elders before the musicians.	
320 Right horizontal pan.	Shot of dancers who were performing with Mulbah Sumo still together and dancing on the side.	
322 Left horizontal pan.	Pan back to the main dancers.	
323 Medium zoom in.	Close-up of dancers, one of the dance elders walks off-camera to the right of field. Camera remains on dancers.	
325 Left horizontal pan.	Shot of the three Poro Zo sitting together on bench.	
326 Right horizontal pan.	Pan back to the dancers.	
328 Zoom in and then all way out (quickly).	Long shot of the two dancers and on either side of them the first two dance elders. The second elder still has the medicine bundle balanced on her head.	
330 Long shot, left horizontal pan.	Music reduces to a single beat. Pan to Zo women on the side dancing. Main dancers at far right of field.	
335 Off/on. Close up (mid-zoom).	Close-up of musicians playing. Shot shows all musicians from mid-sections to heads.	
337 Zoom in another turn. Left horizontal pan. Stop. Right horizontal pan.	Close-up and pan to first musician (on left of musician line). Pan to second musician.	
338 Quick right horizontal pan. Zoom out.	Pan of all musicians in line. Long shot of all musicians playing.	
345 Right horizontal pan.	Pan to both dancers performing next to the second elder.	

Cademic Markers	*Event*	*Narrative*
351 Middle zoom in.	Music picks up beat. Dancers dance more intensely. Close-up shot of them performing. The second dancer touches the hand of the first musician.	
354 Zoom out.	Music stops to single beat. Zoom out to full shot of musicians and dancers.	
359 Right horizontal pan.	Music picks up beat. Pan to far right where Zo women are sitting. Camera moves to the two little girls who were subject of earlier shot.	
362 Zoom in (close).	Close-up shot of the two girls sitting on the laps of elder women Zo.	
364 Left horizontal pan, zoom out to full shot.	Pan back to dancers, zoom out to long shot of them performing in front of musicians.	
368 Long shot.	An elder woman comes in front of dancers from right of field. The two dancers move to the right side of musicians allowing her to perform. The third dance elder takes both of her hands in her own, holds them out and lets them drop. She then stands back allowing the old woman to dance. The musicians begin a slow rhythmic beat. The old woman dances before them with long possessed movements. The third dance elder walks up to her quickly and wipes her forehead and then the head of the first musician. The elder then moves back smiling. The music gets more intense.	
374 Camera holds long shot.	The old woman keeps up with each beat. Yangaw, Mulbah Sumo's head wife, comes up from the right of field and wipes the old woman's head with a shawl, and then wipes her own.	
378 Camera holds long shot.	The two main Sande dancers dance in between camera and the possessed woman.	A: high pitched laugh (hehehe).
379 Left horizontal pan.	Camera follows the two main dancers as they dance away from the old woman and musicians. The first dancer points her baton at musicians, signaling for them to stop the dance.	
380 Right horizontal pan.	Another elder Zo woman from Yamii walks up to the musicians and signals for them to stop. Camera pans over to the	

Cademic Markers	*Event*	*Narrative*
	woman as she gives musicians the instruction. The music slows to the single beat. The old woman comes out of her trance.	
381 Left horizontal pan.	Pan to the two main dancers. The first dancer is still calling over to the musicians shaking her baton (her talk is not recorded).	
382 Slight left horizontal pan—follows shots.	The first dancer faces in opposite direction of musicians and moves with the other dancer to left of area. As they dance the third and fourth dance elders come up from behind accompanied by the woman who was possessed. All are crouched low.	
385 Slow left horizontal pan as follow shot. Camera stops, long shot of action.	An elder woman from Yamii enters from left field. The two dancers move over to her, crouched low. They are followed by the four other women who were in front of the musicians and the possessed woman. The camera follows their action.	
387 Long shot of action. Camera turned to left.	When the two main dancers reach the woman on the left, they crouch below them and face away from her. As the first and third dance elders approach the three women, the old possessed woman comes in between them and crouches down next to the two main dancers. The second dance elder comes in behind the other two dance elders. All are crouched, but not as low as the two main dancers and the previously possessed old woman. When the second dance elder reaches the area, she taps the previously possessed woman's head. The woman was facing the standing woman. When the old woman was tapped, she turned in the same direction as the two main dancers. The standing woman reaches into her lappa and takes out some money. She reaches her hand out, and the second dance elder moves her hand in between hers and the previously possessed old woman. She then guides the standing woman's hand to the first dancer. The woman gives the first dancer the money. The first dancer begins to stand (still in a crouched position) and begins to move	

Cademic Markers	*Event*	*Narrative*
	away. The previously possessed woman moves up to her with her hand outstretched. The first dancer then moves back on her rear foot, turns to the previously possessed woman, and hands her the money. The second dance elder then points to the old woman to leave the area. The woman begins to leave to the left of the field. The group moves to the right field.	
392 Slow right horizontal pan—follow shot.	Camera follows group as they move to right of area ... back to area in front of musicians. As they move, the second dance elder points to previous area and tells the old woman to leave the area. The first dance elder points in that direction with her.	
396 Off/on. Position change in front of musicians. Long shot of action. Camera held unsteady.	Shot of two main dancers performing next to the first and third dance elders.	
398 Long shot of action.	The second dance elder passes in back of the two dancers separating them from the Zo women in front of Kokulah's house. She is carrying the medicine bundle on her head.	
400 Left horizontal pan.	Music slows to a single beat, camera pans to the fourth and a new fifth dance elder. They are in front of the musicians.	
409 Right horizontal pan.	Pan to Zo women sitting in front of Kokulah's house. Camera moves to the end of line of women.	
411 Left horizontal pan.	Pan back to the two main dancers. The women are dancing very intensely and seem to be taking cues from the dance elders. Music slows to a single beat.	
415 Long right horizontal pan.	Pan moves past the Zo women in front of Kokulah's house, makes a full sweep to a group of men standing in front of Folpahzoi's house. They are the members of the men's dance society, the *ngamunea* (*ngamu*'s wife's society). Two of the members greet each other with the finger-snap handshake.	

Cademic Markers	*Event*	*Narrative*
419 Long left horizontal pan.	Pan moves back to dancers and dance elders. The pan follows the same direction as before.	
421 Long shot.	Both dancers are performing with dance elders four and five (the Zo woman who participated in the possessed woman's dance). The second dance elder dances in front of them with the medicine bundle on her head.	
429 Short left horizontal pan.		
429 Short left horizontal pan.	Pan to the three Poro Zo sitting watching the performance.	
432 Short right horizontal pan.	Pan back to the dancers.	
436 Off/on. Position change on side of musicians (same position as when Zo woman presented her grandaughters).	Side shot of musicians playing, dancers perform in front of them. Music ends, then begins.	
440 Left horizontal pan.	Pan to Bellman who was standing on opposite side of performance area. Bellman takes James' picture, James focuses on Bellman while he does it.	
442 Right horizontal pan.	Pan back to the dancers.	
451 Right horizontal pan camera downward tilt (vertical down pan).	Pan to dancers and the first and third dance elders. The dancers come up to James, crouch low before him, and ask for *kola*.	*in Kpelle:* A: Let me give *kola* after we have finished.
453 Vertical upward pan.	Dancers move away from James and continue their performance. Dancers in front of musicians; the first dance elder is directly in back of them. The second dance elder moves in front of the three with the medicine bundle on her head.	
455 Low right horizontal pan.	Camera drops and pans to second dance elder.	
457 Upward left horizontal pan.	Camera pans back to the two main dancers.	
460 Short right horizontal pan.	Pan from both dancers to the second dancer and second dance elder. First dance elder moves in behind the second dancer.	

Cademic Markers	*Event*	*Narrative*
465 Left horizontal pan.	Pan to musicians and shot of Kokulah. An elder Zo woman comes from inside of Mulbahzua's house (Mulbah's head wife) with money in her right hand. She hands the money to the first dancer and thanks her. Two elder Zo women dance in front of the two main dancers.	
476 Long shot.	Mulbahzua gets up and walks into his house.	
478 Right horizontal pan.	Pan to dancers and dance elders. Dancers are doing a hanging baton dance in a straight line, accompanied by the dance elders and various Zo women from Yamii.	*in Kpelle:* B: I think they are moving now.
487 Long shot.	The elder woman who introduced her granddaughters earlier walks in front of the camera. THE TAPE BREAKS.	

2. The Rice Stealing Palaver

Cademic Markers	*Visual Field*	*Narrative*
Long shot.	Shot of accused.	B: Where is she?
Right horizontal pan. Followed by immediate vertical tilt down.	Pan to medicine on floor.	ACCUSED (A): She is at the house. B: You should buy us some cane juice.
Vertical up to left horizontal pan.	Pan to court clerk.	CLERK (C): Are you able to write your name?
Long shot.	Shot of clerk writing in notebook.	A: I am able. Give me your pen.
Right horizontal pan.	Pan to one of observers. Shot of lap, holding hat.	C: Where is the 15 dollars? A: When she finishes cooking rice she will come.
Left horizontal pan.	Pan to door.	D: Who is that?
Left horizontal pan.	Pan to clerk.	C: I did my part of the writing now you must do your part.
Right horizontal pan. Vertical down tilt.	Pan to medicine.	A: Father Mulbah (nang Mulbah) let the matter reach to you.
Long shot.	Shot of medicine.	MULBAH (M): I have said this one thing over and over. Nang Kpa, let me to find the money and give it to you.
Vertical up tilt. Right horizontal pan.	Pan to a man sitting at left of hut.	

Cademic Markers	*Visual Field*	*Narrative*
Right horizontal pan.	Pan to man in center of area—the accused.	B: Someone has to take the bond.
Right horizontal pan.	Pan to chief and clerk.	C: 25¢ is the bond. This kind of business (*meni*) . . .
Left horizontal pan.	Pan to observers to left of hut.	A: The person's name is Bakolee if you do good for someone ehhh. You go in *kuu* and they don't appreciate it good. I worked on his farm. Just for 50¢ business. And the person turns against you. And the chief didn't know anything about it. If I put my hand in it I am going to tell the chief everything that is going on.
Right horizontal pan.	Shot of accused.	
Right horizontal pan.	Shot of chief.	B: The chief is sitting there.
Left follow pan.	Chief leaves the hut.	A: I cannot do it. I do you think anyone can do that. I bought something three times.
Short right pan.	Shot of accused.	D: You are the one who knocked on the door. That is what I am saying.

3. The July 26th Fighting Palaver

Cademic Markers	*Visual Field*	*Narrative*
166 Zoom in, vertical tilt down.	Shot of medicine.	The first part of transcript is in the Loma language.
Vertical tilt up.	Up pan to Zo sitting on bench.	Generally the witness spoke about how he was inside his house and heard loud arguing outside. When he went outside, he saw the three men fighting. He told them that the matter would have to be heard. They first went to the quarter chief of Zoman quarter where the fight took place. They explained the matter to the chief. The men said they were only playing and shouldn't be tried for fighting. At this point the witness switched to the Kpelle language.
Right horizontal pan.	Pan of all Zo sitting in front of Kokulah's house. Shot ends at Kokulah sitting by self to the far right of group.	
Vertical down tilt, fast left horizontal pan.		

Cademic Markers	Visual Field	Narrative
Vertical up tilt.	Witness talking facing the town chief and elders from Zokolomii quarter. Next to them are two of the accused.	Transcript begins at appropriate location on tape.
Mid-zoom.	Close up of above group.	
174 Vertical pan down.	Shot of witness's body.	
Right horizontal pan.	Pan across group to left of witness (those with chief). Pan continues to Folpahzoi's house, and moves to those in front of Tokpahlongwolo's house.	
175 Left horizontal pan.	Pan back to witness.	
Left horizontal pan.	Pan to the two accused and their quarter chief. Pan continues to show whole group. Stops at end—Yapkazua.	In the evening the old man did something. In my mind he wasn't satisfied. And I said, "Old man, how can we solve this kind of problem?"
183 Left horizontal pan.	Pan to adjudicating Zo (Bellman sits with them next to cameraman).	
Vertical down. Right horizontal pan.	Camera drops to Mulbah Sumo's foot, pans to medicine.	It is the truth.
Vertical up and right horizontal pan.	Pan to witness.	
188 Long shot.	Witness points to the two accused next to town chief.	So I told this one and said "OK, but I don't like this kind of business."
Vertical shots up and down.	Vertical study of witness.	It is the truth.
Long shot.	Shot of witness talking to Mulbah Sumo.	
Camera vertical down.	Shot of witness' feet.	
206 Right horizontal pan.	Full pan of all in attendance, pans stop slightly at various groups. At end of group (where James Flumo, the schoolmaster is sitting with group). Camera pauses.	Witness switches to Loma (indecipherable).

Cademic Markers	*Visual Field*	*Narrative*
214 Camera down tilt shows ground, fast left horizontal pan, tilt up.	Pan down and up back to witness.	
221 Long shot.	Witness hits stomach in swearing over medicine.	It is the truth!
229 Left horizontal pan.	Shot of various Zo sitting in front of Kokulah's house.	Laughter (from audience). So he said we are playing and I said is that a way to play? So I told him that you people were fighting, if you start this kind of fighting in a small town like this it is not right. Then they said they were playing. This is a way to play? (hits chest) I don't know if there were four people fighting and I know something about it and I am not saying then let the medicine catch me.
231 Right horizontal pan.	Pan of Kokulah laughing.	
234 Left horizontal pan, down tilt.	Pan to medicine.	
248 Up tilt and right horizontal pan.	Pan back to witness.	(hits stomach)
250 Vertical tilt down.	Shot of witness' feet.	(off to side) That is true. (laughter)
Left horizontal pan.	Pan to Zo in front of Kokulah's house.	Is there any questions? ACCUSED (A): You say you weren't there when the fighting began. How do you know?
Left horizontal pan.	Pan to Mulbah Sumo Jakolii.	W: I said I wasn't there. The medicine should kill me if I lie.
Vertical down tilt.	Tilt to his feet.	A: You said you weren't there?
Vertical up tilt.	Shot of his face.	W: It should kill me, it should kill me.
256 Right horizontal pan.	Pan to witness.	MSJ: The devil cannot chase the owl. (laughter)
262 Long shot.		W: (in English) They all the people ... my head hurts ohhh. I am coming to leave. (laughter)
262 Tilt down, tilt up, right horizontal pan.	Shot of feet, back up to body, pan follows witness to right of field.	(witness holds out hand) Give me my money! I am going to drink today. (walks off jovially) Witness walks next to James Flumo and says: Give me a chair (kicks stool).
268 Slight left pan.	Camera picks up entering new witness.	JAMES: Move your foot from there. (off camera: he has been in the house all day)

Cademic Markers	Visual Field	Narrative
Left horizontal pan.	Camera follows witness to area in front of Zo.	W #2: (to son), Sit down there. (points to bench)
Right tilt down pan.	Shot to medicine.	I was in the house and I heard my oldest brother saying (chicken crows) "Are you home?" and I said, "Hello." He said, the people outside they call my name "Mulbah" are fighting behind the house. I went outside and went to one of the fighters, my namesake (*ndoma*) and said "this thing you are doing is not good." I said "you are not fighting but look at all the blood all over your body." Then he said "Go to the other side" (in Loma). I said "No, that is not right." I told my *molo* (brother-in-law), "You see what they are doing?" He said, "I see." We said "We saw you between the houses and you still say you are not fighting." They have lied until a witness came and proved they were fighting. If I am lying may the medicine kill me (hits chest). Because I saw them on the spot. Who are the relatives (*kala*), you have any questions to ask me?
Left up tilt pan.	Shot of witness and son.	
280 Long shot.	Shot of witness testifying.	
283 Mid-zoom.	Mid-zoom of witness.	
Tilt to feet.	Shot of witness' feet.	
303 Left horizontal pan.	Pan to Mulbah Sumo.	
313 BATTERY ENDS		

4.   The Snake Zo Palaver

Cademic Markers and Visual Field	Narrative
893 Tilt up. Long shot of MK.	And then you sitting down and say I threw snake on the child before I went to cure her.
908 Left horizontal pan to BG listening.	GB: Uh hum.
909 Tilt down to GB's feet, tilt up as he answers.	MK: You spoil my name (*e naa ma shia*).
	GB: Do you have a witness?
	MK: Flumo.
	GB: Do you have a different witness?

Cademic Markers and Visual Field	*Narrative*

Left horizontal to MS with GB to right of field.

MK: Uh huh. It is the truth. So since they took the girl to the hospital they say you must have patience until she returns. So they came from there and they said to me . . .

920   Shot of MS and GB camera tilt to their feet.

MS: I should take it!

MK: Take it.

As MS talks right horizontal pan to MK camera tilts to their feet.

MS: OK, the matter reaches to you (referring to Gbanya).

GB: Did the woman ask you to cure the child?

MK: Finished. I don't know.

Left horizontal pan (MS talking).

MS: You have a sharp mouth!

GB: (finger gestures to MS) I will explain everything.

MS: OK.

GB: You saw them?

937   Right horizontal pan to MK (as MS refers to him).

MS: The thing that happened I told him. Since this thing happened now only I. I want to be clear about it. I want herself to be here. You cannot say anything behind her. I cannot pay for her when she is not here. Everything must go by law. So he told me (refer to MK). I don't know her, I know only you. Since you say you know me, we have to wait. So I called Mulbah to come. When I called Mulbah I said, "Mulbah, Gamai asked me—that's my *ngala* (mother's brother)—that's better, the two of us." So I said, "Father Mulbah, the matter reaches to you." Father Mulbah told me, "You are acting frisky, give me *siling saaba*, NOW!" So I just sat there and said no. So since you said it that way I will try and give it to you and I will give you a chicken as cold water. So the matter continues. The child is in the hospital and took it to Mulbah. They took the child to the big hospital and told me the next morning. So when I want they said, "Father Mulbah was here last night." (MK laughs). So I told him the only thing about the whole thing I got to wait until Gamai comes because she is in the hospital. They took the child to the hospital. Before I pay anything for Gamai or she pays for me, we both must be there. So he told me I hear it. So he went and reported me to Folpah. Before I do it unless Gamai is here. Folpah said that was true. You cannot pay unless they are there to say it is true. If you want to help your *ngala* I will give you three dollars and do it in the *kala meni* (family manner). Do not demand more money from me. People will never believe me if I give money in that way. So the thing continues till Gamai returns.

940   Left horizontal pan to MS (he accentuates point).

Right horizontal pan to MK laughing.

Cademic Markers and Visual Field	*Narrative*
943 Left horizontal pan to MS, tilt to feet, then back to faces.	
949 Left horizontal pan to owner of bar (at pause in talk).	So I went to him and said, ''Gamai came yesterday and this evening you should come so we can go there.''
Camera lifts, right horizontal pan to MS and GB.	GB: Before you talk may *Xala* (God) bless everything so there won't be confusion. Let no trouble come to this house. Let there be peace.
	ALL PRESENT: *Maynaa* (Amen).
	GB: May peace be between the relatives (*kala*) The medicine should work so the child will get better.
	So you told the owner of the house to have medicine fixed.
952 Right horizontal pan to Flumo (next to MK).	MS: She didn't say anything.
	GB: Yes, he fixed the medicine . . . Folpahzoi?
	FOLPAH: Uh.
	GB: (undecipherable)
	FOLPAH: Gbanya.
Left pan to MS and GB (GB talking)	
962 Right horizontal pan to Flumo (next to MK) who speaks.	FLUMO: We leave the matter here with Folpah and we (hits his umbrella) will go and hang head (discuss the matter outside of the room).
	GB: I want to ask you.
Slow left horizontal to GB, then left pan to owner of store.	MS: Ask me.
	GB: Did you put a rock in the mud to hit Folpah with it?
Camera lifts to show bottles on shelf and writing above door to back room.	TOKPAH: You want to fix the matter just to please one person?
	MK: Laughs.
Camera tilts down to MS and GB.	T: You don't know what is in the next person's mind. If you know you could judge the palaver.
	MS: He is doing it.
	GB: Folpah, you cut the matter short.
973 Shot of MS and GB.	F: Uh.
	GB: I want to tell you a different thing.
	MS: I don't want to hear anything else. The same thing I keep telling him is you reach to the woman you can't reach it to me.

Cademic Markers and Visual Field   *Narrative*

982 As Folpah responds camera   FOLPAH: Father Mulbah can't do his own business, some one
     moves up and down.   must do it for him (i.e., MK can't praise himself.)

                                     MS: Uh.

                                     F: You go and call the woman's parents. Father Mulbah is
                                          right here and you all give him the blessing.

                                     MS: Kai?

                                     F: I just hear you. I say the human being.

                                     GB: All right where will it end or begin?

990 Left horizontal to MK.   MK: Folpah, it is just like the *Zotaa wo* (the Zotaa dialect of
                                          Kpelle). Gbanya, the story that I am telling you. Gbanya,
                                          they are just playing with me.

                                     TOKPAH: (in English) The man is lying. If thing like this
                                          happens there is no head or tail.

                                     MK: Uh huh.

999 Two men enter shop and go   TOKPAH: My book is about the two of us. You come and
     to back room. Camera   apologize to Father Mulbah before he gets nasty. You
     moves to right to follow   think we are stupid. Thing like this before you say some-
     their entry.   thing you cannot say "pay" without knowing what people
                                          around are saying.

                                     FOLPAH: Gbanya you must ask your little brother (*nexe*) be-
                                          cause things must come to an ending.

004 Left horizontal back to MS.   MS: If I don't feel like talking I won't say anything. The only
     Then left to owner.   thing I told him which is my idea.

                                     GB: Are the people in here?

     Then back to MS, tilts   F: Who is Gbanya to you? All these things you are doing, all
     down to his legs.   this we are doing, you didn't thank Mulbah or did you
                                          reach it to the woman's parents? Someone should tell the
                                          woman's people to come here.

008 Camera turned off.

009 NEW CAMERAPER-   FOLPAH: Your eyes are big over food.
     SON. Camera shows Fol-
     pah talking.   . . .

     Left to MS.

     . . .

5

Bapostolo Films: Informant and Documentary Uses of the Camera

By contrasting informants' and outside ethnographers' approaches to film, an insight may be gained into variations in perception and the visual vocabularies used to describe events. While we were concerned in Chapter 4 with demonstrating the format structure of events as revealed through visual materials, in this chapter we will use a similar procedure to demonstrate the contrasting approaches of informants and student ethnographers to the same event. The ethnographer's relationship to a community is evident in his filming behavior and the ability to follow the structure of a given event. Inferences about the relationship between filmmakers and subjects may be drawn by examining the intent of their films (Byers, 1964, 1966). The ten informant films that are the subject matter for this discussion will be compared with the products of Western student filmmakers shot at the same time and will also be analyzed in terms of the informants' developing expertise. A full listing of the films and their complete transcripts appear in the appendix to this chapter.

AN APPLICATION OF METHOD

Several factors influence how meaning is conveyed through film, including the very terminology in which filmed events and behavior are described. We have selected cademic markers as viable units through which participants' orientations are reflected. These units provide a basis for examining participants' accounts of settings, but they are neutral to any particular setting and do not explain either the cultural or the idiosyncratic orientations of a particular filmmaker. Crucial to our argument is the assumption that all accounts, whether verbal or visual, are derived within a social context and rely on it for their interpretation. While the descriptions share this characteristic, their styles and expression differ. These

118

variations may be traced to cultural learning, differences in the biographies of filmmakers, and the actual contexts of filming.

Edmund Carpenter (1972) suggests that cultural variations in the use of media have been grossly exaggerated. He asserts:

> Surely the significant point is that media permit little experimentation and only a person of enormous power and sophistication is capable of escaping their binding power. A very naive person may stumble across some interesting technique, though I think such stories are told more frequently than documented. The trend is otherwise. (p. 188)

In addition to presupposing the identical use of a universal film grammar, Carpenter's statement is tantamount to saying that any artistic medium is predetermined by its technology and components. This is certainly not the case in oral traditions, the written word, or the plastic arts. While Bapostolo informant-made films employed a simple film grammar, consisting largely of the horizontal pan, the variations in its use revealed a possibly unique conception of social interactions and notions of visual display. Most notably, interactions were viewed synchronically rather than developmentally. Although one or two activities generally emerged as thematic in the informant-made films, a central activity was not selected to the exclusion of others. The films were also characterized by minimal use of close-up and zoom. Their overall effect was often dizzying to the Western audience.

Each filmed sequence may be treated as an attempt to translate lived experiences through a communicative medium. The ten informant films selected were made in July and August of 1974 and portray secular and ritual settings. They will be compared with the first and earlier informant-made product filmed by Dinanga Jérémie in 1971.[1] Three of the ten segments, that we shall refer to as Yeshaie's play, were directed by an Apostle who wanted to put his message of evangelism in theatrical form. The remaining seven informant films are characterized by a possibly unique combination of camera movements. These movements contrast with ideal techniques for Western filmmaking. They do not focus on a single activity or a sequence of related shots of extended duration.

Instead, panning is used as a method of emphasis. While it became more controlled as the informant filmmakers learned about camera use, panning was retained as the most common way of creating a focal point of interest within a film segment. Panning relied on the proxemic arrangement of the filmed scene and was employed to include several simultaneous activities at once and to indicate the presence of diverse persons at an event. This use contrasts with Roberts and Sharples' (1971, p. 67) assertion that panning from a single camera position is among "the most common faults found in the work of beginning filmmakers." While the Maranke informants were novices, their filming contrasted with that of American novices and showed an evolution of its own with regard to the intentional use of panning and its integration with other camera

---

[1]*The Bapostolo* is a 16 mm film of which Jérémie's segment forms the first half.

techniques. This prevalence of panning in informant-made films suggests a film grammar that was peculiar to them.

SOME AMBIGUITIES IN INTERPRETING INFORMANT FILMMAKING TECHNIQUES

The uniqueness of a film grammar and its meaningful units does not imply that these units can be positively located when the observer reviews a film. There are occasions on which informants seem to hesitate and virtually attempt to erase or modify what they have done previously. A hesitation includes a rapid pan to the right, a pan left, a pause, and a pan right again, as it did in one informant's film. It is difficult to say whether these rapid pans, the content of which is often barely visible, are meaningful in their own right. However, they do point to a choice between the filming of two alternative, often simultaneous, activities, particularly when one of these activities is viewed as peripheral to the other.

Thus, we can assert that the description of meaningful portions of camera units is partially an artifact of how they are seen and transcribed by the observer. To the professional Western filmmaker, hesitations, like pans, would stand as indications of poor filming technique. They would suggest that the cameraperson is unable to follow the action consistently or that he is unsure of the equipment. However, many of the sequences surrounding hesitations in the informant-made materials suggest that the filmmaker is choosing among significant alternative subjects to be recorded. Furthermore, in a more "sophisticated" situation, these scenes might be shot simultaneously by two or three cameras and made into a composite through post hoc editing. Even with this technique, the aim of Western filming is often not to capture the extent of an interaction with its multiple participants but rather to narrow down the focus of action to maintain continuity, reserving panning only for dramatic relief and special thematic emphasis.

Several technically accurate accounts may also be furnished in the transcription of a single filming.[2] For example, discrepancies exist between an informant's account of what he intended to film on a given occasion, a transcript of the camera movements appearing in the scene, and a "narrative" transcript of the content of what is filmed. When he filmed the Kabanana Sabbath ceremony, Ezekiel, one of the informant filmmakers, stated that he intended to "get everything." His pans between the seated congregation and those waiting to enter the place of prayer were rapid. Four of the six times that Ezekiel turned the camera on in this short sequence coincided with songs. He seemed to be describing the kerek as a time for singing. This was Ezekiel's first film. It is also possible to view its rapid pans as indicative of a lack of knowledge about how the camera operated. Although he had been given six three-minute cartridges, Ezekiel used

---

[2]Cf. Turner's (1970) discussion of alternative verbal transcripts.

only two during a three-hour kerek. His filming of the songs took place over a two-hour period.

It is possible that the character of Ezekiel's filming was due to confusion about the brief instructions that he had received. He had been shown how to load the camera, adjust focal distance, use zoom, and turn the camera on and off. He had also been briefly instructed to use the film wisely, since we did not have a great deal of it. When asked why he had used only two 8 mm cartridges for the entire ceremony, Ezekiel answered that he thought that "we did not have much film." By using only one roll for over half of the ceremony, he could save film and could still live up to his ideal of "getting everything" that was important by panning and using the camera only at critical moments. Rather than revealing a lack of instruction, Ezekiel's argument indicated a careful decision with regard to in-camera editing. The narrative transcript of Ezekiel's film (including the sound track) stressed the participation of the entire congregation in singing. He did not spend time focusing on a song leader, and made sure that both female and male singers, respectively, were included in the picture by panning from left (the women) to right (the men). He used a similar technique later in his film of preaching at a retreat ceremony, but by this time he had modified and decreased his use of horizontal panning. While the professional filmmaker might view Ezekiel's evolution as a minimal step toward standardized and unobtrusive filming techniques, the later sequences may be viewed as the development of more subtle techniques for conveying a larger repertoire of meanings through film.

Yeshaie, another Bapostolo filmmaker, leaves the viewer with many questions about the intent of what he recorded. In all four of the segments that he filmed (as distinct from the three that he directed), hesitations and increasingly ornate film sequences abound. Although Yeshaie had less exposure to Western films than Ezekiel, he was far more concerned with learning about the technical features of the camera. Both used zoom once each out of the total seven filmed segments. However, Yeshaie developed a technique of pivoting in which he rotated the camera a full 360° during a three-minute segment. This circular pivot was combined with a rotation of his hand, creating spiraling camera movements. The spiral and a circular dip (a combined pan–tilt) were used to punctuate side activities, much as a pan would be used in conventional Western filming.

These techniques were particularly evident in Yeshaie's film of the Mandevu market next to Marrapodi. Yeshaie's attention was drawn to several objects above and below eye level at the market. We began in the vegetable section. While Yeshaie was filming, he informed Jules-Rosette that he wanted to include several types of seeds on the ground as well as vegetables in bins. He was also interested in filming vegetable vendors inside a closed pavilion. Yeshaie had filmed them on a previous day, but apparently his cartridge had run out. Yeshaie's desire to include objects at different levels accounts for some of the ambiguities in his filming of the market scene. In one sequence, he panned from right to left, lowering the camera to focus on a group of children. Then he panned up right across seeds for sale on the ground, looped the camera up in a circular motion, and returned left to a young woman and Jules-Rosette. As Jules-Rosette walked forward left, Yeshaie panned to follow her, then turned to pan right to a group of girls who were watching us. The effect is unsettling. As Jules-Rosette walked left, Yeshaie had already begun to move the camera right, making it difficult to distinguish between camera motion and her own walking. Treating the camera unit as an intentional act in this case posed difficulties, the most basic of which is discerning what the initial camera movement was and how it related to the sequence that follows.

A similar ambiguity arose in Yeshaie's pan right from a group of girls to a vegetable vendor's table in the same film. As he moved toward the vendor's table, he walked forward rapidly. At first glance, the movement looked almost as if it were a zoom in on the table. But Yeshaie was dollying straight toward the table. From his shifted position, he panned right to a woman standing above the seeds and to a man posing in the aisle beside them. The dolly allowed Yeshaie to change the filming area, pulling away from the young woman and girls to the lower left in front of a furniture business and back to the initial focus of filming, the area covered with seeds. Quite literally, Yeshaie's film came full circle from its beginning to end, placing most emphasis on the area covered with seeds and those who walked the path through it. As in his film about tinsmithing, in which he also employed the pivoting technique, Yeshaie's market film created a sense of completion as his last pan returned to the initial point of departure.

THE HYPOTHESIS OF EQUIVALENCE

Most research conducted on cross-cultural factors involved in perception has been experimental.[3] Even when the most careful precautions and experimental controls have been placed upon these studies, they have often failed to establish an equivalence among Western and non-Western subjects. In Rivers' experiments on color, for example, Murray Islanders were shown color samples in a dimly lit hut, while British subjects were presented colors in an electrically lighted laboratory (Segall et al., 1966, p. 43). It was difficult to tell the extent to which equivalence could be established across experimental conditions, let alone between the two types of subjects. In this study, we have assumed equivalence between Bapostolo informant filmers and a team of Western student filmers. Although both groups were novices, the same problems of equivalence that faced experimenters like Rivers remain in the natural setting: Can the two classes of novice cameramen be compared or contrasted? Can it be assumed that the differences between them are important enough to warrant contrasting and that the

---

[3]For descriptions of this experimental literature, see Segall et al. (1966), Cole et al. (1971), and Cole and Scribner (1974).

similarities are strong enough to establish the equivalence of their products as visual accounts?

INTRODUCING MEDIA TO THE APOSTLES

In the field setting, no effort was made to differentiate between the American and the Maranke camerapersons by substantially varying the tasks or specific instructions that they received. The American informants did tend to handle videotaping and 16 mm filming, while the Maranke informants, with one exception, worked with 8 mm equipment. However, it can be argued that comparable filmed and taped accounts were produced. A team consisting of Jules-Rosette, two American students (Chris and Peter), and Yeshaie set out to film a walkabout survey encompassing the area bounded by the Ncube tinsmith shop, the main thoroughfare, and the Mandevu market.[4]

Walkabouts were used to encourage informants in developing a visual survey of the Marrapodi community. These materials were supplemented by films of ritual events by Ezekiel and by the American students. The overall aim of these films was to create a composite picture of the ritual and social life of the Bapostolo in their community from a member's perspective. The informants were all members of the Maranke church but filmed members of several other groups. This filming was unusual in that it increased the normal contact between the Apostles and several other local groups in the community.

Yeshaie was asked to make a short film of tinsmithing at Ncube's, while the American team began by videotaping street activities in the thoroughfare just south of the shop. Yeshaie had previously expressed a desire to film Ncube's and set himself up at the shop quickly, while Chris, the American videoist, taped people and cars passing on the street. A group of young onlookers gathered around both Chris and Yeshaie. While the presence of the children in response to the camera was apparent in Yeshaie's film, his rapid panning with continual returns to the working smiths created the impression of ''business as usual'' and of an active interplay between street life and the shop (see Fig. 8 below). However, when Chris returned to tape the smithing a few minutes later, attention focused on him more pointedly than it did on Yeshaie. He used zoom to film the two smiths from a distance rather than placing himself in the arena created by the edge of the yard and the work space.

The effect was one of greater distance from the workers. In addition, for the duration of the taping, the workers stopped hammering and pretended to hammer

---

[4]Chris had been trained in sociological field research but was inexperienced in field situations. He viewed his role in the field primarily as that of a researcher. Peter was an advanced sociology student and a member of the church. As Jules-Rosette's husband, he was viewed as a leader of the research team. Jules-Rosette took still photographs on several occasions while members of the research team filmed. She also ''debriefed'' the informants and the student researchers after each filming session.

instead, lifting their hands in exaggerated movements to make sure that they were captured on the camera. This pretense at work was intensified by Chris' steady focus on the workers rather than the scene as an entirety. The spectators and passersby were *not* smoothly integrated into Chris' tape. Instead, they appeared as an intrusion on the main activity. Panning was minimal on Chris' tape, and the centrality of smithing was established by a steady hold on the hammering.

It is impossible to present conclusive evidence that the American and Maranke camerapersons were in fact doing "the same thing." Both had received few instructions about the filming tasks, and both freely developed their own interpretations of the event. Each filmer included at least one shot of the other in his presentation. That is, each was in some way monitoring and keying off the activities of the other without explicit verbal directives or indications that he would do so. This nonverbal interplay culminated in Chris shooting the same scene that was recorded by Yeshaie. The basis of comparison resides in their attempt to shoot "the same activity" with minimal cuing and prior instruction. The saliency and major interest to be found in the contrast is the fact that their formulation of the scenes through the cademic structure of each account is of an entirely different order. The remaining discussion will focus on some of these similarities and differences (Cole & Scribner, 1974, p. 198).[5]

PROFILES OF THE PRINCIPAL FILMMAKERS

All of the informant filmmakers were Tshiluba speakers of either Luba or Lulua descent.[6] *Dinanga Jérémie,* a Muena Lulua, was the youngest. He was 19 years old when he made his first ethnographic film. He was born in 1952 at Kamina in the Shaba Province of Zaire and came to Kananga in the Kasai with his parents in 1960. He lived by his own choice with Tshilumbu, an Apostolic prophet, sharing this household with the American ethnographers. He was fluent in three languages: Tshiluba, Zaire Kiswahili, and French and used all three almost equally in daily conversation. The Apostolic elders considered Jérémie progressive and highly educated. Although he was often asked to read the Bible in kerek, the elders were generally dissatisfied with his performance. When he read the Bible in French, he did not retain Tshiluba tones and oratorical style but instead adopted a French accent. This was regarded as poor ritual performance. Jérémie's participation as an informant ethnographer was also viewed with skepticism by some members. Although they generally responded favorably to his

---

[5]Cole and Scribner stress that intergroup comparisons can and should be made to help validate data on cross-cultural comparison.

[6]The Baluba-Kasai and Bena Lulua are related peoples of the Kasai Province of Zaire. They speak distinguishable but mutually intelligible dialects of Tshiluba. Members of both tribes have migrated extensively to the urban centers of Zaire and Zambia. They represent one of the larger single language groupings in the Apostolic church outside of Rhodesia.

interviewing, some considered it a sign of lack of faith and an over concern with secular affairs.

When Jérémie began filming, he was in his last year of secondary school (*lycée*) and was taking a course in psychology and pedagogy. Jérémie shared his own small adobe house with another student behind Tshilumbu's home. For the most part, the two students spoke French rather than Tshiluba and led a life focused around their studies. Jérémie's roommate, Joseph, was a Catholic relative of the prophet's wife, and the two had long and lively discussions about religion. The walls of their flat were covered with large color photographs of French and American celebrities, travel-brochure scenes from around the world, and wildlife scenes. Jérémie himself was baptized an Apostle when he was eight years old, in 1960, the same year that he came to Kananga. He was among the younger second generation of Apostles in Kananga and had been brought up in an Apostolic household with little direct contact with traditional Lulua religion. He had never lived for an extended period in a rural area and was both critical of and curious about rural life and customs.

Jérémie was relatively sophisticated both in his knowledge of the written word and his familiarity with visual media. At the time of filming, he had had considerable exposure to Western cinema and was an amateur photographer. The films that Jérémie frequented were mostly French and American adventure stories. He expressed his interest in the value of these films despite the disapproval of some Apostolic elders. When he was given a 16 mm camera, Jérémie had already acquired extensive experience photographing ritual events as a member of our research team. He owned a still camera and had used it in assembling material for photo interview sessions. At our suggestion, he had taken additional photographs of each weekly kerek on the basis of what interested him and according to a typology of ritual events derived from interview responses. Jérémie possessed an overall sense of what he wanted to show. When photographing, he paid particular attention to obtaining close-ups of the insignia of office of each member and to capturing some aspect of various types of ritual events.

Generally, Jérémie made his own decisions about what to photograph and film. His instructions were fairly loose. He would merely suggest that he focus on aspects of the ceremony that did not show up sufficiently when we examined the previous week's photographs. When he began filming, Jérémie knew of our interest in recording and cataloging ritual parts such as keti or confession. He also wanted to film one ceremony from start (his household's departure for the kerek) to finish (their return home). Although Jérémie did this in a film that will be discussed later, technical problems and overexposure ruined much of his footage. Nevertheless, Jérémie's filming process and subject selection are of interest whether or not they emerged in the final product.[7]

---

[7]John Collier, in a discussion (American Anthroplogical Association, November, 1973), similarly stressed that the loss of footage may be an advantage in helping the filmmaker recall how and why certain events were filmed.

Kongolo Yeshaie was born in 1949 at Kazumba in southwest Kasai, Zaire, and at the time of filming was 25 years old. He went to primary school at Lambombo mission in Zaire and had no formal schooling after that. He migrated from Zaire to Lusaka, Zambia in 1970 and lived in the northern part of the Marrapodi compound with his wife and another Apostolic family. Yeshaie could speak and was literate in Tshiluba, was fairly fluent in Chishona and Kiswahili, and could speak some Chinyanja. However, he could neither speak nor was literate in a European language.

Yeshaie joined the Maranke Apostolic Church in 1967 and held the office of junior baptist. He was also known for his extraordinary singing abilities in the church and was a candidate harikros or special singer. As such, Yeshaie initiated songs in kerek and was an enthusiastic ritual leader. He led the opening hymn and was often called upon as a preacher and reader in kerek. Yeshaie's knowledge of ritual was detailed, and he insisted on ceremonial perfection. Yeshaie's head was always clean shaven according to Apostolic rulings. He was active and enthusiastic in church business and aggressively insisted that everyone who associated with him follow ritual practices closely. This concern with correct ritual interpretation led Yeshaie to volunteer his services as an informant and to work meticulously in teaching ethnographers the correct interpretation of Apostolic practices. He often traveled with Jacob, a prophet who was equally concerned with church law and enforced it to detect sinful acts and hidden medicines.

Yeshaie had minimal exposure to both written and visual media. His main contact with reading consisted of Bible study and recitation in the weekly Sabbath service. Although he had seen a few Western films, Yeshaie's attitude toward them was negative. He viewed the cinema as the work of Satan.[8] Upon seeing Jérémie's final film and some videotapes of ceremonies, Yeshaie conceded that when used for religious purposes, movies were "not so bad after all."

Yeshaie's interest in the camera was spontaneous. He wanted to join the researchers in filming, the first time that cameras were introduced in Marrapodi. He also used this occasion to direct (rather than film) his own play based on the format of Apostolic preaching. Although Yeshaie's initial use of the camera seemed "awkward," he soon became skilled, developing a careful personal style for capturing the extent of a scene and its simultaneous parts. While there are definite resemblances between Yeshaie's and Jérémie's films, the completeness of Yeshaie's work and his attempts to give it thematic unity distinguish it from the other informant films.

Mwamba Ezekiel is a MuLuba born in 1942 in Bunkonde, in the East Kasai, Zaire. He was 32 years old at the time of filming and had lived in Lusaka with his family fairly regularly since 1967. Ezekiel had five years of Presbyterian primary

---

[8]That is, he initially referred to the cinema as a "worldly" activity like drinking and dancing, both of which are forbidden to Apostles.

education at the mission schools of Bunkonde and Lubondai in the East Kasai and had previously lived in Likasi, a railroad town in Shaba. He later lived in Lubumbashi with his family and moved with them to Lusaka. He joined the Apostles there in 1971. Ezekiel describes himself as a former lover of drink and dance. In his small, one-and-a-half room adobe home in Chaisa, he still displays a photograph of himself dressed formally, holding a large cigar at a Lubumbashi bar. When he joined the church, Ezekiel stated, he left all of his worldly concerns behind. But, he asserted, if it were necessary to return to a bar to convert sinners, he would. In general, Ezekiel's orientation toward church doctrine was more liberal and open than Yeshaie's.

Ezekiel's attitude toward Western media was also more positive than Yeshaie's. He had seen Western films but had rejected them because of their excessive violence. Ezekiel viewed film as a way of communicating the important emotional aspect of events. He thought that the limitations imposed by a film cartridge required him to film as much as possible in a three-minute interval and felt comfortable turning the camera on and off at short intervals. He wanted to both film and be filmed in ritual events and used them, as did Jérémie, to create a special order of reality or environment for action. In one sequence, Ezekiel made a particular effort to film the Sabbath ceremony from the vantage point of a woman's position and used the camera as a vehicle to approach this part of the kerek. Gradually, Ezekiel learned the use of zoom but, like Yeshaie, continued to use constant camera motion as a means of conveying the fullness of a setting. In replay sessions, Ezekiel was particularly concerned about whether his participation as a singer or a reader in kerek had been captured. When his song was absent from a tape, he emphasized the point at which it *would have* taken place if the camera had been left on. On the other hand, Ezekiel filmed daily events far less than Yeshaie. He accompanied the American team on only one walkabout, during which he took still photographs. It might be argued that the combination of Ezekiel's interest in and liberalism toward ritual led him to concentrate on recording those events. Yeshaie, on the other hand, found that intensive participation in ritual did not allow him to film the events.

Ezekiel's interest in visual recording exceeded that of the other informant ethnographers. He was given a Polaroid camera to photograph in the community and used it afterward to start his own business. He would take portrait photos at a fixed price and eventually hoped to open his own photographic studio in the local Marrapodi market. Even before we introduced film and photography to our informants, Ezekiel had learned to take and develop his own photographs and had purchased a camera of his own. Most of the photographs that he took outside of ceremonies were intended for profit, unlike his voluntary filming of ritual events.

Chris, the younger member of the American research team, was born in 1952 in Annapolis, Maryland and was 21 years old during the period of research. An undergraduate student, he had had considerable exposure to commercial media since the age of two, and had some previous filming experience. He had twice used 8 mm silent film before coming to the field and had been videotaped but never before used a video camera. He also had some experience with still photography from taking tourist pictures and documenting everyday events, though he had not followed this as a regular hobby.

Chris had never been to Africa or to a field setting. He was not fluent in any African language, although he had begun to learn Kiswahili. In many ways, the field setting was novel for Chris, and filming provided a major vehicle for him to learn about it. Once in the field, Chris found the videotape to be his major interest, and he quickly developed an effective style for use of the camera, emphasizing zoom close-ups of selected participants alternating with wide angle shots. As a student, he came to the media with an academic interest as well as the practical task of participating in the visual recording. He was interested in the mechanics and aesthetics of looking, emphasizing the differences in perspective from one onlooker to another to yet another. He considered the video technician to be interpreting a scene by his recording of it, not merely relaying an objective report of the scene that would stand by itself. This attitude toward the "active" role of the camera operator was reflected in his technique that, although very different from that of the Maranke filmmakers, showed a similar interest in using the properties of the camera as ways to search actively in the scene for its central events.

For months prior to the field research, Chris had become a member of the Maranke church and had some familiarity with the rituals and their format. However, he knew only a few of the church songs and was uncertain of their exact translation. While he knew the meaning of ritual segments, he was not fluent enough to initiate parts of the ceremony in the vernacular. In describing his intentions in recording, Chris said that, like Ezekiel, he wished to conserve his videotape in order to capture events from different parts of the service. As in Ezekiel's case, this accentuated his use of in-camera editing.

On certain occasions, Chris had difficulty locating what other Maranke members would have seen as central ritual activities. For example, he shot a night ceremony at random in which members considered exorcism to be the main activity. On another occasion, he felt it more important to tape a sermon given in English for our benefit than to alternate between the other preaching and singing activities in the kerek. Chris explained that he wanted to save tape for the conclusion of the ceremony but was unable to do so. Part of his selection of shots may be explained in terms of Chris' aesthetic preferences concerning what to film. However, his filming was also influenced by his minimal basic familiarity with vernacular languages. Lack of linguistic knowledge made it difficult for him to follow the course of events in some cases. Only Chris' prior knowledge about the format of ritual scenes and his personal selection of pleasing shots guided his response to many events.

Peter, the second of the student researchers, had media experience with still

photographs and 16 mm film. He was born in 1946 in Chicago, Illinois, and was 27 years old at the time of filming. He had watched movies from the age of four and television from the age of six. As an undergraduate student, he had taken some 16 mm footage and some still photographs and had augmented his experience on a previous research trip to Zambia in 1971, when he took a number of still photographs and worked with Jérémie in 16 mm. On the present trip, Peter concentrated on 8 mm and 16 mm filming and left the videotaping to Chris.

Peter was fairly fluent in Tshiluba and had a large repertoire of Chishona songs. He had joined the Apostolic Church in 1971, a few months after Ezekiel, and had "obtained the gift" of senior baptist.[9] Members, however, still instructed him in church doctrine while regarding him as a potential harikros and a competent baptist. He was asked to preach, initiate songs, and perform curing and exorcism ceremonies. While Peter's experience with church rituals was not as extensive as Yeshaie's in certain respects, his in-depth study of them as an ethnographer and his performance in a number of ritual settings allowed him to identify and follow key events.

Like Yeshaie, Peter tended to give church doctrine and ritual a strict interpretation, while Chris, who had just joined the group, resembled Ezekiel in his inclination to reflect on the personal implications of ritual participation. Peter enjoyed singing and learning to lead the church's songs. His interest in singing was reflected in one film sequence that devoted twelve minutes to a single song performance. He stated afterward that he found it interesting in musical terms, although the other American researchers considered it repetitive. As Jules-Rosette's husband, Peter was viewed as a principal researcher and on certain occasions spoke on behalf of the research team. Many persons had difficulty discerning the relationships among the researchers. They were most directly influenced by Peter's description of the use of equipment and his filming style. Church elders also viewed Peter as a technician. When tape recorders and other modern machinery broke down, they came to him for repairs and advice. In this critical sense, he was regarded quite differently from the other members of the team.

WHAT DO WE HAVE?: SOME GENERAL FEATURES OF INFORMANTS' FILMING

The ten informant films represent in situ interpretations of ritual and everyday events. They show ways in which informants provide an intentional portrait of each setting. However, it is not possible to speak of the informant productions as a unified piece of research because of the differences among the filmmakers'

---

[9]He thus held a higher position than either Yeshaie, a junior baptist, or Ezekiel, who, despite his experience in the church, had not yet received a formal grade.

backgrounds and orientations. They differ in terms of the events selected to film, individual filming style, expertise with the equipment, and the expressed message to be communicated. There is also a definite progression within an individual informant's products from the first attempt at filming to the later sequences, during which the informant had already developed a confidence and skill in using the equipment.

However, all of the informant products were characterized by the following similarities: (1) extensive use of horizontal panning to establish the filming "field" and emphasize what the cameraperson determined to be focal activities; (2) the emergence of a combination of slow pans with momentary pauses to cover the expanse of activities and incorporate relevant side events; (3) the development of transitional markers or hesitation pauses to mark the transitions from one event to another; (4) the relative absence of zoom; and (5) the use of pivot and dolly to follow emerging activities. In short, the major cademic markers employed in the Bapostolo informant films were a combination of horizontal panning and holds. This panning was often done on a 180° pivot by the cameraperson and was embellished by dolly to follow activities. Situational and stylistic differences created variations, but the basic cademic units were nonetheless visible.

By contrast, the American camerapersons used zoom in almost the same proportion that the local filmmakers used the horizontal pan. Their films were invariably "easier" for an American audience to follow and established the "themes" or "topics" of filming by a combination of long shots and close-ups, with long holds on central activities. The manipulation of the element of time was important. The informants viewed their task as the communication of an ongoing simultaneity. By focusing on a single activity, the American filmmakers defined their aims as the recording of an event's sequential structure. Time for the Americans was emergent and linear; for the Maranke informants, it was synchronic and simultaneous.

As Ezekiel's filming progressed, he modified his technique in response to the American team's comments. He lengthened the duration of holds on specific activities and introduced the use of zoom on two occasions. In addition, he decreased the frequency with which he turned the camera on and off. Yeshaie similarly modified his technique by centering his holds on focal activities. However, his use of horizontal panning did not decrease but instead became more elaborate and adapted to the movements and activities of filmed subjects. To understand the differences among informant films, it is necessary to examine the filmed segments in detail.

THE INFORMANT-MADE FILMS

The films will be divided into those concerning ritual and those about everyday events. Each informant film will be compared to an American ethnographer's film of the same event. The absence of a directional microphone for a variety of the activities filmed resulted in a minimal soundtrack on many of the films, with the exception of some of the ritual sequences and Yeshaie's play. This variation of sound quality made the task of transcription difficult. Each informant film was transcribed at least twice: once on the basis of its cademic structure (i.e., a purely visual transcript) and once with respect to its content including the soundtrack. There was necessarily some overlap in the transcribing process, since certain activities could not be mentioned without referring to how they were captured on film, and certain camera movements were clarified by content and sound as further indications of how to locate them.

Segment 1: Ezekiel's Film at Kabanana

Ezekiel filmed an entire two-hour kerek using a single three-minute cartridge by turning the camera on several times for a few seconds when key songs were initiated. This film was Ezekiel's first. In his opinion, it was a successful attempt to capture the spiritual aspect of kerek. He viewed it as superior to the half-hour videotaped excerpt by Chris in which no singing was included.

The setting. Kabanana is an Apostolic farm about ten miles from Lusaka, Zambia. It is covered with tall weeds and stubble from last year's crops. Each Saturday afternoon at 1:00 p.m., approximately 80 Apostles meet there for worship lasting until early evening. These services consist of prophecy, preaching, singing, and a concluding healing ceremony. Men are seated to the east and women to the west with a sacred aisle for preaching formed between them. Ezekiel's account of this ceremony primarily contained singing.

Description of the filmed segment: The Kabanana Kerek. Ezekiel turned the camera on six times during this film. Four out of the six camera starts were marked by songs. The prevalent camera movement each time was the horizontal pan. The camera was very seldom held on a single activity. Ezekiel used filming as an excuse to rise, cross the sacred path, and stand behind the women's side of the congregation. The camera was used to establish a "filmic order of reality" and a legitimate place for him to create a filmed impression of the ceremony. The camera was in constant motion as Ezekiel alternated between the congregation and peripheral events.

The first shot framed three men in red robes. The camera then moved to the congregation as a whole. Ezekiel focused on the women seated in the congregation and then moved to the prophetic examination (keti) preceding worship. Side conversations were audible in the background. Ezekiel turned the camera off and then resumed filming as singing began. Each time that the camera was switched on, a new song was in progress. Although Ezekiel's film was spaced across a two-hour period, it seemed to capture a single song with numerous variations. Initially, it seemed to be more of a collage than a film.

An excerpt of the principal markers. The following transcript includes several camera movements within each cademic unit. It describes the two opening markers. Three of the following four begin with song.

Cademic Markers	Events
The camera begins on hold.	Three men in red robes are seated on the ground west of the ceremony. The main ceremony has not yet begun.
Pan right, pause.	The women of the congregation are sitting on the ground and singing.
Pan right, pausing twice,	to people standing next to the congregation. Singing continues.
Pan right	to open field. Singing continues.
Pan left, camera off	over field
. . .	. . .
Camera on, hold.	People stand in lines to be examined by prophets in *keti*. Singing is taking place.
Pan right	past *keti* to seated congregation.
Pause	on men's side.
Pan right	to women's side.
Pause	on women's side.
Pan right	past woman walking toward kerek.
Pan right	to open field.
Pan left	to center this woman.
Pause very slightly	on her.
Pan left	to congregation.
Slow slight pan left	to congregation.
Slow slightly	at women's and men's side (barely visible).
Pan left	to and past *keti* to men seated on ground and past child walking left.
Camera off . . .	. . .

Segment 2: Matero Preaching by Ezekiel

This segment might be viewed as a developmental progression from Ezekiel's first film of kerek. It includes less use of pan but includes long shots and zoom. Ezekiel was, in part, responding to the American filmmakers in modifying his approach to shooting. He also changed his orientation toward the activities filmed, concentrating on a mixture of preaching and song that was more representative of the structure of the real time event than the earlier film of kerek singing. The film sequence concludes with a curing ceremony that suggests some interesting interactions between the filmmaker and subjects. They seemed to be subtly orienting to the cameraperson's movements without explicitly paying attention to the filming activity. In this sequence, like the first, Ezekiel used the camera to establish his own order of reality apart from that of kerek by approaching the women's side of the congregation, panning to the sacred path and the men's side from that vantage point, and returning to focus on the women. This film gave a fuller portrait of the flow of the ceremony than the previous segment insofar as it accounted for more of the linear progression of the event.

The segment contained two continuous shots, or camera units, in comparison to six in the previous segment. The first was a symmetrical presentation of the arrangement of the central worship ceremony, beginning with the preacher standing in the aisle between the men and women, who sat facing each other on the ground. Ezekiel then panned left over the women, then right over the men, ending the sequence by zooming in on the speaker. Both segments show Ezekiel's preferences for panning symmetrically back and forth, as well as his growing willingness to use zooms and holds on central activities.

The setting.   Matero is a secluded village about fifty miles west of Lusaka. Its chief is an Apostle, and the spot is chosen for the annual Feast of Tabernacles, a church conference held in early August. During this time, Maranke Apostles live for a week to ten days in a bush retreat near the village and devote full time to worship. Although the major ceremonies have the format of the Sabbath kerek, many take place at night and are supplemented by intensive healing and exorcism rites. Ezekiel's film records a Sabbath kerek during the retreat. This ceremony is crucial because it is the final Sabbath service to take place during the retreat. It is at this time that prophets present visions relevant to the entire congregation. Matero retreat is a setting at which attendance is largely restricted to church members. While local villagers and some townspeople attend, this and other ceremonies are performed principally to instruct and strengthen members rather than outsiders.

Description of the filmed segment.   Ezekiel opened this segment with a wide-angle shot of the congregation that centered on the speaker in the sacred path. He stood on the men's side of the congregation, facing west. The preacher continued to explain the importance of the worship event in Chishona. As he welcomed the congregation to the retreat, the speaker held his staff upright, remaining stationary. Ezekiel panned left slowly to the women's side of the congregation and centered on a group of girls. He then panned further left across the women's side and returned right with a rapid motion to a hold on the speaker. He panned right, across the men's side to the back row. After a hesitation, he panned left to center on the speaker and zoomed in as he gesticulated. The preacher faced the men's side and emphasized several points, nodding his head to the speech cadence and dipping his staff twice. Ezekiel turned the camera off and terminated this sequence.

When he switched the camera on again, he had moved to the place of healing after the kerek. The main ceremony was over and members had broken up into small groups to discuss what was taking place. Ezekiel stood in the rear of what was formerly the men's side of the worship area and faced west. Men were circulating in the foreground. In the background, singing was taking place. By now, the late afternoon sun had noticeably altered the lighting of the scene.

Ezekiel panned left to several men standing in the foreground talking, then right to a man leaving the place of prayer. He hesitated and then continued to pan right over the groups of people, then left again. In so doing, Ezekiel emphasized the fact that the congregation had split into several groups. He panned right to the place of healing. The setting initially contained two people, one man healing another. A third was seated, waiting to be healed while others gathered around. Ezekiel centered on the third man who wore a red robe symbolizing his need to be healed. The first man to be healed stood and began to walk up left, after picking up his Bible. Ezekiel adjusted and centered the camera on the curing activity as one man sat down and another prepared to leave. A woman arrived to be healed with her child and knelt down behind the others. The first healer continued and the man with the Bible knelt down to heal others.

An excerpt of the principal markers.

Cademic Markers	Events
Camera on, hold, centering preacher in the center aisle.	Preacher stands facing east. Holding his staff upright and remaining fairly still, he preaches in Chishona, welcoming the congregation.
Slow pan left	over women's side and center on girls. They sit, looking at preacher and at camera.
Slow pan left	across women's side . . .
Hesitate, pan left	to center speaker.
Hold	on speaker, who stands and preaches, moving his staff silently from left to right and up and down. He turns to face the men's side and emphasizes points, nodding his head to the speech cadence and dipping his staff twice. . . .
. . .	
Center.	Healing is taking place in the space behind Chris. The patient is sitting on the ground facing left (east) and the healer is kneeling behind him to perform the ceremony. The tripod of the video camera is in front of and to the left of this healing ceremony. Other men move around the healing scene.
Pan left. Pan right.	Same
Pan left. Pan right.	Same
Center	on healing. Another man sits down to be healed. He is wearing red to show that he has already been healed or has been sick. The first man picks up his Bible, stands, and walks off left.

Segment 3: Singing and Preaching at Matero by Ezekiel

While segment 2 marked a definite increase in hold shots, and a concession to the use of zoom, segment 3, filmed during the early part of the same ceremony, was a continuation of Ezekiel's recording of song in kerek. This segment was shot with three camera units and consisted largely of horizontal panning from the women's to the men's section of the group. Preaching was interspersed with singing which constitutes the main kerek activity filmed. During the last portion of the film, preaching took place, but the sound was lost.

Ezekiel's three ritual films contained a progression toward a closer representation of real-time events in kerek. In his Kabanana film, he concentrated on singing, while his first Matero segment emphasized preaching. In segment 3, song was the main activity, but preaching was present as well, and at one point we observe the alternation between preaching and song. This segment thus struck a balance between the other two and portrayed the alternation of ritual activities. His treatment of the spatial ordering of kerek was similar in segments 2 and 3 with a marked difference from the Kabanana film. In the latter, he shifted his position after each shot, resulting in a series of different camera angles. In the Matero films, all the shooting was done from the east end of the center aisle. Ezekiel panned symmetrically between the men's and women's sides, pausing in the center to show the speaker or singer. Segment 3 thus shows most clearly the kerek's arrangement in time and space through the creation of a filmed order of reality.

The setting.   The scene was the same as in segment 2. Several thousand people were sitting in rows on the ground. It was the Sabbath afternoon kerek, the major service to be held in the five-day conference. Ritual participation was intense, but side activities such as child care, walking about, and fidgeting by young people were also parts of the conference setting that appear on the film.

Description of the filmed segment.   The opening shot panned slowly across the women's side to the aisle as a song began, then panned left over the women's side and held on the front row during the first part of the song: "We have seen there in Jerusalem. . . ." Slowly, Ezekiel panned right to the men's side as the singing continued. He hesitated and then panned back left across the men as they sang, then across the women as they sang. He then panned right from the women's side to the center aisle where a man was leading the song, hesitated, panned left to the women, and held on the women. Similar panning from the women's to the men's sides of the ceremony took place during the following two cademes. At one point, Ezekiel held the camera on the preacher who had been interrupted by a singer. In the background, the singer gesticulated and the preacher again entered the center aisle to continue the sermon.

An excerpt of the principal markers.   The only cademic markers appearing in this sequence were horizontal pans, pauses, and holds. On three occasions Ezekiel hesitated in the midst of a horizontal pan. Unlike the first segment, the horizontal panning in this one did *not* extend beyond the area of the ceremony. Panning covered the reactions of men and women in the congregation. The holds on the center aisle showed the viewer a partial progression of the activities there and a shift from preaching to song.

Segment 4 (a) and (b): The Marrapodi Confession Film by Yeshaie

This was the first of Yeshaie's films, and as such it has an "awkward" appearance. However, upon closer examination, these techniques reveal social conventions that Yeshaie was observing, for instance, a ritual order of speakers and ritual rules concerning eye contact. Among the few at-home ceremonies to be filmed, this event mediated between a full ritual performance and daily private worship. Several members of the church had gathered to meet with a visiting prophet. They were anxious to have him perform a curing ceremony and at the same time give them personal prophecies. After two of the members of the American team had participated in the curing ceremony, Peter began to film. Yeshaie observed his camera technique closely and then asked to film a short sequence himself. Since he was particularly concerned with recording Chris' response to the curing and confession, Yeshaie chose this as a point of departure. When Yeshaie centered the camera on Chris standing before the prophet, he included only Chris' torso. It is interesting to note that facial close-ups were absent from all but the very last segment that Yeshaie filmed. The confession and curing, like the other informant films, was characterized by its alternation of the pan, hold, and hesitate markers. During the process of panning, Yeshaie had already begun to develop the semicircular pivoting motion that he exploited more fully in later films.

The setting.   The confession took place in the home of Mama Eva, a Zairean Maranke Apostle. She provided lodging for many itinerant Apostles in Lusaka. On Saturday mornings, the Apostles would gather at her home with other local members for prekerek discussions and confession. By confessing before the main ceremony those gathered at Mama Eva's could avoid a lengthy ceremony at the afternoon kerek. The presence of the visitor, Baba Yowane, a special baptist with prophetic abilities, drew a larger crowd than usual. Apostles with sick children and with work or domestic disputes waited for his advice. Everyone took part in the curing ceremony. Jules-Rosette was the first to be healed and was asked to confess her problems before Baba Yowane would lay hands on her head. A Zairean woman followed and was recalled to confess three times before Baba Yowane prayed for healing. With her, he established a pattern of recalling subsequent patients.

The incident was unusual enough to inspire laughter.[10] Although each candidate confessed several times, everyone hoped that the multiple confession would be only for others and that he or she would be found free from sin. As each candidate was put through the same routine, awe increased for Baba Yowane's powers.

Description of the filmed segment.   This segment was lively and contained dialogue that will be summarized here. The first reel began with Peter, as

---

[10]Laughter is generally not allowed during confession ceremonies. The judges tried to control it.

cameraperson, holding on Chris who was sitting on the floor. He turned the
camera toward Baba Yowane and the women in the background then panned left
toward Chris who stood with hands at his sides to confess. The camera angled
upward to follow Chris' movements, then panned down right as Baba Yowane
whispered in his ear. He told Chris that he would have visions and prophecies.
These visions would be very clear and forceful for a period of two or three
months. Then Chris would meet a woman who would distract him from religious
concerns. She would be a *mambo muntu,* or mermaid spirit, and would lure him
with promises of riches and joy.[11] Although he would temporarily lose his
prophetic ability, he would regain it. After presenting the prophecy, Baba
Yowane asked Chris to confess and to verify it.

Peter panned up left, following Chris as he stood and resumed the confession,
hands at his sides and palms turned outward. As Baba Yowane advised Chris,
Peter panned down right to follow him. He held the camera on Yowane as he
continued to speak and then centered it on him. Then Peter handed the camera to
Yeshaie. He hesitated and centered on Chris' waist, then tilted the camera up
left, focusing on Chris' torso. Chris' head was not visible. The camera wobbled
and tilted slightly as Chris confessed, then Yeshaie gained control and panned
down left to Peter's hands and head. From there, he panned up and right to Chris'
legs, stomach, and face. Yeshaie paused on Chris' face and then panned slowly
down right to Chris, who was still confessing.

At this time, Ba'Kazadi, the officiating evangelist, questioned him in French:

BA'KAZADI:	C'est tout que vous avez?
	(Is that all you have to say?)
CHRIS:	Oui.
	(Yes.)
BA'KAZADI:	Donc, vous êtes un Apôtre....
	(Now then, you are an Apostle) ... The sound fades out.

[The sense of this is that Chris' status has been reinstated after confession.]

Yeshaie held the camera on Baba Yowane and shifted it slightly to the left to frame
two women in the back of the room. He panned left to Chris and up along his
body, until his face was visible though not his whole head. Chris sat down.
Yeshaie panned down to follow him. He panned right to frame Baba Yowane as
he prepared to lay hands on Chris for healing. The singing started. Yeshaie
panned left to Peter and up to another evangelist. Everyone was praying. Yeshaie
panned right, framing Baba Yowane and Chris, and held the camera on them
during the laying on of hands. The prophet laid his hands on the top of Chris'
head. Chris then moved toward the wall to the left, still sitting down. He sat
against the wall next to the author. Yeshaie panned left to follow him.

---

[11]These spirits (called Mammy Water or Mami Wata in West Africa) are found in folk beliefs
across subSaharan Africa and are often considered the cause of insecurity and unhappiness.

Yeshaie raised the camera gradually, and as soon as he reached Chris' face, he lowered it. Among Apostles, for both men and women, staring is a sign of disrespect. Women customarily kneel to greet men, and at this time they turn their heads and eyes down, so as not to stare at or challenge the person whom they greet.[12] He studied Chris' stance and reactions with vertical panning and used horizontal panning to follow the course of talk. The prophet Yowane standing to the right of Chris prayed over him and made predictions.

While Yowane prophesied, Yeshaie held the camera directly on his face. Seated on a stool, Yeshaie was at approximately the same level that Yowane was when he knelt. Chris' face and entire body entered the frame as he sat down in front of Yowane for the concluding prophecies and curing ceremonies. As Yeshaie came to feel more at ease with the camera, he followed Chris' motions closely. He also used panning to show the presence of others in the scene, including Peter, the judging evangelists, and the women in the background in that order. He highlighted Baba Yowane's advice and healing activities by panning from Chris to Yowane and by framing the two together at the culminating point of healing.

Yeshaie then inserted a second reel and filmed Ba'Kazadi's confession before the other evangelists. This reel is a single shot, consisting chiefly of horizontal and vertical panning. The jerkiness of the camera disappeared as Yeshaie began to space his pans and holds more evenly and to handle the camera more steadily. Again, he spaced his pans across Baba Yowane, Ba'Kazadi, and the audience, taking particular care to include the reactions of Chris, Peter, and the author. This segment also marked the termination of Baba Yowane's healing activities. He rose and sprinkled the room with holy water as Yeshaie panned to follow him. At the conclusion of the segment, everyone present knelt to pray as Yeshaie held the camera on the women. Yeshaie then put aside the camera to pray himself. This segment was both one of his earliest efforts and the last time he filmed ritual.

Segment 4(a):   An excerpt of the principal markers.

Cademic Markers	*Events*
Wobble, tilt (probably not intentional markers since the camera is being passed to Yeshaie for the first time)	Chris' head is not visible. His waist is shown.
Hold (still rocking)	Chris' waist. He is speaking.
Pan down left	Peter's hands and head.
Hesitate, hold	Chris' body as he confesses; not visible above shoulders.
Tilt up	Chris confesses; his chest is visible.
Slow pan up right	to Chris' shoulders.

[12]Albert (1964) reports similar postures among the Barundi.

Cademic Markers	Events
Slow pan down right	across women in background to Baba Yowane.

Dialogue:	BA'KAZADI:	C'est tout que vous avez? (Is that all you have to say?)
	CHRIS:	Oui. (Yes.)
	BA'KAZADI:	Donc, vous êtes un Apôtre . . . (Now then, you are an Apostle . . .)

Cademic Markers	Events
Hold	Baba Yowane listening.
Slow pan left	to Chris
Pan up	to Chris' shoulders
Pan down to follow	Chris as he sits down to be healed. Baba Yowane begins to sing.
Hold	Chris is sitting. Baba Yowane prepares to ''lay on hands'' for healing.

Segment 4(b):   An excerpt of the principal markers.

The camera has already been on throughout the previous segments. Yeshaie keeps it on for the duration of the filming.

Cademic markers	Events
Pan down	to water cup on the floor as Baba Yowane starts to sing.
Pan left and up	to frame Chris and the author as Yowane sings.
Pan right	to Baba Yowane as he sings.
Slow pan left	to Chris and the author, then to the evangelists.
Pan down right	to Peter coughing.
Pan right	Baba Yowane is standing and sprinkling the holy water to terminate the healing ceremonies.

An Overview of the Films of Ritual

Although the individual shooting styles varied, each of these films was influenced by and reinterpreted the basic format of the ritual filmed. Ezekiel first provided a ''mystical'' interpretation of kerek as ''song.'' Then he proceeded to film preaching and singing as more equally interspersed, placing emphasis on both the preacher's activities and congregational response. However, in the first film, no one in the congregation was shown at length, in part as a result of the number of times that the camera was switched on and off. The distribution of activities in Ezekiel's second and third segments filmed at Matero resembled Jérémie's earlier shooting, with the inclusion of close-ups and cutaways and an interest in the balance of activities. Our post hoc editing of Jérémie's film attempted to simulate the ''real time'' format by combining preaching and singing segments in a manner that he had not.

In Ezekiel's film segments, the reactions of the participants to the camera were indirect. In the curing segment, participants seemed to flock to the curer who was being filmed in preference to others, although they did not overtly pose for the camera. By contrast, in Yeshaie's segment, little attention was paid to the camera, in part as a result of the compelling and novel character of Yowane's confession-cures. Yeshaie followed interactions through more thoroughly than Ezekiel. From the beginning he tended to use fewer cademic markers, although he used the same horizontal panning consistently throughout each segment. His filming, therefore, followed the structure of the event as it unfolded. He emphasized personal reactions and used them to highlight significant portions of the ritual, for example, the relationship between confession, the presentation of judgment by the evangelists, and the laying on of hands by Baba Yowane. Panning was rarely used to follow action. Instead, it created its own arena of activity. In each case, Yeshaie wished to convey personal reactions, and through them he presented the progression of events. Since the verbal presentation and judgment of cases was also important, Yeshaie's shots were more continuous in order to reveal the substance of the matter rather than simply impressions of the scene.

Everyday Events on Film

In contrast to the ritual events, the mundane events, although structured, did not follow a specific format. Yeshaie's film of tinsmithing came the closest to portraying a bounded activity, but in this case much of the unity was created through his filming technique. The walkabout and the film of Mandevu Market captured people engaged in ordinary activities. However, these two films, to a greater extent than those of ritual, clearly interrupted the activities at hand. Participants posed for the movie camera as though for a still photograph to portray everyday activities. Yeshaie made the pose an integral part of his latter two films.

Yeshaie's use of the camera became increasingly self-assured and elaborate the more he filmed. He added to panning the 360° pivot and was sensitive to following through motions and entire activities. The use of the pivot as a way of returning to a central activity gives each filmed sequence a sense of thematic unity and completeness. Yeshaie rarely used zoom or continuous hold on a single incident for emphasis. Instead, repetition created the narrative link for his communication.

Segment 5: The Marrapodi Tinsmith by Yeshaie

Yeshaie began this walkabout at Ncube's tinsmith shop where he filmed three young men making buckets and chicken feeders. Ncube, the owner and a member of the Masowe church, was absent. On the previous day, he had given permission to film his shop at an indefinite time. Ncube's wife had been washing clothes and left this activity to watch the filmmakers. Yeshaie turned the camera on once for the duration of the reel. He used a 360° pivot to cover the corner where the tinsmiths worked, returning to emphasize their activities by horizontal panning. At certain moments, Yeshaie seemed to be in the throes of a decision, hesitating in making a horizontal pan. This marker was labeled "hesitate." Throughout the film, Yeshaie returned to the tinsmiths six times while panning across the work scene, and held on them for four out of the six occasions. It is through this return pan and hold that Yeshaie established tinsmithing as a central activity.

Yeshaie's tinsmith film was made as part of the community visual survey and revealed his sense of artistry and form. His 360° pivot during the shooting allowed him to pick up all aspects of the scene. Yeshaie stood in the middle of the shop and gave the feeling of relating closely to the workers and spectators. Although many children and young people had gathered to observe Yeshaie, he captured them naturally in the film, panning regularly from the workers to the onlookers. The workers continued, occasionally glancing at the camera but not allowing it to interfere with their routine. Poses interrupted their activity rather than stopping it as they did for the Americans. The workers, who had known in advance that Yeshaie would be filming, were prepared for us.

The setting.   The young men were working near the protective awning of the shop. When Yeshaie began to film, other youths joined the tinsmiths, and neighborhood children flocked to watch both the smithing and the filming. In Chris' video sequence at Ncube's, these groups of children grew ever larger. The poses that interrupted the smiths' activities increased during Chris' taping and began to interfere with their work routine.

As Yeshaie filmed, several passersby moved along the throughfare. None stopped to greet Ncube's workers, perhaps as a result of the filming. In fact, with the exception of glancing at Yeshaie, they did not interact with the scene. On the other hand, there was more direct interplay between the videoist and the observers in Chris' tape, as we shall see later.

Description of the filmed segment.   In this segment, the camera was turned on once for the duration of the reel. Yeshaie opened by focusing on the two men working with the tin. One man hit the tin with a hammer, another stood to his right, and another was behind them. Only the sound of hammering was audible. Yeshaie panned left past some children who were watching to Peter. He then returned to the smiths by panning right and held momentarily on them. He slowly panned further right past the work scene and up the street to a taxi. Then he panned left to the edge of the shop and right past the taxi to a woman walking. He paused to center the children and panned right to follow the woman as she walked down the street. With a slow pan right, he aimed the camera across the street and held it on some women washing at the faucet. He centered the young spectators then panned right across the yard and left to the intersection where Chris was taping.

After panning right to follow a truck down the street, he moved left, stopping at the working men, then past a group of men in front of the first doorway of the house to show Ncube's wife at the second doorway. This marked his second return to the smiths.

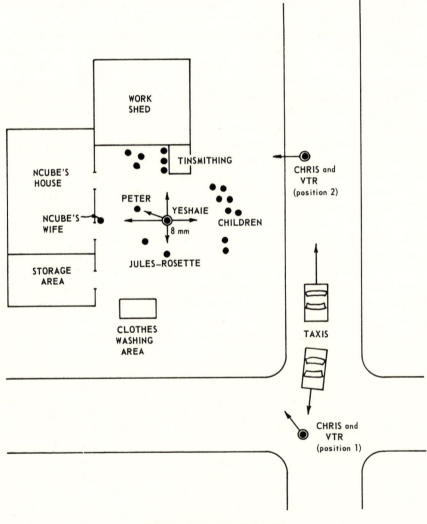

FIG. 8   The Marrapodi tinsmith.

Yeshaie then reversed his circular pivot, returning right past the group of men to the smiths. He continued a slow pan right to show children with a bicycle and moved left to center a young boy and right to the rest of the children. A youth walked up playing with a chain. Yeshaie panned right and centered him and then left to a clothes vendor as he walked down the street. He panned left several times to follow the children at play, then panned left and centered the tinsmiths. He continued to pan counterclockwise with the camera, passing Peter near Ncube's doorway, angling down toward some children, and moving left again to follow Ncube's wife. As she moved right, Yeshaie panned to follow her back to the second doorway of the house. A fast pan right, intended to bring the author into the picture, ended the reel. Throughout the film, Yeshaie returned to the tinworkers six times while panning across the scene and held on them at length for four out of the six occasions, establishing their work as a central activity.

An excerpt of the principal markers.

Cademic markers	*Events*
Hold, medium close-up	on children in front of camera; behind them are tinsmiths working.
Slow pan left	over children, Peter's hands.
Pan right	over children to workmen.
Hold.	three workmen standing at bench; one is hammering; heads are omitted.
Short pan right	brings hammering into full view, road on side.
Hesitate	same
Pan right	across road to taxi parked on side of road, kids.
Pan left	covers hammering (same as short pan right above); passes to men standing above hammerer.
Pan right	to two men standing in the street . . .

This sequence demonstrates the presence of smithing in the context of neighborhood activities.

Pan right	to group of men in work places.
Slow	at tin work.
Slow	at children with bicycle.
Pan left and center	on boy.
Pan right and hold	on children.
Pan fast right	Youth enters playing with a chain.
Pan left	to clothes vendor.
Slow pan right	following clothes vendor to group of spectators.
Pan left	to tin work.

Segment 6: The Marrapodi Walkabout by Yeshaie

Members of the John Masowe Apostolic Church occupy much of the southern portion of the Marrapodi community. Ncube is a member of this group and so are many tinsmiths and cabinetmakers. In the light of the overwhelming presence of Masowe members in the community, it is not unusual that Yeshaie's walkabout began as a record of their workplaces. Yeshaie chose to film a cluster of houses across from the Marrapodi bus station. He knew and was friendly with the residents. Yeshaie stopped by the side of the road and filmed from that vantage point.

The setting.   Only women and children were at the Masowe homes. It was midday and everyone seemed to be relaxing. Groups of young girls amused themselves and were ready to pose and mimic for the camera. The interaction with Yeshaie was friendly. One young woman started a conversation as he continued to film her. Yeshaie approached her in a friendly manner and continued to converse with the camera in hand. Two women awaited the departure of a bus at the station. As the segment closed, persons who had just left taxis or who had come from the market moved along the main street.

Description of the filmed segment.   Yeshaie opened by focusing on a large house on the left side of a lot. He then panned right across the lot to some smaller houses. He panned right past some women and children and left again to show a girl raising a tin stove in the air to display it to him. He moved the camera left and right across the houses several times and then panned left to the main street, holding the camera down on sewage water by the side of the road. He then panned slightly to the left and centered on the author talking with a group of passersby. He paused and panned left to Chris, who was taping across the street, and then turned slowly farther left to the bus station. Two women were sitting in front of the station. He then panned left and held as two cars passed. The local bar and other larger buildings were in the background. He panned left from the street to the edge of the yard. Clothes were hanging out to dry, and the carcass of a white car sat in the yard. Boys played near the car. Yeshaie panned left to the woman who sat in front of the large house, looking startled. He panned back to the center of the lot and held on it. The lot was nearly deserted. He panned left and right across the lot twice, turned to the right, and held as the young woman approached the fence to talk to him. She was still talking as he turned the camera left to the lot. Children ran to enter the picture. Yeshaie turned further left to the thoroughfare as the author walked out of the frame.

Yeshaie held the camera steadily on the thoroughfare. Three men walked toward it. Still focusing on the street, Yeshaie moved the camera left and centered it. A group of Masowe girls jumped into the frame. They vied for Yeshaie's attention as he turned the camera left toward Chris and right toward the author. Simultaneously, a man in a dark suit walked up the thoroughfare.

An excerpt of the principal markers.   A single cademe is employed.
(a)   Opening markers:

Cademic markers	Events
Initial hold	on the large house to the left of the lot.
Pan right	to smaller houses and to the center of the lot.
Pan right	to houses on the right side of the lot and white junked car.
Slow pan left	to a young girl waving a charcoal stove in the air. She speaks to Yeshaie but what she says is inaudible.
Pan left	to the houses on the left side.
Pan right.	The girl with the stove walks away and then turns to lift the stove.
Pan right	to the white car.
Pan left	to the house on the right side of the lot and the children.
Pan left, hold	to the center of the lot.
Pan left	past the houses up the thoroughfare.
Hesitate and hold	on the sewage water.

(b)   Yeshaie increasingly uses the camera as a means to interact with persons in the scene.

Hold	on the right side of the lot.
Pan right	to a house on the right side.
Hold	same
Hold.	Again, as the girl walks forward to the fence approaching the camera.
Pan left.	She talks, Yeshaie pans to the center of the lot.

Segment 7: The Mandevu Market by Yeshaie

This segment was a continuation of the Marrapodi walkabout. Like Yeshaie's choice of the Masowe households, the open market between Mandevu and Marrapodi was a representative gathering place recognized by members of several subgroups in the community. The market film, like the walkabout, showed several persons who posed for the camera or seemed somewhat disturbed by its presence. However, rather than remaining distant from his subjects, Yeshaie approached them with a friendly attitude and panned from one to another. The effect was one of a staged presentation displaying tableaux of people at work. Yet, most of the poses were explicitly intended to recreate life at the market and to represent habitual work settings.

Yeshaie created a feeling of completeness among his shots by using the 360° pivot and choosing a focal thoroughfare as his point of return. But in this segment, he did not follow through a single activity such as tinsmithing. Instead, he presented an impressionistic portrait of various persons and activities at the market place.

The setting.   The Mandevu Market was an open area divided into several sections: the tinsmiths' display, the cabinetmakers' workshops, the stalls for hardware, clothes, vegetables, meat, and fish vendors. The southeast portion was devoted to cabinetmakers, and it is here that both Yeshaie and Chris began to record. To the north of this area, there were several vegetable stalls. On the ground below the furniture and the vegetables were several canvases full of edible seeds.

Description of the filmed segment.   Yeshaie again placed himself in the center of the arena that he wished to film and pivoted 360°, panning to follow action. He chose as a focal spot the lane between the cabinetmakers and vegetable vendors. Many of the persons filmed posed, forming a tableau as Yeshaie panned across them. The movements of the camera were so rapid that the posing is not immediately visible. The film opened with a shot of a woman and child to the right of the lane. The child, a toddler, was hitting an object on the ground with a hammer. Yeshaie panned left to a man posing in a blue smock. He was a worker from one of the businesses. As he posed, he stood akimbo and shifted his weight. Yeshaie panned left and paused at another worker and from there to a man posing with hands raised in the position of a boxer. As Yeshaie panned left toward Chris, the man abandoned his pose and laughed. Yeshaie paused at Chris who was adjusting the video camera. He panned right to a doorway in the building facing the camera and right again to children and women in the lane. Yeshaie retained this image as a man walked in front of the camera, brusquely pushing two of the children aside as he passed across the thoroughfare.

At this time, Yeshaie had returned to his point of departure and here panned left and right between the woman in the lane and the man in the blue smock who was gesturing to the children. Yeshaie rapidly shifted his orientation, panning right to Chris and down left to some children who were watching the scene. He held on the childrens' faces and then panned left to a woman behind the author. Then he panned left to Jules-Rosette, paused, and panned left to the women behind who were staring with some distrust at both of us. Jules-Rosette walked to the right. Yeshaie panned slowly, first right and then left, lowering the camera to film the seeds. He then panned right to a young woman behind the school girls.

For the first time, Yeshaie dollied forward and zoomed in on a table in front of the furniture business across the lane and centered it. This was Yeshaie's first and only use of zoom. He hesitated, panned left and right to follow two children, then he panned down right to a set of chairs. Yeshaie turned to pan up left on a young woman with a child and then further left to make a horizontal pan on one of three girls in a group. The workmen entered, carrying a large board, and Yeshaie panned left to follow them and held on the doorway.

From there, he gradually began the return counterclockwise pivot to his point of departure. He panned left past the group of girls and right again back to the doorway. Then he panned left to a vegetable stand and further left to a group of people. He moved right again, filming a woman's torso without her head. She stepped back and her face came into view. He panned right to a group of children and then left again across the seeds and back to the central lane. A woman walked by and several children entered the scene to pose. The entire effect was one of constant yet calculated and directed camera movements. Yeshaie made the poses into natural and meaningful displays within the scene. The market appeared to be cluttered and bustling. In order to include seeds and vegetables spread on the ground, a tilt downward was used along with a spiraling vertical pan up to objects and persons on a higher level. This pan/tilt downward was more than a random combination of two camera movements. It was intended to emphasize a specific relationship among the objects filmed. This movement allowed him to eliminate objects that were not relevant to his account.

An excerpt of the principal markers.

(a)   Opening markers:

Cademic markers	Events
Hold.	A woman and child are standing right of the lane.
Pan left to the lane.	A little girl plays with a hammer.
Pan further left.	A cabinetmaker poses in a blue smock.
Pan left and center.	The chairs being made are being shown.
Hold	on chairs.
Hesitate, pan left.	Stops at a man who is observing a man in shirtsleeves.
Pause	at this onlooker.
Pan left.	toward the man in shirtsleeves, posing like a boxer. He lets
Pause	down the pose as the camera pans away.
Pan left	to Chris with the video recorder.
Pause	at Chris.

(b)   This scene contains Yeshaie's first use of zoom. The zoom is contained with a dolly and is used to orient toward a furniture business. The dolly is followed by a use of vertical panning for emphasis.

Slow pan right	past the school girls.
Pan down left	to the seeds.
Hesitate	after the seeds.
Pan right	to the young woman behind the school girls. She walks right.

Dolly forward and zoom directly in	on the furniture business. The girls move right.
Center	on booth across the lane.
. . .	. . .
Pan down right	to chairs.
Pan left and up left	to young woman with a child.
Pan right, down and up	on a girl in the group of three.

(c)   Another torso focus appears toward the end of the segment.

Cademic Markers	Events
Pan right	to follow some people across the path.
Pan down left	to woman's torso.
Vertical pan.	The woman steps back and reveals her face.
Pan right and hold.	Yeshaie returns to children who are standing in the initial lane.

The Structure of the Everyday Settings

The reasons for which certain events were highlighted in the everyday settings were ambiguous on many occasions. Since only Yeshaie's films were chosen to represent the informant's view of these settings, more similarity of structure is available in the filming than in the character of the settings themselves. Above all, Yeshaie stressed the simultaneity of events. He incorporated posing as an expected feature of his films.[13] He did not stop or hesitate when he noticed posing and interacted freely with the persons filmed.

It is difficult to explain why Yeshaie seemed to hesitate with the camera. He did not recall these movements as anything other than an attempt to follow the entire scene. In all three film segments, he panned to follow individuals and presented their activities in a more continuous manner than Ezekiel did in his first films of kerek. His pans also create a composite picture of a scene in ongoing interaction. He was also less able than Ezekiel was to rely on his own and the viewer's foreknowledge of what was to come. In the only ritual scene that Yeshaie filmed, the final decision or content was so important that continuous following was also necessary.

The market scene was the least "personal" of Yeshaie's films. Although he interacted openly with the individuals filmed, their posing, while not disruptive, created a distance between the cameraperson and the filmed subjects. This interpersonal distance was manifested through the expressions of the subjects and the

---

[13]One may infer that for Yeshaie's purposes there was no distinction between the artificial or posed setting and the capturing of the "natural event." For a discussion of the use of posing by photographic subjects to give an idealized version of a scene, see Sudnow (1972).

angles from which Yeshaie filmed. Yeshaie seemed equally concerned with portraying objects and persons. He returned three times to the seeds on the ground, used vertical pan to portray individuals in much the same way that he used zoom to highlight objects, and he filmed (for whatever reason) another torso shot.

There are sociological reasons for Yeshaie's filming behavior. His status as an Apostle had provided him entrée into the two John Masowe settings, but it did not validate his presence in the market. While he maintained a jovial attitude, several of the women and young girls viewed Yeshaie and the rest of the American team with suspicion. His film segment in the market and, to a lesser extent, the two others as well, were portraits of everyday life created for the camera and, above all, they revealed the relationship of the Maranke cameraperson to the scene.

COMPARISON OF INFORMANTS' AND AMERICAN STUDENTS' FILMS

Like the informant-made films, the students' films deal with both everyday and ritual settings. They differ from the informant films in style, interactional distance from filmed subjects, and the combination of camera techniques or markers used to convey meaning. Even when the students attempted to avoid selectivity by leaving the camera on the tripod and letting it run, their very placement of the camera and decisions to move it created a particular recording perspective. The composite of all of these differences will be referred to as a filming perspective. While we maintain that these differences in perspective rely upon contrasting perceptions and experience with visual media, it is also necessary to consider idiosyncratic differences in filming style. Therefore, intergroup comparisons will prove as helpful as cross-cultural parallels that can be used to investigate how film expresses meaning. The context of filming is, furthermore, much more than a mere background factor to be brought in for more conclusive analysis. Each film is a product and expression of the social context in which it was made. As such, each of the informants' and students' films must be approached differently. Transcription and analysis have been modified to meet the particular specifications of each segment. Despite these methodological differences, some broad equivalences and contrasts may be drawn.

Rather than describing each of the American students' tapes in detail, the tapes will be discussed in comparison with the seven informant films. Once that is done, we shall examine Yeshaie's play as a joint product of informant and researcher participation.

Peter filmed the main ritual segments while Chris taped both ritual and everyday events. While their presence as observers and recorders at scenes was equal, Peter's concentration on 8 mm and 16 mm film and his close familiarity with ritual objects led him to produce more comparable film segments. By employing several half-hour videotapes to record three different ceremonies, Chris created substantially different documents of ritual. While taping he used a tripod, in contrast to Peter's hand-held camera. The use of the tripod led Chris to leave the camera or to adjust it minimally while he watched and participated in the event. It also permitted him to capture segments of worship, for example, the Mwari Komborera, or invocation of the Holy Spirit, that could not be recorded by film since total participation was required. Yet, the tripod meant that perspectival unity and distance would be maintained. As a result, Chris' principal cademic markers were zoom, hold, and pan.

Although Peter had considerably more freedom than Chris in the use of the hand-held cameras, he used dolly and zoom more than did the local informants. In filming everyday events such as tinsmithing, Peter would place himself at a distance of about ten feet from the activity, zoom in on it, and carefully follow the work of the tinsmith rather than work from the center of the activity as Yeshaie had done. He would show the motions of the smith's hands and the linear process used to make a tin bucket. He attempted to capture the researcher's orientation toward construction of an object without violating what he considered to be a comfortable and appropriate distance to film the activity. When filming ritual events, Peter would generally shoot from his seated position and would often remain there, panning back and forth to follow the speaker when he was in motion or framing speakers and readers together. Rather than create his own order of reality by moving through the kerek, Peter attempted to present an "insider's" view by shooting over people's heads and angling the camera upward to capture the preachers and singers. Informant filmers tended to avoid upward shots in their filming practice. Yeshaie's confession film, the only one made from that vantage point, cut off Chris' head when he was standing and contained a series of pans between full height level (Chris) and floor level (the evangelists and Baba Yowane).

The Researchers' Films of Ritual

The Matero Films by Peter: Segments 1 and 2

Peter's films of the Matero kerek placed equal emphasis on preaching and song. He followed the line of movement down the sacred path, included the speaker's gesticulations, and then zoomed in on him preaching. Peter used dolly and pan to follow, panning from left to right in constant motion. However, this continuous panning's resemblance to Yeshaie's is deceptive, since Peter used this marker only when a speaker or singer was running back and forth in the aisle and then only to follow him rather than to alternate between him and other subjects. Peter's filming reflects his foreknowledge of the format of ritual and an effort to present his own participation through film. In two of his 8 mm sequences, the night kerek and a dawn instruction session at Matero, he held the camera steadily at the event and made no attempt to interfere with it. In the instruction session, just as in his segment of the Sabbath kerek, Peter filmed the baptist's face and upper torso from the seated position.[14] This angle gave a "larger than life" impression of the instructor leaning forward over the circle of elders.

This instruction session also marked an important choice of occasions to film. Members did not volunteer to use the camera at this time and, in fact, felt that the setting was private. They were dealing with disputes, decisions, and interpretations that were considered especially relevant for discussion by the baptists before being raised among the other elders. Peter filmed the instruction session in his role as a baptist, yet he did not film the scene as a local member would. We did not have a film by Yeshaie or Ezekiel of a comparable scene, since they held different grades and were not participants.

Another sequence shot by Peter at a Matero worship service reveals his attempt to follow the preacher's movements from the perspective of a congregational spectator. He used panning to follow the preacher's movements but paused considerably more than Ezekiel did during his film of the same event. Peter used zoom rarely and its absence was an intentional omission. Slow panning was intended to provide an interpretive view of the scene. Peter's technique during this scene contrasted sharply with Chris' heavy use of zoom with the stationary camera.

Cademic Markers	Events
Hold.	Magora, the preacher, is walking left in the aisle, speaking. The camera is held from seated position on the men's side about three rows back, facing aisle. Magora stops walking and talking, turns his head to face the camera, gesturing with his right hand.
Hold (midshot, centered).	He raises both hands, speaks, brings both hands back to his chest. The congregation responds, "Alleluia!"
Pan right to follow.	He turns further toward our right, hands raised, walks right, speaking and gesturing with both hands.
Pan right, faster	as he begins to run. He greets the congregation, "Vana va Africa!" (Children of Africa). They respond. He slows to a walk. One member: "Alleluia!" He stops.
Pan right to follow.	He starts walking left. He says one phrase. One member: "Yezu Mambo" (Lord Jesus).
Pan left to follow.	Speaking, gesturing, moving faster, he continues to move left. He says one phrase, stopping in front of the camera and facing camera while speaking.
Hold.	Magora speaking.

[14]A baptist, as indicated earlier, is one of the higher ranking members of the Apostolic Church and is charged with the baptism of new members and the organization of the congregation.

Overall, the cademic markers found in Peter's film reflected an attention to the ritual event in terms of those activities that literally followed one another: preaching and song, with a slight emphasis on the former. His movements were inhibited. He stated that he felt conspicuous with the camera, and he generally preferred to remain either seated or on the periphery of the ceremony. An observable difference between Peter's and Ezekiel's Matero footage lies in Ezekiel's preoccupation with the women's side and the women's reactions. In his Matero preaching and singing segments, he faced the women directly and filmed them. He is also concerned with maintaining a balance of shots across the men's and women's sides of the worship area through constant panning. On the other hand, Peter's films concentrated on the central activity of preaching which was oriented largely to the men. Since he was filming while seated, Peter readily captured the facial reactions and expressions of nearby men rather than women in his shots. On the whole, the number of cademes employed, the cademic markers used, and the interaction displayed through film stood in distinct contrast for the informants and the researchers' productions.

The Matero and Kabanana Tapes by Chris: Segments 4 and 5

Chris made a videotape of the same Matero Sabbath ceremony that was filmed by Ezekiel and Peter, providing another contrasting document. Chris left this tape on from the opening prophetic examination to the concluding sermon. The inclusion of the opening invocation was achieved by leaving the camera unattended. During this interval, Chris joined in song and prayer. Each time he thought that the preaching portion of the ceremony was about to end, another speaker arose. Chris switched the camera on for each of these occasions, hoping to tape the closing healing ceremony but instead obtained another sermon. Part of his difficulty in determining shots for in-camera editing resulted from his inability to understand the language and the announcement of an order of speakers. Just as Ezekiel presented an impressionistic account of kerek as ecstatic singing performed chiefly in Chishona, Chris presented a taped description of the ceremony as a sermon, translated into English. Ezekiel and Chris recorded the parts of the ceremony that were the most comfortable for them. Chris translated the ceremony into terms that he could understand during the course of taping and thereby created a preinterpreted ethnographic account within the natural setting (cf. Bergum, 1974).[15]

---

[15]Bergum presents the major problem of the ethnographic filmmaker as one of translation from one cultural idiom into another. He states: "In this cross-cultural problem, the filmmaker is akin to a translator and the film a translation. Note that the translator is concerned with equalizing meanings from one system to another. Furthermore, the meanings of the same perceptual object may differ between cultures, as meaning is rooted in cultural experience and it is just the lack of shared experience that blocks the translation process" (p. 8). It is through focusing on events that he can most readily understand that Chris accomplishes this translation while shooting in the natural setting as opposed to post-hoc editing and transliteration.

The Kabanana kerek was Chris' first. In it, he used the camera on a tripod but shifted the camera angle and focused several times. He used zoom extensively to highlight activities, for example, the beginning of prophecies and of antiphonal readings, and to record facial expressions. He held the camera on the keti as several candidates, including the congregation's leader, received prophecies. Chris then switched the camera from a side view of the prophecy to an angle directly behind the prophets, close to where the candidates stood. The effect was a simulation of the candidate's position through the camera angle. The camera was, however, still clearly on a tripod. It was steady and stationary. Although Chris panned to follow the candidates as they entered the kerek, there were few pans and they were placed at long intervals.

Chris then moved the camera to the north side of the place of prayer where it remained. He stayed with the camera to follow the opening prayers and the initiation of preaching. With the exception of switching the camera on and off at the moment when the opening prayers and hymns end, Chris followed through the entire sermon. This tape of kerek is the closest that we possess to "real time" filming of the ritual. It contains all of the "structural properties" of the kerek described in Chapter 3: antiphonal preaching, preacher–reader exchange, and song interruption. This tape provides a "documentary" account that stands in contrast to both Ezekiel's and Peter's films and Chris' later taped account of kerek as preaching.

At Matero, Chris taped a sermon given in Chishona and simultaneously translated into English but did not tape substantial portions of other sermons and neglected to record any songs. He kept the camera stationary, using zoom to emphasize the movements of the preacher and his translator. They, in turn, faced the camera and spoke into it, announcing that since they were unable to reach the American audience directly, they would do so indirectly through the medium of the camera. At one point, the preacher formulated this process by announcing: "This is for you, the whites." This admission explained their peculiar structuring of activities and the absence of spontaneous song within this segment. They wanted Chris to focus upon this segment and he did so at the expense of other activities. This segment is recorded in the Appendix (pp. 181–182).

Segment 6: The Marrapodi Confession by Peter

Peter began the filming of Baba Yowane's confession and curing ceremony. His familiarity with the ritual allowed him to capture its central features. Peter's filming preceded Yeshaie's. He shot upward from the corner of the room, capturing the faces of each member who confessed. Yeshaie watched him, but others did not seem particularly aware of the camera. After filming two reels, including Yeshaie's own confession, Peter gave the camera to him. Like the Matero films, these two segments are relevant for their content, format, and filming style. It is interesting that Peter filmed Yeshaie, and Yeshaie, in turn, filmed Chris. Peter used the standard filming technique of allowing an individual to respond, then turning the camera toward him a few seconds later. He used panning to follow action in this manner and otherwise held the camera directly on the person speaking. He did not use zoom and kept the camera on a full wide angle.

Description of the filmed segment. Peter opened on hold and then panned down left to the evangelists talking. He panned to follow Baba Yowane as he sang and leaned forward to advise Yeshaie. He panned up to Yeshaie's upper torso, a movement that Yeshaie would perform differently later. He held the camera steadily on Yeshaie as he shrugged and began to confess. A woman and child walked out to the left in the background as Yeshaie continued to talk. Yowane gave Yeshaie God's direct message. Yeshaie confessed about a quarrel that he had at work about leaving for Zaire.

Baba Yowane prayed for Yeshaie, and Peter panned up right and held on this activity. He placed his hand on Yeshaie's head twice and then put his staff back in his right hand. Both leaned forward simultaneously. Yeshaie prepared to rise. Baba Yowane shifted his weight as he sang. Everyone present sang the healing song together.[16]

An excerpt of the principal markers. Although panning from the evangelists to Baba Yowane and Yeshaie was present, the use of hold was more frequent than in Yeshaie's confessing segment.

Cademic Markers	Events
Hold	on woman in yellow shirt framed from head to waist, just right of center frame; she speaks, folding her belt as she does so. An evangelist answers her briefly (not visible); she continues. Baba Yowane's staff leans left in front of her.
Hold	on staff pulled away to right. Woman puts hand to her forehead and pulls it down quickly. She is speaking.
Slight pan down left.	Her arms and belt are also visible.
Pan down left, hold	to close-up of men seated on floor, facing her. Profile, facing right; their heads, shoulders, and staffs on shoulders are visible. One evangelist leans forward, speaking.
Hold.	Woman begins to answer.
Pan up right to her, hold.	Woman speaking.
	Evangelist speaks again, she looks down left at him.
Pan down left	to evangelist.
Hold	on evangelist speaking. He nods, as in assent, saying "A-ah." Kazadi (a child) sits down with the men, left background of frame.
Pan right.	Woman sits down. . . .

[16]The healing ceremony is short and routine. The healer kneels behind the patient and touches his head and limbs in a standard fashion while singing the song, "I heal in the name of God in Heaven."

The Students' Films of Ordinary Events

Both Peter's and Chris' films of ritual revealed a different conception of the event and their relationship to it than that of the informants. Neither used ritual space in the same way as informants to create an arena for filming, with the possible exception of Peter and Yeshaie in the confession segment. Their choices of what and how to film also contrasted. In everyday settings, the choice of scenes to film was more comparable. In this case, Chris tended to follow Yeshaie's lead rather than vice versa. However, the differences in the use of filmed markers remained equally salient in the everyday segments. These differences were compounded by noticeable contrasts in filmed subjects' reactions to informant and researcher cameraperson.

Chris' Marrapodi Film Segments

Chris followed Yeshaie from Ncube's to the Mandevu market, taping the activities that Yeshaie filmed on several occasions. He began with a tape of the thoroughfare behind Ncube's. He first taped women washing clothes across from Ncube's for about ten minutes. Then he moved toward Ncube's. It is this segment, the following walk toward the market, and the concluding market sequence that the author has transcribed and contrasted with Yeshaie's films.

Segment 7: The Marrapodi Tinsmith by Chris

The setting of Ncube's is the same. Yeshaie had just completed his filming and is seen in Chris' tape leaving Ncube's toward the main thoroughfare. About six minutes after Yeshaie had terminated, Chris walked northeast to the shop and began to tape. He turned the camera off and repositioned it once during this segment. He videotaped most of the events that Yeshaie had filmed. The camera remained on a tripod and Chris repositioned himself with it once.

Description of the filmed segment.   Chris approached the shop, zoomed in on it and on the principal worker smithing. The worker was uneasy at Chris's presence, stared at him, but continued to work as Yeshaie moved away. Chris then panned out toward the road, held on the road, and returned the camera to its initial position. He turned the camera off and turned it on again to hold on three smiths working. They exaggerated their movements and two finally stopped working, while the other continued in mime. Chris taped them until one resumed work, and then turned away to the thoroughfare. He maintained a distance of approximately 15 feet during the taping. This reluctance to approach the scene is reflected in Chris' choice of shots and his interaction with the workers.

An excerpt of the principal markers.

Cademic Markers	Events
Slow full zoom in, hold	on "Tinsmith" sign.
Slow full zoom out.	Same.

Center and hold.	In corner of the frame there is one person hammering and another standing. One continues to hammer.
	Man on right stops hammering.
	Man in middle continues haphazardly.
	Man on left continues but with exaggerated movements.
Camera off.	

Segment 8: Chris' Marrapodi Walkabout

Shortly after Yeshaie left Ncube's, Chris followed him south toward the Mandevu market. He placed his camera across the main thoroughfare where he could pan out to the road, the playground, and the partially completed Catholic Church. Chris kept his back toward Yeshaie and the other on the road. As passerby walked up the thoroughfare, they glanced at him, but he was not watching. The shots that Chris took on the walkabout were devoid of interaction, that is, they did not flow through a particular activity. His taping did not reveal that he was aware of or interested in what Yeshaie was doing, although Yeshaie included Chris in his filmed segment.

The setting.   The setting was the crosswalk exactly parallel to Yeshaie's Marrapodi walkabout location. Chris was about 20 feet from the main bus station and was on a grassy island between two thoroughfares. Although he was centrally located in terms of community traffic, few people watched Chris. The Masowe girls were preoccupied with posing for Yeshaie and for Peter's Polaroid shots.

An excerpt of the principal markers.   There is little content to describe in Chris' walkabout. This segment includes shots of the playground, the garbage heap next to it, and the bus station. The comparatively high use of zoom characterizes this sequence.

Cademic Markers	Events
Long shot, hold.	A woman walking down the road.
Zoom in	on the woman.
Pan left, zoom out	away from the woman.
Zoom out and zoom in to focus	on the playground.
Hold	on the playground.
Zoom out and pan left	away from the playground.
Zoom in	on the woman.
Pan left	to a metal enclosure (to a partially completed church) next to the garbage heap.
Pan right	over the enclosure.
Hold, zoom in	on the bus station.

Segment 9: The Mandevu Market by Chris

Chris and Yeshaie walked together to the Mandevu Market. There, Chris set his camera up and remained in the northeast corner of the market in front of some cabinetmaking shops. While Yeshaie faced south toward the carpentry shop, Chris faced north toward another set of cabinetmaking businesses and the market thoroughfare. He turned the camera around in an 180° pivot and also changed its position during the course of taping. Chris turned the camera off once and used this opportunity to focus on a vegetable stand. He used panning to link different filmed subjects. At one point, however, he panned quickly across several businesses and repositioned himself, creating a segment that is more transitional and a little dizzying. With this exception, Chris' taping was more characterized by comparative prevalence of zooming and steady camera holds.

Cademic Markers	Events
Camera on	several children in foreground; a man stands behind them to left, more children in background to right; booths behind them.
Slow pan right	over booths and merchandise as a woman walks right; centering a man standing in front of wood products.
Slow pan right and zoom in, hold	on a man, centered, lifting and showing a wooden object to cameraman.
Hold	same. He puts it down and picks up a larger pole. Turning to right, he holds it at an angle, turns it and lays it down.
Zoom out.	He finishes laying down the pole; a boy walks into foreground, facing away from camera.
Zoom out, pan right	as boy walks out of frame, left. Man is bending over wood, away from camera to left. Carpentry shop is to right.
Pan right	to carpentry shop, a big open doorway with corrugated roof. A table extends out front. A second table is visible inside with men beside it.
Hold	on shop; man works inside.

Each of the above segments reflects a striking difference between informant and researcher choice of shots, use of the camera, and interpretation of scenes. Chris, because of the technological limitations placed on his work as well as his own preference, used zoom and hold the most. While Peter panned more frequently, his choice of shots revealed a different orientation to the scenes filmed.

Yeshaie's Play: An Experiment in Ritual and Theater

Yeshaie instructed Chris, Peter, and the author to read from the Gospel of Mark and explain the true baptism to the American audience. Chris was selected as the main ''student'' and received all of the instruction while the author and Peter alternated in filming the scene.

The play was a spontaneous production in which rhetorical devices common to Apostolic preaching were adapted to film. Yeshaie announced that he was the director and confidently told the three American researchers where to stand. Of these, Peter was initially holding the camera, and Chris and the author were "actors." Yeshaie passed out Bibles and indicated when Peter should start filming. He then began to address questions to Jules-Rosette for translation to Chris, involving what we were to do as Apostles on our return to the United States. "Is the baptism real?" he asked. At each point after the questions were related to Chris, Yeshaie read him biblical passages and told him to use the passages as the basis of his answer. Other members of the household stood around as Chris repeated the answers.

Peter held the camera steadily on the scene, which opened with Yeshaie instructing the author to translate for Chris. Once an agreement was established, the scenario developed along the pattern of kerek readings. The reading and biblical interpretations were modified for presentation. For the closing segment, the author then took the camera and began filming, and Peter took Chris' place as the "respondent." Again, Yeshaie asked long rhetorical questions on the Apostolate in the United States. When had we arrived? How long would it be before we would undertake any other activities? If we wished the church to be strong, what procedures should we follow? Yeshaie asked each question in a declaratory way, and Peter replied to each one in slow Tshiluba.

The techniques used to film the episode consisted mostly of short pans between the participants and holds on one speaker or, more frequently, on at least two participants, the speaker and listener. There was little attention to the surrounding scene or the other parties, although at some points the camera shifted position, simultaneously panning and dollying to reach a new angle that included more of the people present. However, the careful attention to the entire social context found in Yeshaie's everyday films is absent. Instead, the camera concentrates on the narrative flow of the event, marking its questions and answers and holding on the immediate participants. In this case, Yeshaie structured the event's content but did not supervise the filming procedures.

FILM AND THE CROSS-CULTURAL STUDY OF PERCEPTION: SOME CONCLUDING INFERENCES

The differences in filming style among the participants are not idiosyncratic. The informant filmers view zooming as a way of making transitions, while the American students treat panning in this way. Horizontal panning for informants is a form of indirect emphasis. By returning to an object in the same way that Nawezi returned to the list of participants in the scene he described, the informant camerapersons established centrality through repetition.

While the American students made ethnographic interpretations of settings, their goals and orientations were different. Peter was interested in *simulating* a member's interpretation of a setting on the basis of his organization of shots and access to settings. However, these simulations contrasted with actual informant products. The informants, for example, did not film rituals from a participant's perspective. Jérémie and Ezekiel used the camera to create new realms of action. The informants thus wanted to portray aspects of a setting that were most relevant to them without regard for the boundaries imposed by real time, the sequencing of events, or the spatial and kinesic restrictions *normally* imposed by ritual. They were, in effect, asserting that the camera was and did "something special" in a setting. It freed them from the constraints of regular participation. Nevertheless, informants did not feel that these "special" effects of the camera were disconcerting. Within the everyday setting of the Mandevu Market, Yeshaie turned posing into a resource to convey the natural activities of buyers and sellers. He panned rapidly among these poses, creating an effect of animated activity.

Overall, however, the problem of equivalencies with which we began was not completely resolved by the presentation of data. While it is possible to establish comparability among filmed and taped events on the basis of the occasion of recording and with respect to a shared ethnographic intent on the part of informants and researchers, neither the structure nor the perceived context of filming remains constant. Despite intragroup differences among Maranke informants and the American students, a communicative difference persists in the use and interpretation of film language. While panning was used by the Americans to establish key transitions in activities, it was used by the Maranke informants to establish the salient features of events. Some indecision of the type found in most novice filmmakers was present. However, Chris expressed this visual hesitation by zooming in and out on an activity, while Yeshaie did so by beginning abortive pans. There were, of course, technological differences between film and tape equipment. But even when the same equipment was used in identical settings, as it was by Peter and Ezekiel at Matero, the importance of panning for the informants and zoom-hold for the American students remained.

If existing categories of film practice were applied to the American students, it might be possible to say that Peter's style approached that of "cinéma verité," while Chris' approach was more documentary (Bergum, 1974, pp. 2–3). Peter was interested in sharing in the order of reality or structure of the event through film and conveyed his intensity of participation. He attempted to show subjective reactions and movements from the perspective of the filmed subject as well (e.g., following Magora closely). Although Chris wished to capture events as fully as possible, he did so in a documentary manner, attempting to hold the camera steadily on an activity as it unfolded. The major difficulty with the latter approach was that its "objectivity" in capturing events simultaneously generated a great deal of self-consciousness on the part of those taped.

In addition to drawing upon different camera movements to convey what they see, informants wanted to present an image of themselves. The recognition: "That's me" on the screen or while being filmed makes a difference in how one orients to the process of filming and of observing. For example, Ezekiel stated that he was displeased with Chris' tape because he had sung several lively songs on that day and they did not appear on the tape. He had come to the special screening in part to see himself singing. Maranke Apostles have used the tape recorder as a means of perfecting their singing. Ezekiel expected to use videotape in the same way. The informant films and the home movie are similar with respect to these self-revealing properties of film. In each case, the cameraperson and subjects look at the films in order to see and recall themselves in a situation.

When examining the informant and American films, the following conclusions can be drawn:

1. *Filming as an order of reality differed for informants and researchers.* Although both groups were "members" of the same church and shared a community of knowledge, the members of each filming team conceptualized the possibilities of filming differently. The Americans viewed filming as more nearly a part of regular ritual participation, while the informants differentiated it as a special activity.

2. *The choice of shots was different.* The informants filmed either activities in which they had already participated and wanted to preserve or activities that they would not have otherwise observed (e.g., Yeshaie's film of the Masowe household and lot). They did not film activities in which they were deeply involved as participants. The American filmmakers were more willing to combine participation and filming.

3. *Their conception of social events differed.* Americans were content to focus on a single activity and its flow. The informants insisted on multiple activities and filming events in a broader social context.

4. *Their filming behavior contrasted.* Informants used filming as an occasion for intensive interaction with the people filmed. The Americans tended to view the persons filmed or taped as "subjects" engaged in particular activities. They maintained a greater physical distance from participants. Informants found this element of depersonalization in films humorous. One Maranke member even commented on a taped replay that it made the subjects "seem more primitive" than they actually were.

5. *The visual repertoires of informants and researchers contrasted sharply.* While this statement might be regarded as an obvious causal factor creating the principal film differences, we regard it as a finding. The visual histories of informants were often complex, and it was difficult to judge the differential impact of previous media exposure on them. However, a salient difference was to be found in the conception of timing and in the acceptance and use of film languages that had previously been introduced.

6. *The use of film language and technique varied.* The Americans used panning to establish a setting or create transitions from one setting to another.

They employed it for relative emphasis but viewed its constant use as poor and disconcerting film technique. They found zooming in and out of activities to be far more effective in emphasizing them. On the other hand, informants used panning to establish the importance of an activity and zoomed to make transitions from one aspect of an event to another. However, zoom and facial close-ups were used only a handful of times. When a full transition or change of position was desired, the informant would use panning as well, or if a fuller break was necessary, he would simply turn off the camera.

MEDIATED COMMUNICATION AS A VEHICLE FOR CROSS-CULTURAL RESEARCH

Worth and Adair have already established the fact that sharing the English language as a lingua franca does not assure a common film language. Johnny Nelson was able to film both in "English" and "Navajo." Ezekiel, when told what it meant to film to the researcher's satisfaction, was able to modify his filming style even before he viewed a completed informant-made film. Certainly, the existence of such differences does not leave us with invariant aspects of communication that set one group off against another. However, the immediate differences among techniques and styles point to the dependence of *perception* upon the social context of an event, and the very construction of accounts of these events is inextricably tied to participation in the event itself. In this chapter, we have stressed the relationship of filming practices to the individual biographies of camerapersons but more significantly to the very settings in which the films were made. That one is a participant in a ritual scene, for example, may lead to the production of a *filmed account* (as opposed to a videotape) very different from that scene as conceived in "real time." These informant accounts were more apparently awkward and impressionistic earlier on and became more subtle in their portrayal of various aspects of a social environment later.

We have seen that the informant and researchers' films combine diverse techniques, often on an individual basis, while retaining certain idiomatic features. One of our principal findings is that these variations also occur within the context of membership in a voluntary social group. The filmed products reflect the specific interests and purposes of the camerapersons in the settings recorded *as* they were filmed. These concerns were developed and varied in the case of all the informant filmmakers. They involved the use of a filmic order of reality as an opportunity to expand the expected perspectives of membership. Just as the position of the informant–ethnographers gave them the opportunity to ask questions about which they would otherwise have been inhibited or that would have appeared irrelevant, filming allowed them to take visual perspectives that would not otherwise have been available. In other cases, assumed features of church membership became topics for discovery and expression through film.

The subjects of filming and filming techniques provide avenues of access to much more than the camerapersons' perspective. They offer culturally related ways of accounting for social settings, the interaction of all participants in a living situation, and the conventions used to express these settings. In contrast to Carpenter's earlier assertion, our data lead to the conclusion that the cross-cultural use of media is far from uniform. It varies in the intent and in the codes employed. Just as the tonal qualities of African languages introduce new units of meaning and nuances into verbal communication, so too do the assumptions and techniques that the Maranke informants used to film.

A comparison of student and informant films reveals unique types of involvement in social settings and the expression of this involvement filmically. The American and African filmed and taped sequences presented here provide an illustrative example and point of departure for future research. Examining the informants' view and expression of a situation offers a mirror for our own research and is the first step toward uncovering the logic of description.

APPENDIX: BAPOSTOLO FILMS

This appendix contains transcripts of the following segments analyzed in Chapter 5:

1. Informants' Films.
    A. *Ritual Events:*
        Kerek, Kabanana by Ezekiel.
        Matero Preaching by Ezekiel.
        Singing and Preaching at Matero by Ezekiel.
        Confession and Curing by Yeshaie.
    B. *Everyday Events:*
        The Marrapodi Tinsmith by Yeshaie.
        The Marrapodi Walkabout by Yeshaie.
        The Mandevu Market by Yeshaie.
2. American Students' Films.
    A. *Ritual Events:*
        Matero Preaching by Peter.
        The Matero Tape by Chris.
        Confession and Curing by Peter.
    B. *Everyday Events:*
        The Marrapodi Tinsmith by Chris.
        The Marrapodi Walkabout by Chris.
        The Mandevu Market by Chris.

Kerek, Kabanana by Ezekiel

Cademic Markers	Events	Sound
Camera on. Hold	Three men in red robes sitting on the ground.	Talking.
Pan right, medium fast	to congregation, people standing in line for keti, all heads cut off. Sweeps past keti line over ground with occasional shots of people's feet.	Singing.
Pause.	People sitting on ground, heads are cut off.	
Pan right	across ground to open field.	
Pan left	back across ground, woman's back; view of people sitting in kerek singing, then keti area and beyond keti, all in one smooth pan.	
Camera off/on, position shift. Hold.	Keti, people sitting on ground (congregation).	Song: "... Jehovah, (Lord) Une masimba Jehovah, (Yours is the power, Lord) Une masimba Jehovah.
Pan right	past keti to congregation.	
Pause	on men's side.	
Pause	on women's side.	
Pan right	past woman walking left toward kerek, to open field.	(Jehovah) Une masimba Jehovah Une masimba Jehovah Une ma—..."
Pan left	to center woman.	
Pause very slightly.	Same.	
Fast pan left	to congregation.	
Pan slows very slightly (barely visible)	at women's and men's sides.	
Pan left	to and past keti to men seated on ground and past child, child walking to left.	
Camera off/on, position shift	looking from kerek to keti.	Talking, in Tshiluba. (Side conversation)
Pan right	past women's side.	
Hesitate.	Congregation.	
Pan right	to open field.	
Pan left	to congregation, centering men standing to be seated.	

Cademic Markers	Events	Sound
Pan left	to and past keti in background.	
Camera off/on, position shift.	Full congregation seated.	Song: (Kwese, Kwese)
Hold.	Men's side.	"Tizwe tino mu—" (Hear us)
Pan left slowly	to and past side.	
Camera off/on, position shift.	View of area behind women's side in kerek.	Song: (Kwese, Kwese)
Pan right slowly	to full view of kerek, past men's side and women's side, then beyond kerek to the right where trees and bushes are all that can be seen.	"Asi isu Baba wedu—" (But we, our Father)
Camera off/on, position shift. Hold.	Men's backs and heads seated in kerek.	Song:
Pan right and slightly up	to song leader standing in center aisle.	"Vanoera mu denga (Saints in Heaven)
Pause	centering song leader.	Vanoera mu denga, Vanoera mu denga,
Slow pan right and slightly down	past women's side where women are singing, and video camera, to edge of congregation.	St. Jonyi. (St. John)
Pan left	across women singing and song leader.	Tuakamona mu Jerusalema, (We have seen in Jerusalem)
Pause slightly	with song leader to right and men's side to left.	
Pan left	across men's side.	Vanoera—"
Reel ends.	. . .	

Preaching in kerek, Matero by Ezekiel

Opening shot: wide angle shot of congregation centering on speaker in the center aisle. Camera position initially, east end of aisle, from MS, facing approximately west.

Cademic Markers	Events
Hold	on preacher, standing in the center of the aisle, facing east, toward camera. Holding his staff upright and standing relatively still, he preaches in Chishona, welcoming people to the musankano.
Slow pan left	over women's side and center on girls. They sit, looking at the preacher and at the camera.

Cademic Markers	*Events*
Slow pan left	across women's side.
Slow pan right	up across women to center on speaker.
Hold and tilt	on speaker, who walks toward the camera. He greets the congregation, who respond, then he continues to preach.
Pan right	to tree standing in the kerek ground (on men's side near the aisle)
Pause, pan right	to men's side to show the men in back. Women in upper right move heads.
Hesitate, pan left	to center speaker.
Hold	on speaker. He stands and preaches, moving his staff slightly from left to right and up and down.
Zoom to close-up of speaker.	He turns to men's side and emphasizes points, nodding his head to the speech cadence and dipping his staff twice.
Camera off.	
Camera on.	Healing place, after kerek, still facing approximately west, in a place hear the back of where the men's side was and toward the right (i.e., west) of the side. The members stand around singly and in small groups.
Pan left, pan right, pause at each group.	Close-up of several men standing in foreground, other members in background talking. It is later in the afternoon, as the yellow sunlight slants in. In the background, singing takes place.
Pan left	to follow man walking left.
Hesitate	on man walking left.
Pan right	over people standing in the background.
Pause	on people in background, walking and standing.
Pan right	over background, and pause.
Pan left.	over background.
Hesitate.	Same.
Pan left.	Same. *Sound:* singing is going on in the background, not too audible.
Pan right.	People are still standing in background.
Slow pan right	to Chris in close-up. He backs away right out of the camera.
Center	on healing taking place in the space behind where Chris was. The patient is sitting on the ground facing left (east), and the healer is kneeling behind him to perform the ceremony. The tripod is in front of and to the left of this healing group which begins as two people, one man healing another. Other men move around the healing scene.
Pan left, pan right.	Same.

Cademic Markers	*Events*
Pan left, pan right.	Same.
Center	on healing. Another man sits down to be healed. He is wearing red. The first man stands and walks off, up left, after picking up his Bible.
Center and hold, shift camera position right, still centering	on Chris as he removes the tripod to the right.
Hold and center.	Another man sits down, healer continues to work, one man gets up to leave, another man and women sit down, first healer continues to work while man with Bible now kneels down to heal others.
Still centering. End of reel.	

Singing in Kerek, Matero by Ezekiel

Taken from east end of aisle, facing west.

Cademic Markers	*Events*
Camera on	back row of women at left of women's side. Women are seated.
Slow pan right	across women's side to aisle and video setup. Some of the women in front look back. A song begins:

> Tuakamona kuna Jerusalema uko—
> Amkiroswe
> Amkiroswe
> Amkiroswe
> Amkiroswe ku denga—

Pan left	to front of women's side and
Hold	on women.
Pan right	to video set in the aisle.
Hesitate	
Hold	on the aisle between men's and women's sides.
Pan right	to men's side.
Slow pan right	to middle of men's side and people standing in the background for keti. Men sit down in the back rows. The men are seated and singing.
Hesitate.	
Hold	on men's side.
Hesitate	left and right several times on men's side.
Pan left	across men.
Pause	just before the aisle, including the videotape deck.

Cademic Markers	*Events*
Slow pan left	to aisle. Men are singing.
Slow pan left	across women's side to back. Women without robes sit in the back in plain dresses. Everyone is singing.
Pan right	across women's side to frame the aisle. A woman in front jiggles her baby with a knitted hat up and down. A man walks right across the aisle.
Hold	on aisle, where song leader is singing.
Hesitate left	to women.
Hold	on women.
Pan left	to back, two women out of uniform in the back. Behind them is a group of people in the back.
Pause.	
Pan right	across women's side (main group).
Hold	on a few women in the front.
Pan right	across aisle, across men's side to far side, a man sits down in the back, other men walk to sit down.
Short hold	on men walking.
Pan left	to center aisle.
Pan left	to women, without stopping. Dip down on a few women for emphasis.
Pan left	to women in back without garments.
Camera off/on.	Back of the women's side, same angle as before. Sound is off.
Pan right	across women's side to aisle.
Hold	on aisle, where a soloist at end of aisle is leading.
Shift camera angle	from right to left, centering soloist.
Slow pan right	across men's side to the back where men move to the seated area and another man sits down.
Pan left	across men to center aisle, where man in a pink *mutambo* (ritual garment) moves down and out of aisle.
Camera off/on.	Position has shifted to right side of aisle, framing back of the women's side, women in dresses.
Pan right	across women from those without uniform to the aisle. Sound back on again. Women sit. Young girls in front fidget.
Hold	on aisle, where preacher continues. A man behind preacher is gesturing and singing. Since camera has shifted to the right, more visibility behind preacher.
Slow pan right	across men's side to back, two more men walk forward and one sits down. Sound off.

Cademic Markers	Events
Slow pan left	across men's side to center preacher, who moves his staff back and forth.
Hold	on preacher until end of reel.

The Confession and Curing Sequence by Yeshaie

Camera is in the northeast corner of the front room, on full wide angle, facing southwest across the room. Peter on camera initially. (Left and right directions refer to visual field.) To avoid confusion, note that *Ba*Kazadi (an evangelist) and his wife (*Ma*Kazadi) were both present at the confession and were called upon to confess later.

Cademic Markers	Events
Camera on, hold.	Baba Yowane speaking, leans forward briefly and back right. Chris' left arm in an out of frame to left. MaKazadi turns her head in the background. Baba Yowane is speaking. Woman in background speaks.
Wobble, tilt up and left (camera passed to Yeshaie).	Chris' body.
Rocking motion, tilting up and left.	Chris' midsection. He is speaking.
Slight pan down	as Peter gets up in front of camera.
Hesitate left, right, still rocking slightly.	Chris' body as he confesses. Not visible above shoulders.
Same.	BJR leans right to look at camera from behind Chris' stomach.
More rocking motion, tilting up.	Chris confesses (his chest).
Hold.	Peter sits down in front of camera, scene is blocked.
Hold.	Chris' side, arm, and hand. Hand is in a fist.
Pan left slightly.	Chris' left hand gesturing to chest.
Pan down and left	to close-up of Peter, sitting next to Yeshaie.
Slight pan up and right	to Chris (face not visible).
Hold.	Same.
Slight pan up	to shoulders.
Slight pan down right	across women in background.
	Dialogue:
	BABA YOWANE: C'est tout ce que vous avez? (Is that all you have to say?)
	CHRIS: Oui. (Yes)
Continue panning right	to Baba Yowane.

Cademic Markers	*Events*
Hold.	Baba Yowane listening. MaKazadi in background puts face in hand.
Slow pan left	across women in background to Chris.
Pan up	along Chris till shoulders are visible.
Pan down to follow	as Chris sits down. BJR in background. Baba Yowane begins to sing.
Hold.	Chris sitting.
	Singing: "Ndi rapire Mambo mudi mudenga," (I heal in the Name of God in Heaven.)
Pan left	to evangelists sitting to left (front of room).
	"Ndi rapire Mambo mudi mudenga,"
Hold	on evangelist.
	"Ndi rapire Mambo mudi mudenga—"
Same.	Baba Yowane begins praying:
	BABA YOWANE: Mambo (Lord) mera . . . di revelation Jehovah . . .
Pan right	to Chris. People begin to sing second verse.
Pan up and hold	to center Chris' face as he sits being healed. Baba Yowane lays hand on his head, once long, once short.
Hold.	Baba Yowane takes hand off and takes staff. Chris looks briefly at camera, looks to left, moves over to left and sits down as second verse of song continues.
Pan down slightly	to Chris' legs and feet as he sits back. Second verse ends.
Slow pan right and up	to close-up of Baba Yowane as he speaks, pointing with finger.
Hesitate left and right, hold.	Same.
Pan down left.	Extreme close-up of Peter's shirt.
Pan up.	Evangelists.
Slow pan right.	Chris.
Slight pan right.	Chris and BJR. Evenagelists and Baba Yowane are discussing.
Hold.	Chris, BJR. They discuss. BJR looks down.
	Dialogue:
	AN EVANGELIST: . . . kumumvuishe diyi. Mumvuish—mumvuishes. (to explain the word to him. Explain to him—explain to him.)
Slight pan right	to include woman in background. Mama Eva fixes her scarf.
Slow pan right	over women in background and Baba Yowane.

Cademic Markers	*Events*
Pan up and left	over Baba Yowane and women.
Pan up and left to follow.	Peter gets up and walks out.
Hold	on Chris' face. He looks at evangelists.

Dialogue:

BaKazadi: Si vous voulez gagner, n'est pas, chez . . . (If you want to win, isn't it, at your home.)

| Camera off/on | (end of reel). |
| Pan left | across Chris to woman. Chris is now sitting down for healing again. |

"Sûr, toujours. (Surely, always.)"

| Pan right | to Baba Yowane. |

"Si vous—si vous voulez faîtes (inaudible) . . . (If you, if you want to do.)"

| Pan left | to Chris. |
| Pan right | to Baba Yowane. |

(Chris?):   Hunh?

| Hold. | Baba Yowane. |
| Pan left | to Chris. |

Chris: Hunh?

Chris looks at camera.
Baba Yowane prays again:

". . . section spied . . ."

| Pan left, hold | to frame Chris and Baba Yowane. |

"Revelation spied a tenzi section spied. Mambo mera sipa section spied."

Baba Yowane looks to left at camera and says two phrases.

| Hold. | Baba Yowane, praying. |

"Revelation spied ah Tenzi Jehovah sarpo section spied. Mambo mera, tipa section spied a . . ." (Speaks, two phrases.)

| Pan down right | To BaKazadi to right: |

"Ah, votre coeur, ce n'est pas tout à fait pur" (Ah, your heart, it isn't completely pure). (gestures, one hand)

Daniel: C'est tout à fait court. (It is very "short.")

| Pan right slightly | to Baba Yowane. Discussion in French and Tshiluba. |

BJR: You get angry very quickly.
Peter: You get angry very quickly.
BaKazadi: Votre coeur fache toujours. (Your heart always gets angry.)

Cademic Markers	*Events*
	CHRIS: Hmmm?
Pan left	to Chris. He looks up and over at BaKazadi.
Hold	on Chris.
	BAKAZADI: Vous connaissez bien—vous connaissez bien... (You know well—you know well).
Pan left	to Chris, who leans over right to hear.
Hold	on BJR.
	BJR: You get angry a lot.
Same.	Chris turns head around to look at her.
Pan left	to frame BJR and Chris. She explains to him. He looks forward.
	PETER: You get irritated.
Pan right	to BaKazadi.
Pan up	to Baba Yowane talking to BaKazadi.
Hold, pan up slowly.	Baba Yowane leans down, up, he prays.
	BABA YOWANE: Revelation spied, tenzi... section spied.
Same.	Baba Yowane looks down.
	BABA YOWANE: Asei unaambia... (He is telling you) mubi ya pale, moyo yake, miniona (that you have sins in your heart, I see) inakamata moto (it catches fire)
Hold	on Baba Yowane. BaKazadi is speaking, he speaks again.
Pan down and right slightly, hold	on BaKazadi. Sits down.
Pan left	from Chris and Baba Yowane to BJR and Chris. The evangelists translate: "... et pour vous donner le conseil." (and to give you advice.)
Fast pan right	to Baba Yowane, who talks.
Hold.	Framing Chris and Baba Yowane.
	BABA YOWANE: ... ambia. (tell him)
Hold	on Baba Yowane.
	BABA YOWANE: We baba muvanger. (You, evangelist.) Ashikiya (explain to him).
Hold.	Baba Yowane looks at camera.
	BABA YOWANE: When you come, babatiza asked you, you come to—you come to one your homes, in America. Of course we should see, but Jesus he say, before he ask you, you must, do that, do that, who can... do... this? You are a... or are you not?
	CHRIS: I still don't understand.

Cademic Markers	*Events*
	BJR: I think it's that . . .
Camera off/on.	Chris is sitting down again. A man walks across scene to left. "Sijambo baba" (Hello, father).
Pan up left	to BaKazadi, standing at door. His face is not visible. He gestures with two hands.
Hold.	on BaKazadi.
	BAKAZADI: Musique, eh? (Music, eh?) Baba Jambo (Hello, Father).
Hold.	A man gets up in front of BaKazadi and walks up left.
End of reel.	

The Marrapodi Tinsmith by Yeshaie

Cademic Markers	*Events*
Close-up.	Children in front of camera.
Slow pan left.	Children, Peter's hands.
Pan right.	Same.
Hold	on three workmen standing at bench; one is hammering; heads cut off.
Short pan right	brings hammering into full view; road on side.
Hesitate.	
Pan right	across road to taxi parked on side of road, kids.
Pan left	covers hammering; passes to men standing behind hammerer.
Pan right	to two men standing in street.
Hesitate	on men in street.
Fast pan right	past taxi to view of street; woman walking; kids.
Slow pan right	follows woman and children walking down street.
Fast pan left	two boys close-up.
Fast pan right	past woman to view of street corner.
Hold	on view of street corner where Ncube sign is.
Slow pan right	to cross street; man walking; view of street.
Hold	on houses across street; children running.
Pan right.	Same.
Hold.	Same.
Pan right.	Children and corner of Ncube's yard.
Hold	on laundry in yard next to Ncube's.

Cademic Markers	*Events*
Pan left.	Same.
Hesitate.	Laundry in yard.
Pan left	past street view, houses, to corner where Chris is setting up video.
Hold	on Chris.
Pan left, hesitate	to view of street, kids' heads in foreground.
Pan right	back to Chris setting up video.
Hold	on Chris.
Pan left	follows car going up street.
Hold	on car going up side street.
Pan left, hold	up street to kids in front of camera; car drives past.
Fast pan left, hesitate	up street past kids.
Pan left	to yard where men are hammering.
Short hold	on men hammering.
Short pan left.	Same.
Short pan right, hold.	Same (centers on hammering).
Pan left	past men standing around shop.
Hesitate, pan right.	Not discernable.
Hold	on young Masowe woman.
Wiggle back and forth.	Masowe woman in and out of view.
Pan right	across shop past man hammering to man on bicycle.
Pan left	to group of men around hammerer.
Hold.	Same.
Pan right	to man on bicycle and two boys.
Pan down	to boys in front of bicycle.
Hold.	Same.
Pan right	to children in front of camera.
Pan up	to children in front of camera.
Hold.	Same.
Pan down and right.	Same.
Pan up and right	to street and people.
Fast pan right	to man with some chain in hands.
Pan up	to get man's head.
Pan left	past street and people.

Cademic Markers	*Events*
Hold	on street; men walking.
Slow pan right	follows man walking.
Fast pan left	to hammerer.
Hesitate	on street scene.
Pan left	across shop.
Pan down.	Same.
Pan left.	Same.
Pan up, hesitate	on small child.
Pan left	across shop to yard.
Pan left	to women in yard.
Hesitate, pan down	to women.
Pan up and left	to women.
Pan right	to women's legs.
Hesitate	on woman.
Slow pan right	follows Masowe woman with baby (Ncube's wife).
Hold	on Masowe woman.

The Marrapodi Walkabout by Yeshaie

Cademic Markers	*Events*
Camera on, hold	on big house on left side of street.
Pan right	to smaller houses and to the center of the street.
Pan right	past children, women in center street, to houses on right side of the street and white junked car where girls stand around.
Slow pan left	to right side of street, catching girl raising stove or bucket, she says something that sounds like "kugara."
Pan left	to left side, houses.
Pan right	to center street, where girl with stove walks away, girl turns and lifts stove.
Pan right	to white car.
Pan left	to house on right side of street and children.
Pan left	to center of street and
Hold.	
Pan left	to left side of street and past the houses up the thoroughfare. A dusty street, wide and straight.
Hesitate.	Same.

Cademic Markers	*Events*
Hold	on sewage water down right to the side of the thoroughfare.
Pan slightly left to hold	on BJR talking to two other people and walking slowly toward the camera, down the thoroughfare.
Pan left	to small field across the thoroughfare and trees in background.
Pause.	
Pan left	to Chris videotaping across the thoroughfare, field extends for a long distance with junked cars in the middle background and trees in the far background.
Slow pan left	to bus station, a small cinderblock structure, two women are sitting in front of it.
Hold.	Same.
Slow pan left	to large black and orange bus parked on the street corner to left of the bus station.
Hold and hesitate.	Same.
Pan left, hold	to corner down the thoroughfare, to taxi stand. Two cars come up the thoroughfare toward camera and pass the camera. In the left background behind the corner are larger buildings. To the right, people are sitting on the ground and behind them, more buildings.
Slow pan left	to yards on the left side of the thoroughfare where clothes are hanging out to dry.
Continue panning left	to white car and house on right side of street. Boys are in front of it.
Hold	on house.
Hesitate	Same.
Pan left	to woman at house at left side of street.
Pan right	to center of street.
Hold.	Same.
Pan right	to house at right side of street.
Pan left	to center of street.
Pan right	to right side of street.
Hold.	Same.
Pan right	to house at right side of street.
Hold.	Same.
Hold	as girl walks forward to fence, approaching camera, and leans on fence to talk.
Pan left	to center of street.
Hold and hesitate.	Same.

Cademic Markers	*Events*
Pan left	to left side of street as kids run into the frame at center of street.
Pan right	to girl in front of the house, right side of street, she is talking.
Pan left	to right side of street.
Pan left	up the thoroughfare as BJR walks left out of frame (camera begins to follow left).
Hold	up center of thoroughfare.
Hold	as three men walk down thoroughfare toward camera.
Pan left to center	on BJR as Masowe girls enter scene from right.
Hold	on BJR and girls.
Pan left	to Chris, still videotaping.
Pan right	to BJR.
Hold	on man in a dark suit who walks right, up the thoroughfare.
End of reel.	

The Mandevu Market by Yeshaie

Cademic Markers	*Events*
Camera on, hold	on lane left, woman standing right.
Slow pan left	to chairs.
Hold.	Same.
Pan left.	Man in dark blue suit, left, chairs right.
Pan right	centering front chair.
Hold briefly.	Same.
Pan left	centering on man. One arm is down, one hand on hip.
Pan left	past shed to men posing.
Slow pan left	at posing men.
Continues panning left	to Chris with VTR setup.
Pause	at Chris.
Pan right	to door or work shed.
Pause.	Same.
Pan right quickly	to first lane. Woman holds a pannier to right.
Hold.	Man walks away from camera in center. Two girls stand facing camera to his left; he pushes them aside and walks through.
Slow pan left	to where blue suited man is at left.
Fast pan right	to center man who lifts both arms a little.

Cademic Markers	*Events*
Fast pan right	to lane where people are walking.
Fast pan left	to VTR setup.
Hold briefly	on VTR.
Pan down and slightly left	to child standing in foreground.
Pan downward, tilt right	over seeds.
Pan–upward tilt	over seeds on ground.
Pan left and down	over seeds.
Pan left–upward tilt	over seeds to child.
Pan left and slightly down	over schoolgirls to BJR.
Hold	on BJR.
Pan right	as BJR moves left, over schoolgirls.
Hold	on two schoolgirls.
Pan up right (slight).	One schoolgirl is centered, face not completely visible.
Pan left	to BJR very close-up.
Pan left	to lane behind her where women walk right.
Hold	on women.
Pan down left	to vegetable stand.
Pan up	to vegetable stand.
Pan right	to woman, still walking right and child in foreground.
Hold	on child as woman walks right.
Zoom in	to center counter of carpentry shop across lane.
Pan right (slight).	A woman enters frame, walking to left, close-up, looks at camera.
Hold.	Same.
Pan down left.	Same.
Pan up right.	Same.
Pan left	following child walking left.
Pan down	carpentry shop still in background, centering chairs on display.
Fast pan slightly down and right	to follow girl walking right.
Hold	on other child in front of shop.
Pan up, left, up, left	over children to other children to left.
Pan down	over girl with baby.
Pan up.	Same.
Pan left	to men carrying a board right.

Cademic Markers	Events
Pan right	to follow them as they carry.
Hold	as they carry it into shop away from camera.
Slight pan left	centering girl with baby; she looks at camera.
Pan up and slightly left	to girl with sweater, face not visible.
Long pause.	Same.
Pan left, pause	on other schoolgirls, faces not visible.
Pan up left, pause	on two women in light headscarves.
Pan down right	over Masowe women.
Pan down.	Same. Head of boy is shown, he retreats out of frame.
Pan up	over women.
Pan right.	Same. Back to carpentry shop counter.
Fast pan left	to vegetable stand.
Pan down right	to vegetables; woman behind vegetables.
Pan down	to vegetables.
Zoom in, dolly in	over vegetables.
Slow slight pan up and shift camera position left.	Same.
Pan left	from vegetables to lane.
Hesitate	on lane.
Pan left	to girl standing.
Pan down	over girl. Another girl walks left into frame.
Pan up and left	over girl to boy standing facing camera, arms on hips.
Pan down	to his waist.
Pan left and pause	to show merchandise behind him.
Pan up and left slightly.	Same.
Pan left, hold	side of shed, lane.
Slow pan left, up, left, down left	to lane where boys are posing. One changes position.
Hold	on boys' faces, close-up.
Slow pan right	to boy standing with hands on hips.
Pan right	across shed. Spoken: ''Mama Maria.'' Other lane; a man and boy walk right. Kids in foreground look at camera.
Slow pan right	across kids.
Fast pan right	to woman's torso.
Hold	on woman's torso.
Pan down	over woman.

Cademic Markers	*Events*
Pan up	over woman. She turns to face camera. Two boys enter frame left and right, close-up.
Pan right	to center one boy close-up.
Pan down slightly and pan right	to carpentry shed behind the boy.
Fast pan right and down	over seeds on the ground.
Pan down right	over seeds on the ground.
Pan up left.	Same.
Pan left.	Same. Boy looks into camera from left, very close-up.
Pan left	to follow him left; he retreats out of frame; seeds on the ground.
Pan down	over seeds.
Pan up	over seeds; centering man in white shirt posing in mid-ground, in lane to right of chairs.
Pan right	centering cabinet behind man; man to left, a woman standing to right; a woman walks left.
Pan left.	Same.
Hold.	Same.
Two slight hesitations, pan down slightly.	Man in background, face not visible, seeds in foreground.
Two hesitations, (left–right, up–down).	A boy stands in front of the man and poses; face not visible.
Pan up	to include his face.
End of reel.	

Matero Preaching by Peter

From seated position on men's side, about three rows back and toward left, facing aisle where preacher is walking. Left and right refer to visual field.

Cademic Markers	*Events*
Fast pan left and slightly up.	Magora, the preacher, walks quickly left, speaking. He greets the congregation, "Vana vatendero!" (Faithful children). *Response*. He says one more phrase.
Hold.	He stops walking and talking, turns his head to our right, gesturing with his right hand. Facing camera.
Hold (mid-shot, centered).	He raises both hands. Speaks, brings both hands back to his chest. One phrase. *Response:* "Alleluia."
Pan right to follow.	He turns 3/4 right. Hands raised, walks right, speaking, gesturing with both hands.

Cademic Markers	*Events*
Pan right faster	as he begins to run. "Vana va Africa!" (Children of Africa). *Response*. He slows to walk, walks right. A member: "Alleluia." He stops.
Pan left to follow.	Magora starts walking left. He speaks, one phrase. A member: "Yezu Mambo." (Jesus Lord)
Pan left to follow.	Speaking, gesturing, moving faster. ". . . here?" (Is it?) (One phrase.) Stops in front of camera, faces camera while speaking.
Hold.	Magora is speaking.
Pan right to follow	as he runs right, one phrase: ". . . Mwari we—" (You, Lord)
Hold.	Second phrase while running. Stops running. A member: "Alleluia!"
Hold, mid-long shot.	*Response:* "Imeni." (Amen) Magora is standing, moving slightly to right. He speaks again, one phrase. Same member as before: "Yezu Mambo." (Jesus Lord)
Pan left to follow.	Magora is partially hidden behind heads of members in row in front of the camera. He moves left, speaking. He is walking, swinging his right arm.
Pan left faster to follow.	He speeds up to a run, "Vana va Africa!" (Children of Africa) *Response*. He stops at camera and turns toward it. A member: "Imeni" (Amen) as he walks back right.
Pause.	
Pan right to follow.	Magora walks right.
Pan right to follow.	He walks back right, speaking. Responses in congregation: murmuring and talking. Close-up of heads in front of camera.
Pause, pan left.	He turns around, walks back left.
Swish pan with wobbling, left, large hesitation	
pan, left and up	to trees
to right	to Magora walking left,
left	to reader, standing on men's side toward left,
right	to Magora walking toward reader.
Pan left to follow.	He walks left to reader, turns to 3/4 right, bending slightly, stops.
Hold.	
Pan right to follow.	He walks right, gestures, up in the air, down to chest, up in the air, down to chest. Stops walking. Turns, walks left.
Pause, pan left to follow.	Magora walking left, speaking, stops at camera.
Pause, pan right to follow.	Runs right, speaking: "Vana va Africa!" (Children of Africa) *Response:* "Alleluia." "Amen."

Cademic Markers	*Events*
Pan right slower	as he stops running and walks.
Pan left to follow.	He turns and walks left. He speaks. Congregation: laughter. Magora is gesturing.
Hold.	Magora stops, turns toward camera, gestures. "... wedza." Turns to right.
Pan right to follow.	Magora walks right, speaking. Murmuring, chuckling in congregation. He is in background, heads and staffs show in foreground. He stops.
Hold.	Magora is in upper right of the frame, gesturing and speaking. Heads and staffs in the foreground. He starts to walk left.
Pan right	over men in congregation.
Pan left	to Magora, still speaking.
Pan left to follow	Magora walking left.
Hold.	Magora is stopped, facing men's side, hits chest. Speaking.
Pan right slightly.	He walks right, speaking. Laughter from congregation.
Pan right to follow.	He starts to run, more laughter in congregation, murmuring, he stops and turns.
Slow pan left to follow.	Magora moves left. Reader begins.
Hold	centering on reader as Magora continues to left and out of frame.
Hold on reader	as Magora walks right, back into frame and behind reader. He continues right.
Camera off.	

Matero Preaching by Chris

Cademic Markers	*Events*
Hold, mid-shot.	Two men, standing in center aisle. Camera is looking west along center aisle. Speaker, to right, faces camera, holding staff. Translator to left, faces away from camera, hand behind back. Congregation: *Response*.
Zoom out slightly.	Speaker speaks toward camera. "... ama zangu (my). Wimi nake."
	Translator turns toward camera; the two are centered.
Zoom out	to include view of first two rows of congregation on both sides and reader at front of men's side at right of frame. Congregation is reacting.
Hold.	Same.
	TRANSLATOR: We are all here now gathered eh—to you, the whites.

Cademic Markers	*Events*
Hold.	SPEAKER: . . .edu. (our)
Hold.	TRANSLATOR: For you to observe how we are held by the Holy Spirit.
Hold.	SPEAKER: Vana Africa (children of Africa) *Response*.
	Speaker takes a small step toward camera with each phrase and also pokes his staff on the ground with each step. He says four phrases: ''Vangeri (Gospel) Mweya mutsvene vakubateri (the Holy Spirit comes over you) . . . ne mashav' (have a demon).''
Hold.	TRANSLATOR: Otherwise, if you went to live where you come from, if the Holy Spirit seizes you, people may say you have got demons.
Hold.	SPEAKER: One phrase. (to men's side)
	TRANSLATOR: Or you are drunk.
	A girl gets up and walks off to left.
Hold.	SPEAKER: . . . pera. (finished)
	TRANSLATOR: Otherwise, you are mad.
Hold.	SPEAKER: Funda (kuepi).
	READER: Wakale, (truly?) wakale, (truly?) . . .
	A woman at left gets up and walks off at left.
	READER: . . . here? (Is it?)
Hold.	SPEAKER: Vana Africa! (Children of Africa).
	Facing reader. Begins speaking, turns slowly, faces camera. Says one phrase. Translator faces him (right).
Hold.	SPEAKER: (second phrase) . . . ose. (all)
	Translator turns to face camera.
Hold.	Third phrase to men's side: ''. . . mu sa musoro.'' (on his head).
	Fourth phrase, facing camera, moving body and staff from side to side: ''. . . biwaka . . . dura a manya manye.''
	Fifth phrase, ''tisa tise (lu) musoro wake (his head).''
	Gestures with staff.
Hold.	TRANSLATOR: Now you see what we do here in Africa. When we pray, everyone you find him shaking his head. But there is nothing that affects his body.
	SPEAKER: Vana Africa (Children of Africa).
	RESPONSE: Amen.
	Speaker doesn't move.
End of tape.	

Confession and Curing Sequence by Peter

Cademic Markers	*Events*
Hold.	Yeshaie's upper body and face are visible as he confesses.
Pan down left	to men sitting in the front of the room. They talk.
Pan up right, pan down left.	Men continue to talk.
Pan right to follow.	Yeshaie sits down.
Pan down and hold.	Baba Yowane sings.
Pan right, hold	to center Baba Yowane who puts hand to his forehead and talks. He holds staff to his forehead and talks.
Pan left	to frame 2 (i.e., frame both Baba Yeshaie and Baba Yowane) as Yeshaie stands.
Pan up to follow, center	Yeshaie's face and upper body, as he talks.
Hold.	He shrugs.
Hold	on Yeshaie as men talk.
Hold	on Yeshaie as he talks. A woman and child walk out to left in the background.
Hold	as Yeshaie talks.
Hold and shift slightly	as a man gets up and leaves at left (partly visible).
Pan down, pan right	on Yeshaie. He listens while men talk.
Pan down left	to men as they talk.
Pan right	to frame woman in back between Yeshaie and Baba Yowane as the evangelist talks.
	BABA YOWANE: Mungu anasema . . . (God says)
Pan left	to evangelist. Other evangelist looks at camera. Kazadi coughs and claps his hands.
Hold on men.	Evangelist gestures and talks. Chris is partly in the frame to the right.
Pan right to him.	Baba Yowane speaks.
Frame	Baba Yowane as he prays.
Pan left	to evangelist.
Pan right slightly	to include Chris in frame.
End of reel.	
Camera on, hold.	Yeshaie is standing. He sits.
Pan down to follow, center and hold.	Yeshaie sitting. In the background are, left to right, Mama Esthere, BJR, MaKazadi, Mama Eva. Baba Yowane is at right. Yeshaie sits leaning slightly forward. Baba Yowane leans forward slightly and starts to sing. He rises to high kneeling position.

Cademic Markers	*Events*
Pan up	to frame 2, all sing.
Pan right	to frame heads of Baba Yowane and Yeshaie with Baba Yowane's arm extending between them as Baba Yowane leans back to lower kneeling position with hand on Yeshaie's head and arm straight out. He prays, speaking, putting his hand on Yeshaie's head twice, then puts staff back in his right hand.
	Both lean forward simultaneously. Only their heads are visible but it looks like Yeshaie is preparing to get up and Baba Yowane is shifting his weight. He sings. All sing.
Slight pan right, pan left, pan right, pan down	as Yeshaie gets up and BaKazadi stands, moves around him and sits down.
Center and hold.	Singing continues. A woman walks in from the left and sits down in back. Baba Yowane prays: "Ishe Mwari..." (Lord God). He prays with staff in left hand, right hand up, separate and extended, gestures as he prays. Singing continues.
Pan up right, hold	to center Baba Yowane. He puts his hand to his forehead and up in the air three times, then lets his hand down quickly. He prays: "Alleluia, alleluia..." Singing continues. Baba Yowane leans forward, BaKazadi leans right.
Pan slightly left, hold	to center 2. Singing continues.
Hold.	Baba Yowane leans down left so that his head is level with BaKazadi's and talks to him. Baba Yowane leans back right, prays: "Mambo (Lord) mera, tenza (Lord) rexion spied..."
	Chris comes in and sits down to left.
Center	on Baba Yowane. A lady in a yellow and green outfit walks across the background right and sits down.
Pan right, hold	to follow her and to center Baba Yowane praying. His head is centered as he prays. "Mambo, Mambo teza rexion spied..." (Lord, Lord...). He leans to talk.
Pan left, hold	to frame 2. He gestures as he says, "... ingine. Mungu anasema..." (another. God says)
	Gesturing each stressed word with fingers curved, palm down. End of statement, gestures once with palm up. He leans back to the right.
Pan up right to follow	He puts his staff to his face, his hand out again, starts to talk. He finishes a sentence, hand down. A woman in the back rubs her face.
	BABA YOWANE: Unishikiya... (You understand)
Pan left	to frame 2.
	BABA YOWANE: ...uh huh?
	He leans back up and prays.

Cademic Markers	*Events*
Pan left	to frame 2. Baba Yowane leans forward, puts his hand to BaKazadi's head.
	BABA YOWANE: Alleluia
	(hand on head), further glossolalia (hand on head and holds it there gently). He leans back, gestures, goes smoothly from praying into talking.
Frame 2, hold.	A woman in a purple shirt gets up in the background between and behind Baba Yowane and BaKazadi. BaKazadi starts to get up.
Hold on 3.	
Pan up left	as BaKazadi gets up.
Hold	as he leans down forward toward camera, to sit down.
Pan down	as BaKazadi sits and woman sits in healing place.
Center.	Woman sitting. Baba Yowane is praying throughout the standing and sitting. Baba Yowane stops praying as she finishes sitting, and turns to speak to her.
Pan right slightly	as woman sits down and back. Baba Yowane is speaking.
Center	on woman. Baba Yowane briefly speaks, she stands up to confess.
Pan up right slightly	to frame 2, then
Pan up left, center, and hold.	Woman is centered. Staff is visible momentarily at right.
Holding and centering.	She confesses. One man answers, one man asks a question, she turns her head left and right, pulls at her belt. A third man speaks, she sits down.
Pan down to follow and center, hold.	Baba Yowane speaks, one man answers, woman assents.
Pan up left (as curve)	to follow her getting up to confess again.
Hold.	She confesses, she speaks for a longer time than before. A man asks a question. She demurs and continues to speak. Another man asks a question, she assents.
End of reel.	
Camera on, hold.	Woman in yellow shirt is visible from head to waist, just right of center. She speaks, folding her belt as she does so. An evangelist answers her briefly, she continues. Baba Yowane's staff leans left in front of her.
Hold.	Staff is pulled away to right. She puts hand to her forehead, pulls it down quickly. She is speaking.
Slight pan down left.	Her arms and belt are visible.
Pan down left, hold	to close-up of men seated on floor, facing her. Profile, facing

Cademic Markers	*Events*
	right. Heads, shoulders, staffs are visible. An evangelist leans forward, speaking. Woman begins to answer.
Pan up right to her, hold.	Woman speaking. Evenagelist speaks again, she looks down left at him.
Pan down left, hold.	Close-up of evangelist speaking. He nods, as in assent, says "A-ah." BaKazadi sits down, left background.
Pan right.	Woman sits down.
Pan down slightly.	Woman is sitting down, right center, midback, Baba Yowane visible at right, closer. He speaks (praying): "Revelation spied . . . Amen, revelation spied."
Hold	on Baba Yowane, to right, speaking (Kiswahili): ". . . sema, . . . sema . . ." (says).
	He gestures with right hand as he speaks. Woman looks to her left (our right) toward him. In left background, MaKazadi holds baby, in center background, half visible behind woman is Mama Elizabeth. Woman looks forward, down, says, "Eyo . . ." (yes). Baba Yowane looks forward (left).
Pan up left	following woman as she stands up.
Hold.	Woman speaks.
Hold.	She is speaking. She looks down forward toward evangelists.
Hold	on woman as she listens, evangelist speaks.
Pan down left, hold	to evangelist speaking. He leans down, up, gestures with hand.
Shift left slightly, hold.	Evangelist speaking.
Pan right.	Woman sits down. Yowane starts to sing: "Ndirapire Mambo mudi mudenga." (I heal in the name of God in Heaven.)
Hold.	Woman leans forward.
	GROUP: Ndi rapirere Mambo mudi mudenga. (I heal in the name of God in Heaven.)
Hold.	Woman begins on offbeat, "Ndi—." Baba Yowane looks at her, raises right hand, she looks at him, he says, "Ts."
Hold.	Woman: "Allelu?" He drops hands, nods slightly, then looks forward. She stands up.
Pan up left	as she stands up.
Hold.	She speaks. Smiling. Stops speaking, looks down at evangelists.
Hold on her.	They speak. Hold on her face as she listens. She looks over down left (to our right), maybe at and over camera.
Pan down left	to men, still speaking.
Hold.	She speaks briefly, like assent.

Cademic Markers	*Events*
Pan right	to center Yowane. She is sitting down. When pan reaches him, he leans forward while singing: "Ndi rapire Mambo mudi mudenga," (I heal in the name of God in Heaven), he leans forward.
Pan left to follow.	He kneels up (center close-up).
Hold.	He is kneeling, holds staff with left hand, head resting on arm. One verse of song. He prays, head still on arm. A baby says something. He prays again.
End of reel.	

The Marrapodi Tinsmith by Chris

Cademic Markers	*Events*
Camera on	House, trees (facing east from southwest corner of yard).
Pan right.	Same.
Zoom in (very slight).	Same.
Zoom out (very slight).	Same.
Slow pan right	to UNIP sign: UNIP—Mutambe Central P.O. Box 3340 Lusaka
Hold	centered on UNIP sign.
Zoom in (total) (slow).	UNIP sign.
Center (pan up), hold.	Same.
Mid-zoom out (slow).	Same.
Pan up	to "Tinsmith" sign.
Zoom in (total) (slow), hold	on "Tinsmith" sign.
Total zoom out (slow).	Same.
Pan right	past people grouped in yard, milling around Peter, BJR, Yeshaie, and tin workers, to man hammering, who glances up periodically at the camera.
Zoom in (total)	on man hammering, who glances at camera and then back at his work; keeps hammering.
Hold.	People around hammerer looking at camera.
Quick pan left, then down, then up to original position (more like a wiggle)	to Peter, BJR, and onlookers. People are looking at camera and at Peter and BJR.
Hold.	Same.
Very slight pan right, slow pan left.	Same.

Cademic Markers	*Events*
Hold.	Men in white shirt looking over shoulder.
Medium fast zoom out (total).	Yeshaie with 8 mm camera walks away from the group.
Hold	on children directly in front of camera, looking into lens, come into view. Yeshaie glances at camera while he walks toward it, also at kids in front. The man hammering is not glancing up anymore.
Aperture adjustment, hold.	Same.
Slow pan right	to view up street. Yeshaie says: "Baba Phillipe."
Hold	on view up street.
Medium fast mid-zoom in	on car coming toward camera. A kid runs across the street.
Hold	on car going away; street. Cyclist rides in front of camera; pedestrians; cars pass. Pedestrians don't look back at camera.
Camera off/on	to three men hammering. Men of the left and right looking at work; man in center looking left to where Peter and BJR are filming, then he glances at camera and back to his work. All three are hammering.
Zoom out (slight)	to frame pile of tin buckets.
Pan slightly down	to include all the buckets in frame.
Hold.	Men are hammering. Center man looks up again and back at work.
Hold continues.	Man standing behind wall on right looks out at camera then at workers. Man to left of three workers not looking at the camera.
Hold continues.	Worker on left looks to left briefly, then at camera, keeps hammering, then looks back at work. Man behind wall leans out again to look at camera, smiles. Two women walk in front of camera, both looking into lens, the first fully facing camera, the second looking out of the corner of her eye.
Hold continues.	Man behind wall says something to workers. Middle worker looks up, then right worker looks up at camera. Middle keeps hammering half-heartedly, right stops altogether. Left worker is still working at not looking at camera.
Camera off.	

The Marrapodi Walkabout by Chris

Cademic Markers	*Events*
Camera on.	Looking east along major thoroughfare, on north side of the street. The view shows one man walking away from camera in mid-background. To left background are a field, trees, bushes, banana trees. To right, street stretches straight ahead.
Hold.	Same.

Cademic Markers	*Events*
Zoom in (full) with one slight pan up	on man walking, centering him, and also showing a woman and child, a man, and a child in right background beside the banana trees.
Zoom out, pan left	to field in foreground, trees in background.
Pause.	Same.
Slow pan left	to field with trees.
Zoom out	to include trash heap, foreground.
Pan left	again shows trash heap.
Zoom in	to kids on playground.
Camera off.	

The Mandevu Market by Chris

Cademic Markers	*Events*
Camera on.	About four children in foreground, a man stands behind them to left, children background right, booths behind them.
Slow pan right	over booths and merchandise as a woman walks right at left of frame; end centering a man standing in front of his merchandise (carpentry).
Slight pan right and hold.	Man is centered. He lifts and shows a piece of wood to cameraman. Sheds at right behind him.
Hold.	Same. He puts down the piece and picks up a larger pole. Turning to right, he holds it at an angle. He turns it and lays it down. His back is to the camera.
Zoom out.	Man finishes laying down pole. A boy walks into foreground, facing away from camera.
Zoom out, pan right	as boy walks out of frame, left. Man is bending over wood away from camera to left. Carpentry shop to right.
Pan right	to carpentry shop. Big open doorway with corrugated roof. Table extends out front. Second table visible inside, men are beside it.
Hold	on shop. A man is working inside it (sanding or planing, etc.).
Hold	on same. A woman walks by to right.
Hold.	Man is working in shop. Second man is visible for a moment, also working.
Slow, slight pan right	still on shop (to right). A man walks out of shop to left.
Pan left	past him over sawhorses out front. Man who picked up the pole is sawing.
Pause	centering him; another man walks to left. Two children standing midground, three youths walk right close-up; covering work scene; they walk by.

6

A Paradigm for Looking:
Film and Video in Two
Communities

Both of the studies around which this volume is centered were supplemented by additional audiovisual research in 1975. These follow-up investigations allowed further informant expertise to develop among a number of informant cameraperssons. Yet, the camerapersons maintained a consistency of style and of camera usage that supports the conclusions drawn from the earlier research. The growing involvement of community members with visual media did not bring about major modifications in the respective cultures. Instead, a self-selection process occurred in which those members interested in using media became more involved with videotaping and their own personal usage of audiotapes. Large segments of the communities retained their interest in viewing the media products while remaining relatively unaffected by the recording process. Aspects of the culture were highlighted by visual recording, which was still welcomed as a new perspective on familiar events. We shall examine the responses of the two communities to audiovisual research in some detail, not only illustratively with regard to hypotheses of media effect, but also through analyzing the process of audiovisual production itself and the interaction of cameraperson and subject (Carpenter, 1972; McLuhan, 1964).

PARTICIPATION WITH THE CAMERA: SIMILARITIES
AND DIFFERENCES
IN THE RESPONSES OF THE TWO COMMUNITIES

Our studies demonstrate how media can be used to record social interactions and events that later can be analyzed for their organizational properties. They also point to how informant-produced materials provide valuable data on the reasoning and accounting practices of each of our cultural groups. The various markers we isolated in our investigation offer a paradigm for looking that makes sense of each camera movement as an intentional activity. The basic camera movements can be viewed as a finite number of motions possible with a camera. The studies stress the extent to which each is a constitutive part of the recorded event. Hence, the occurrence of a particular movement does not explain its use, even if the movement was employed by both informant groups and the American camerapersons. Both the Kpelle and Bapostolo used the technique of tilt embedded in horizontal pan. Yet, that movement was different in each case. For the Kpelle, it segmented content within the event, while for the Bapostolo it included specific content in the course of the pan. Likewise, the nonexistence of a technique in one study suggests that other techniques were used to achieve a similar purpose. The Bapostolo used a slight pause in their filming that we have called "hesitation," while the cameraperson made the decision of what to film next. Filming simultaneous events regularly led to the use of hesitation pauses. When the Kpelle camerapersons videotaped simultaneous events, they employed horizontal pan with embedded tilt. When, on the other hand, they wished to include specific content in the course of a shot, they used a combination of horizontal and vertical panning rather than the embedded tilt of the Bapostolo filmmakers.

The two groups also differed significantly in their respective uses of dolly (movement toward action). The Bapostolo used it to segment and focus on subjects, to follow preachers in the ritual path, and to approach objects in secular settings in preference to zoom. The Kpelle dollied only to keep up with a subject moving across the visual field. In order to move in on an action they used partial zoom shots. Their use of in-and-out dolly was almost nonexistent. In many taping sessions, the camerapersons were reluctant to change positions even at the prodding of some of the researchers. When they did so, it was only for an important reason such as the knowledge that some activity was about to occur in a new place. When they wanted to move closer to the action they normally turned the camera off, changed positions, and then turned the camera back on again. While the Bapostolo cameraperson also used this technique in the recording of ritual settings, especially in Ezekiel's early films, they consistently explored the possibilities of a moving camera position.

We mentioned earlier our anticipation that after our informants acquired greater expertise with a camera, they would develop more sophisticated ways of producing the visual effects shown in our materials. This expectation was borne out later through the greater willingness of the informant camerapersons to combine their own techniques with those used by the American researchers, as well as by their greater confidence with and mastery of their own visual styles. In taping bricklayers in Marrapodi in 1975, Ezekiel imitated the long holds and slow pans of an American student researcher. He carefully framed the pile of unused concrete, the men shoveling the concrete into molds, and the activity of setting the bricks in place. Yet, he retained the overall technique of the moving camera that had appeared in his earlier products despite the slower movement and his willingness to focus on fixed scenes. Unlike the American, who in part moved the camera from one still composition to another, Ezekiel continued to treat holds as pauses in the overall flow of camera movement. Like his earlier, "pidginized" use of zoom, Ezekiel's techniques moved toward the greater ability to combine new camera techniques in his own distinctive style.

Because of this consistent development in the informants' techniques, we have been able to determine in many cases what a cameraperson was trying to do with a given technique at a specific time. As in Ezekiel's case, their techniques segmented their productions in significantly different ways from the techniques used by Western filmmakers. We have shown that their films and tapes were organized by many practices similar to those used in verbal accounts. An informant's manner of presenting a filmic idea, his understanding of relevant and tangential topics, and his presentation of subject matter were all aspects of these practices and were observable in the media productions.

Besides exhibiting differences between informant and American recording techniques, each tape and film contains specific information on how our informants and American camerapersons understood and perceived events. We have seen how the segmentation of a scene reflected the cameraperson's intentional position within the scene, as well as the knowledge of what was occurring within it. Consequently, each of our films and tapes points to ways in which informants structure social scenes in different kinds of situations. We have attempted only to present the set of procedures necessary for developing a paradigm for locating the intentional structure of informant-made materials. The implications that these structures have for understanding the nature of cognitive processes can only be alluded to here. A full explication necessitates independent monographs for each group. Our purpose in this work has been to present analyses of the methodological procedures required to carry out these studies.

It is now possible to reexamine the impact of our research assumptions and procedures upon the communities involved. We have already demonstrated the depth and extent of material available to informants. To pursue the question of the effectiveness of informant-produced data, it is also necessary to analyze the impact of the ethnographer's and informant's status upon the research. Another way of posing this question is to ask why use informant filmers and videoists as opposed to outsiders and why use visual methods. This query is somewhat analogous to the problem of using computers. It is often assumed that advanced technology contaminates the phenomenon under inspection. However, there are four major ways in which the use of visual methods can modify research returns: (a) The similarities between naked eye and camera observation can be explored, opening the door to a documented study of intentionality. (b) The process of participant observation can be explored in depth, through recording of its various stages. (c) Immediate research feedback and exchanges between subject, informant, and researcher become possible at early stages in the investigation rather than after the fact. (d) A record can be maintained of the substance of the activities recorded, whether by informants or outside researchers. Our analyses of the Kpelle and the Bapostolo have consistently demonstrated these four methodological and substantive advantages of informant media use.

The informant's access to events relies on his status as a community member. This question of participation recalls the fact that perspectival differences among camerapersons are much more than perceptual variations. They relate to the access of the informant to the organization of social knowledge and social life in the community. The degree of access to this knowledge is based upon the informant/researcher's membership in the group or community and therefore on the way in which he shares a variety of social assumptions with its members.

Throughout this study, we have regarded camera movements as concrete exhibits of the way in which human recorders attend to the world. A great deal of cultural learning is brought to bear in each camera movement. The cameraperson's field of attention is also highly structured by his participation in it. Through combining our findings on perspective and participation, we arrived at a schema of camera movements. The organization of these movements relied on the context to which the respective camerapersons were exposed in the first place. When the American camerapersons in both studies recorded events, their productions differed from those of informant filmmakers. There were also major differences between the films and tapes of outsiders inexperienced with the culture and the American filmmakers who had done extensive ethnographic work in the setting. The type of participation available to camerapersons influenced the way they approached and structured content.[1]

The influence of participation can be examined in terms of who ultimately did most of the filming in the communities and with respect to their camera techniques. For example, the informants' walkabout products were intended to portray their respective communities as they perceived them. In both cases, the camera was a new stimulus. Reactions to media were often the reverse of normally expected behaviors by virtue of the participant's new position as a cameraperson. Kpelle did not recognize the chief's authority over occasions during which media were introduced. In Marrapodi, children followed and swarmed about the camera, leaving their usual games and household tasks in order to appear on film. They entered a playground to swing on an abandoned merry-go-round and pose for the camera. The children's unexpected behavior in both cultural settings pointed to obvious features of the communities' organization that were highlighted by the presence of the camera (cf. Loud & Jackson, 1974).

The camera itself intensified ordinary aspects of participation in daily life. In the Kpelle study there was an immediate identification of the media with *kwii meni* or a Westernized order of reality. The traditional leaders of the community

---

[1]Compare Rouch's (1974) conception of the participating camera, which is selectively present to activities in the scene through the cameraperson's selective involvement in them. Rouch advocates improvisation by the cameraperson within the situation to anticipate and follow its changing character.

had difficulty exerting their authority in this domain. The town chief made vain efforts to drive away interested children when he viewed the videotapes. When a tape was made in the schoolyard, an area considered to be governed by *kwii meni,* the children surrounded the cameraman and mugged in front of the lens. When taping in other settings governed by traditional *meni,* the same cameraman was much more effective in chasing the children from the area. When the orders were given, the camerapersons all shouted *"Ka lii belei mu"* or "Go into your house." It is interesting to note that a similar warning is given before the Poro devil comes into town. It is an order to nonmembers to move from the area and seclude themselves. In this case, however, the society was the *kwii.* In the first case, the children invoked a "modern" order of reality in order to interact freely with the camera. In the second, the cameraperson treated taping as a *meni* with the right to enforce seclusion using the analogy of traditional societies.

Nevertheless, despite the association of cameras with being Western, the Kpelle elders were excited about the equipment. Two of the major elders of the Poro society asked to be instructed in the use of portapacks. This willingness on the part of the elders reflects a general eagerness to accept innovative ideas. In several cases, the elders were more interested in the video project than some of the younger people of the town. In order to learn, they were willing to assume a relatively low order status within the *kwii meni* for making video recordings. That is, the elders were in a sense willing to suspend aspects of their community membership in order to participate in the taping. The joking that took place during their instruction sessions did not denigrate their status in other *meni.* Instead, the younger people maintained the exclusiveness of *kwii* and traditional orders of reality through a modified form of deference that can be observed on the tape. In no case were there direct insults to elders. Even in the case of the town chief, the children did not mock him. They simply protected themselves against his blows as they moved in toward the camera.

The Bapostolo elders differed in their response from the Kpelle elders in that they encouraged the use of media but did not want to participate in the filmmaking process. While this was the case to a certain extent for the Kpelle, it happened without exception among the Bapostolo. They saw this as a young man's function and were content simply to oversee it. On the other hand, all members used tape recorders freely in the ceremonies. Both films and tape recorders were viewed as a source of feedback and a means to evaluate ritual performance. The basic distinction that the elders used in their decisions about media use was the amount of activity needed in each recording process. With their tape recorders, they simply had to turn the machines on and remain passive. Making a film or videotape was different. To record, the filmmaker had to actively participate in the surroundings. This the elders did not want to do. It would have interfered directly with their traditional role in the rituals of supervising with limited intervention except in their own closing formulations.

Both the elders and younger members of the church were very anxious to see the photographs and films of themselves and regarded them as a valuable record. Several women took photographs midway through the study, but they expressed only passing interest in filming. The freedom of movement required to film was virtually impossible for them to acquire in most of the religious events. The status of women as potential filmmakers illustrates the paramount importance of membership as a means of access to media in the Marrapodi setting. On a follow-up field trip, Jules-Rosette found that women were far more interested in videotaping and filmmaking than they had been in 1974. She began to train a young woman healer but found opposition among her male informants who insisted that the woman would not know what to tape or what to do with her recordings once she finished with them. In less extreme ways, the assumptions about the physical mobility of younger men gave them a freedom to select among a wide variety of possible shots. They were limited only by encounters with groups other than the Bapostolo, in respect to which their membership status assumed a new significance.

PERSPECTIVAL DIFFERENCES

We have already explained the occurrence of different camera movements as a function of the recorder's orientation to scenes. The differences that arose among camerapersons could not be explained solely in terms of cultural variations. For example, expertise with the camera is a feature of recording. It might be argued that the novice cameraperson is more absorbed by the mechanics of recording than the more experienced filmmaker or videoist. This absorption was observed in Ezekiel's learning of film and, subsequently, videotape. He imitated all of Peter's movements in an exaggerated fashion. The increased resemblances in their framing of scenes and use of zoom could be remarked in the final product.

Similar findings on physical absorption and body imitation have been presented by students of trance and possession states (Walker, 1972).[2] Much trance behavior is learned by observation and mimicking. Younger devotees begin by exaggerating the movements and gestures associated with deep trance although they may never have been explicitly taught what is involved. Many persons also seem capable of imitating or "faking" key movements during trance ceremonies. All of these forms of learning and the ability to identify them seem more or less indirect. If learning and mastery of a technique are both indirect and context bound, at what level is it valid to speak of group similarities and dif-

---

[2]Walker (1972, p. 31) states that older, more experienced devotees in spirit possession cults tend to be more in control of themselves and aware of their surroundings, while younger participants often become more absorbed in trance.

ferences? When we speak of differences in filming technique, we are in part referring to differences in the use of space and the execution of body movements associated with physical mobility (cf. Hall, 1969; Lomax, 1971).

For example, Yeshaie used his entire body as an instrument of filming. The circular sweep and tilt down were extensions not only of his eye movements but also of the normal ways in which he related to space at Ncube's shop. The conception of the camera as a physically separate entity that must be held on a tripod or the view of the body as a stationary tripod were both alien to him. The camera became an extension of moving and being in the scene. Peter used the camera similarly to follow action from his perspective as a seated member. Ezekiel used the sacred space to which he was entitled as a young man participating in the kerek. The potential for spatial maneuvering was therefore a crucial feature of the filming process. Learned bodily techniques associated with camera movements were also important. These movements contrast with the natural sweep of the eye. Thus, Ezekiel had to learn that the camera could not be used to keep up with rapid eye motion. In so doing, he imitated the way in which Peter held the camera and used zoom in order to decrease his rate of camera movement.

Like learning the movements of a trance-dance, approaching the nuances of camera movement is subtle and indirect. The movement of the hand from arm's length to eye with the camera is never explicitly learned, yet it is this movement that determines what is shot and its frequency. We found that our informants were naturally inclined to throw their entire bodies into the shooting process in ways that are discouraged by Western professional filmmakers. Rouch (1974, pp. 43–44) has referred to this process of becoming absorbed in shooting as "ciné-trance." When explicitly cultivated, this activity creates a unique type of filming behavior that is intended to communicate the cameraperson's presence through what is seen. Most Western film techniques are developed to do the opposite: to remove any traces of the cameraperson's individual participation in the scene that is filmed.

Distinctions must be made between aspects of filming learned through expertise and orientation to the scene based on participation. For example, the upward tilt and panning to follow action that Peter used was a product of effort to preserve his orientation to the ritual and a calculated use of the camera. Nevertheless, Peter's use of the camera proxemically constituted a challenge to the preacher. Filming upward resembled looking upward from the seated position directly into the preacher's face. The contradiction is that the lower status or seated person is expected to look down as a sign of deference. The subtle difference between filming the same scene from the seated as opposed to the standing position is at the heart of the participatory and hence perspectival differences between the informant and the outside ethnographer.

Furthermore, both the student and the professional American cameraperson tend to hold the camera stationary. They do not use it as a means for entering scenes but instead as a way of establishing a boundary between themselves and the scenes. For example, Chris relates to the scenes that he tapes with a visible distance and uneasiness. When he turns the camera toward a group of people and zooms in at a distance, they stop working to stare at the camera. Yeshaie's filming position from within a scene creates another orientation from which he pans outward to encompass surrounding events. The filming techniques that he uses are grounded in his orientation to the scene. Panning is a logical and a meaningful alternative with respect to Yeshaie's relationship to the filmed subjects.

When Ezekiel videotaped some Marrapodi bricklayers during a follow-up period, he used zoom and long shots which did not exploit the physical space from which he shot. This was largely because he taped in concert with an American informant and viewed his instructor's shooting style as correct. It was also the result of a participatory distance from the bricklayers with whom he did *not* share secular or sacred group membership. James Mulbah's tape of the Sande dance ceremony reflects in another way his relationship to the participants and to the structure of the event. He was careful to maintain his distance from the Sande leaders and avoided coming too close to the special medicines on display during the performance. Likewise, Folpah's three palaver tapes demonstrate how his interaction with the events being recorded and his status position or speaking prerogatives within each of the palaver's respective *meni* are revealed in the way he segmented the palavers, framed his shots, and chose what to focus on and when.

The American researchers' visual productions in both studies differed, not only from those of informants, but also between the films and tapes of those inexperienced with the culture and those who had done extensive ethnographic field work in the setting. For example, Peter's accounts differed significantly from Chris' due to his intensive participation and membership in the Apostolic church. Similarly, the differences between Chris and Joan reflected their respective relationships to the events recorded. For example, Chris wanted to obtain a holistic picture of kerek and attempted to assume the role of an omniscient observer.[3] He placed his camera on a tripod and considered it to record most of what took place in the ritual. Logue, on the other hand, was more concerned with following an event and so used only a hand-held camera. She was interested in eventually editing tape together into a documentary program. Consequently, she experimented with shots to achieve various visual effects. As a result of Chris' decision to just "let the camera run," his record of the ceremonies was incom-

---

[3]The so-called "neutral" observer actually assumes that he can completely control his actions in a setting, that he can withdraw from participating in it and that his observations thereby become more accurate. In many cases, the assumption of neutrality is associated with one of omniscience. The observer believes that by withdrawing from and observing a scene, he thereby gains access to everything taking place in it. For a further discussion on the relative influence of objectivity and participation in field study, see Jules-Rosette (in press).

plete as a member's account. It lacked the kerek's core spiritual features. The Kpelle subjects, on the other hand, did not know what Logue wanted but permitted her to tape freely. In the playback sessions the community members were primarily interested in seeing their own tapes.

Both Chris and Joan used a documentary style that was revealed in the distance they maintained from the subjects, the license they took to film certain events, and their selection of shots. They both used zoom extensively and in different ways from either group of informants. Our informants used zoom to make transitions and locate actions embedded in events, while Chris and Joan used zoom to emphasize or study subjects and actions. They often zoomed in on portions of a person's body or parts of an object to achieve an aesthetic effect. For instance, Logue made a videotape of a Kpelle musician playing a stringed instrument known as a *goining*. Most of the shots were of his hands. She made another tape showing a Kpelle elder weaving country cloth. This tape also was full of close zooms on the elder's hands and occasionally on his face. Joan spent much time studying faces without equal attention to what was taking place. However, both groups of informants, in different ways, always attempted to keep an action or individual within its context. Their use of zoom was much more functional and less purposively aesthetic.

In addition to using different camera techniques to convey what they saw, informants also wanted to present a particular image of themselves and their friends. The recognition: "That's me" on the screen or while being filmed was one of the most important and gratifying observations that the informants made. On several occasions during the follow-up period, the Bapostolo gathered to watch films and videotapes of ceremonies from other churches and vice versa. Each group saw itself reflected in the ceremonies of the others. They viewed the other group's activities as valid to the extent that they conformed to the home group's rituals. Thus, even tapes of others were viewed as areas in which observers could legitimately locate themselves and should identify practices with which they were familiar. Ezekiel took this principle seriously. He stated that he was displeased with one of Chris' tapes because he had sung several lively songs on that day and they did not appear on the screen. Ezekiel had come to the special screening to see himself singing and expected to use the videotape as a way to improve the effectiveness of his singing style.

When the Kpelle videotapes were shown to many people from the community, most expressed the same delight at being able to recognize themselves on the monitor. However, some expressed embarrassment when they were the sole subject matter of a particular tape. For instance, Labulah shrank down in his chair as his friends identified him as the one who had tapped the palm wine in Folpah's first palm wine tape. On the other hand, when people were identified in the course of naturally occurring activities (including the ritual performances), they expressed the "that's me" excitement of self-recognition.

THE EFFECTS OF THE STUDIES ON THE TWO COMMUNITIES

After the completion of the initial Sucromu and Marrapodi studies, follow-ups were conducted in each community. In contrasting ways, the people of both Sucromu and Marrapodi moved from a curiosity about media to their own ethnographic uses of film and video. It is important to note that in neither case were media universally adopted nor did they influence the lives of all community members. A sharp distinction must be maintained in this sense between mass media and media as research and community tools. Edmund Carpenter (1972, p. 188) asserts that the impact of media tends to be destructive of existing aspects of traditional culture. Our research suggests that such changes are by no means universal in their extent or direction. Community media use is selective. It is also adapted to the existing communicative styles of the group involved. The parallels between mediated and verbal account segmentation and the salient differences between the two suggest to us that media are the servants of accepted forms of communicative forms rather than their masters. The same conclusion arises with regard to media impact on social organization. For example, the walkabout tapes and films revealed important subgroups in the communities much more than they created them. To be sure, the small children who followed the camera were a new phenomenon that grew out of existing children's play groups. But, by and large, the walkabout routes and the familiar scenes covered in the tapes already existed as parts of social networks that the informants used to maintain community alliances. The media became extensions of their users and a vehicle through which participation in daily events took place. This process of participation must be examined without the assumption that the influence of media was disruptive.

An apt analogy can be drawn between the introduction of piped water to Marrapodi and the use of the camera in the same community. This comparison illustrates that technology in itself does not necessarily introduce new cultural principles. Rather, it is the uses to which community members allow technology to be put and the ways in which they initially conceive of it that influences its cultural effect. In Marrapodi, the older wells required the cooperation of a household or group of households in collecting and storing water. To the extent that kinship ties were preserved within the community itself, they were also maintained in the proprieties of well use. When piped water was introduced to every house in some parts of Marrapodi, the sharing of water supplies did not cease but its character changed. Those who had previously shared wells freely moved to each others faucets if someone was using their own household's water pipe. Nevertheless, to share faucets without such a motivation was physically more difficult. The customary structure of social relations that existed in the time of the waterhole remained but was invoked only under special circumstances.

The technological innovations modified the overt social relationships but did not remove them. Persons using the water tap based their decisions about which social relationships would be appropriate on the existing circumstances, for example, convenience and current use of the water. Behind each circumstantial decision was the participant's alternative social networks within it.

On our return to the communities a year later, we found that certain persons had selected themselves as media users while others were disinterested.[4] Folpah and James Mulbah remained dedicated videoists in Sucromu but had formed definite ideas about the kinds of scenes they considered worth recording. They expressed a desire to record many of the events to take place in the coming Poro initiations. James recognized that since the initiations take place only once in about every 14 years, significant changes may occur the next time they are performed. He even discussed with Bellman the possibility of recording some events which would remain in safekeeping behind the Poro fence without being shown to nonmembers. He also became excited about the prospect of using media in the classroom as a novel way of presenting some class materials.[5]

The Bapostolo were much more publicly divided on the issue of media use during the 1975 follow-up period. Ezekiel and Yeshaie continued as informants, and the reaction of high leaders to their filming in ritual settings was enthusiastic. They were also well received in the community at large. However, certain church members, in particular one of the prophets, felt that filming interfered with the spiritual progression of kerek even though the ceremonies had previously been recorded on several occasions. These persons criticized the movements of the informants on the periphery of the kerek area and claimed that participation lowered their spiritual strength. It was only when higher leaders intervened to announce that photographs could aid evangelizing that their disagreements abated.

The influence of media upon a community involves a multilevel relationship among media users, their knowledge of the community's organization, and their personal decisions about media use. Rather than giving some "overall" picture of either the community at large or reactions to media within it, the informant's and researchers' activities present the detailed record of those very occasions where media were introduced. Unlike the introduction of print and radio, the recording media preserve the history of their own use. The reactions of camera subjects may thus be made salient as their counterparts to media use. This process involves a continual feedback among all those taking part in it (Rouch, 1974, p. 43). Although not limited to audiovisual research, this feedback affords ways of examining media innovations as affecting and being affected by the events recorded. It is through long-range observation of communities to which

----

[4]This is exemplified in the case of the woman discussed earlier who became more interested in filming and some of the elders who were more skeptical of media in the return trip.

[5]Jules-Rosette was present on one of the follow-up visits to Sucromu and was surprised at the calm orientation, even indifference, that media received in their public social scenes.

both informant and mass media have been introduced that we shall accumulate the foundation for making reasonable assessments of how community members have integrated media into their daily framework of understanding.

It has been asserted that visual media allow little experimentation and that cross-cultural differences in filming are actually quite minimal (Carpenter, 1972, pp. 188–189). The investigation of Kpelle, Bapostolo, and American products, however, suggests that we are just beginning to discover the scope and importance of perspectival variations and the influence of the immediate social context upon the structuring of accounts. Differences in perspective and organization do not preclude an underlying similarity in communicative processes across cultural groups. To discover and interpret the extent of variations in visual expression requires investigating the relationship of all persons to the scene and the specific features of the recording process. A structural explanation of the visual outcome will not suffice. Without extensive ethnographic observation, it is not possible to validly decipher and assess informants' materials. A major problem that confronts the study of visual communication once some of these similarities and differences have been assessed is understanding the total process of representation. In everyday communication, we take for granted the semantic equivalence of talk and gesture and the redundancy of verbal and visual representation (cf. Bateson, 1972, pp. 411–426; Cicourel, 1974, p. 163).[6] However, when an equivalence that seems so obvious in direct communication is mediated through the camera, it becomes apparent that a motion toward an object and a description of it are two distinct orders of phenomena. Even when intentional motions are made, the assertion that equivalent types of representation are used connot be substantiated.

We can now suggest a broader research scope for informant media. The caveat must be presented that other domains should not be examined without extensive attention to their ethnographic background and the training and assumptions of media users. Areas for further research include exploring the filming of home movies by persons at various levels of expertise, for example, movies made by inexperienced children and by more seasoned amateur adults. In each case, one could examine the combination of group specific camera practices along with the particular contexts of filming. These scenes might reveal not only unique types of involvement in scenes but also new ways of expressing this involvement visually.[7] The cademic markers can also be regarded as a means to explore how

---

[6]Cicourel's work presents the basic critique of the structuralist and semiotic approaches to language. However, to examine visual expression, one must deal with the conventions it presents and not reduce them to a model of cognitive processes.

[7]In a study of Manhattan day care centers, Bellman and Joseph Glick found significant differences between videotapes made by directors with different philosophies and positions regarding day care. The camerapersons who were in more contact with the children tended to follow the activity rather than attempt to describe the center without regard to the children in it. The camerapersons who had only a formal relationship to the center were unable to locate the sense of the children's behaviors. They spent most of their tape showing the close-ups of "cute" children and several shots of short duration presenting an inventory of the center's facilities.

informant, documentary, and commercial media productions are structured. The uses of camera movements to appeal to and communicate with specific audiences would be considered in this light. For example, the presumed neutrality of news broadcasts, the attraction of children's programming, and the calculated appeal of commercials might be examined with regard to the use of camera movements across these recording contexts.

Finally, drawing upon informant-made materials offers the social scientist one of the most effective avenues for self-examination and for the analysis of representational systems across cultures. Through looking at the informant cameraperson's selection of relevant activities in comparison to his own orientation, the ethnographer is provided with a mirror and a corrective example. By simultaneously addressing the problems of representational and perspectival differences, we have begun to approach the uniqueness of visual accounts and the processes through which they convey messages.[8] The production of visual accounts in a natural setting forms the background for a broad range of filmed and videotaped materials.[9] It is through examining this process in detail that we can discover the logic of description and the complexities of multiple communicative forms.

REFERENCES

Albert, E. "Rhetoric," "logic," and "poetics" in Burundi: Culture patterning of speech behavior. *American Anthropologist,* 1964, **66,** 39–54.

Barrett, D. B. *Schism and renewal in Africa: An analysis of six thousand contemporary religious movements.* Nairobi: Oxford University Press, 1968.

Bateson, G. *Steps to an ecology of mind.* New York: Ballantine, 1972.

Bateson, G., & Mead, M. *Balinese character: A photographic analysis.* New York: The New York Academy of Sciences, 1942.

Bellman, B. L. The hermeneutics of Fala Kpelle secret society rituals. Paper presented at the Third Triennial Symposium on Traditional African Art, Columbia University, April 1974.   (a)

Bellman, B. L. The sociolinguistics of ritual performance. *CORD Research Journal,* 1974, **6,** 136–147.   (b)

Bellman, B. L. Ethnohermeneutics: On the interpretation of intended meaning among the Kpelle of Liberia. In McCormack & Würm (Eds.), *Language and mind.* The Hague: Mouton, 1975.   (a)

Bellman, B. L. *Village of curers and assassins: On the production of Kpelle cosmological categories.* Approaches to Semiotics Series No. 32, Thomas Sebeok (Ed.). The Hague: Mouton, 1975.   (b)

Bergum, C. Defining interpretive film practice. Unpublished paper presented at the Sixth Annual Meetings of the Conference on Visual Anthropology, Temple University, 1974. Pp. 2–12.

[8]Both verbal and visual elicitation could be used to uncover the assumptions behind categorization systems. Elsewhere, I have suggested examining instruction in certain activities (e.g., ritual practices) as one way to approach the problem of different perspectives toward learning about describing scenes (see Jules-Rosette, 1974).

[9]Goffman (1971) distinguishes natural settings from a variety of experimental and staged social occasions. He suggests the former as a location for the study of basic forms of ordinary social interaction.

Boas, F.   *The mind of primitive man*. New York: The Free Press, 1965.

Brinkley, A. B.   Toward a phenomenological aesthetic of cinema. *Tulane Studies in Philosophy*, 1971, **20**, 5.

Burling, R.   Cognition and componential analysis: God's truth or hocus pocus? *American Anthropologist*, 1964, **66**, 20–28.

Byers, P.   Still photography in the systematic recording of an analysis of behavioral data. *Human Organization*, 1964, **23**, 78–84.

Byers, P.   Cameras don't take pictures. *Columbia University Forum*, 1966, **2**, 27–31.

Carpenter, E.   *Oh, what a blow that phantom gave me!* New York: Bantam Books, 1972.

Castaneda, C.   *The teachings of Don Juan: A Yaqui way of knowledge*. New York: Ballantine Books, 1968.

Cicourel, A. V.   Basic and normative rules in the negotiation of status and role. In D. Sudnow (Ed.), *Studies in social interaction*. New York: Free Press, 1972.

Cicourel, A. V.   *Cognitive sociology*. New York: Free Press, 1974.

Colby, B. N.   A partial grammar of Eskimo folk tales. *American Anthropologist*, 1973, **75**, 645–662.

Colby, B. N., & Cole, M.   A cross-cultural analysis of memory and narrative. In Robin Horton & Ruth Finney (Eds.), *Modes of thought*. London: Faber & Faber, 1973.

Colby, B. N., & Peacock, J.   Narrative. In John J. Honigmann, (Ed.), *Handbook of social and cultural anthropology*. Chicago: Rand McNally, 1973.

Cole, M., Gay, J., Glick, J. A., & Sharp, W.   *The cultural context of learning and thinking: An exploration in experimental anthropology*. New York: Basic Books, 1971.

Cole, M., & Scribner, S.   *Culture and thought: A psychological introduction*. New York: Wiley, 1974.

Collier, J., Jr.   Photography in anthropology: A report on two experiments. *American Anthropologist*, 1957, **59**, 843–859.

Collier, J., Jr.   *Visual anthropology: Photography as a research method*. New York: Holt, Rinehart & Winston, 1967.

Doob, L. W.   *Communication in Africa: A search for boundaries*. New Haven: Yale University Press, 1961. Pp. 102–103.

Fabian, J.   Genres in an emerging tradition: An anthropological approach to religious communication. In Allan W. Eister (Ed.), *Changing perspectives in the scientific study of religion*. New York: Wiley, 1974.

Faïk-Nzuji, C.   *Enigmes Lubas: Nshinga: Etude Structurale*. Kinshasa: Editions de l'Université Lovanium, 1970.

Fitzgerald, D. K.   *Prophetic speech in Ga spirit mediumship*. Monograph No. 36, Language-Behavior Research Laboratory, January 1970.

Fulton, R. M.   The political structures of Poro in Kpelle society. *American Anthropologist*, 1972, **74**, 1218–1233.

Garfinkel, H.   *Studies in ethnomethodology*. Englewood Cliffs, N.J.: Prentice-Hall, 1967.

Garfinkel, H.   Lecture Notes, 1970–1971.

Garfinkel, H., & Sacks, H.   On formal structures of practical actions. In J. C. McKinney & E. A. Tirakian (Eds.), *Theoretical sociology: Perspectives and developments*. New York: Appleton-Century-Crofts, 1970.

Gay, J. & Cole, M.   *The new mathematics in an old culture*. New York: Holt, Rinehart & Winston, 1967.

Gibbs, J. L., Jr.   Marital instability among the Kpelle: Towards a theory of Epainogamy. *American Anthropologist*, 1963, **65**, 552–573.

Gibbs, J. L., Jr.   The Kpelle of Liberia. In J. L. Gibbs, Jr. (Ed.), *Peoples of Africa*. New York: Holt, Rinehart & Winston, 1965.

Goffman, E.   *Relations in public*. New York: Harper, 1971.

Gurwitsch, A. *The field of consciousness*. Pittsburgh: The Duquesne University Press, 1964. Pp. 386–387.

Hall, E. *The hidden dimension*. Garden City: Anchor Books, 1969.

Harley, G. W. *Notes on the Poro in Liberia*. Cambridge, Mass.: Papers of the Peabody Museum of American Archaeology and Ethnology, 1941. Vol. 19, No. 2.

Jules-Rosette, B. Reflexive ethnography I: Instructions as data: The apostolic case. Paper presented at the UCLA Ethnomethodology Symposium, June 1974.

Jules-Rosette, B. *African apostles: Ritual and conversion in the Church of John Maranke*. Myth, Symbol, and Ritual Series, V. Turner (Ed.). Ithaca: Cornell University Press, 1975. (a)

Jules-Rosette, B. Song and spirit: The use of songs in the management of ritual settings. *Africa*, 1975, **45**, No. 2. (b)

Jules-Rosette, B. The conversion experience. *Journal of Religion in Africa*, 1976. (a)

Jules-Rosette, B. Verbal and visual accounts of a ritual setting. In F. Sack, J. Schenkein, & E. Weingarten (Eds.), *Ethnomethodologie*. Frankfurt: Suhrkamp, 1976. (b)

Jules-Rosette, B. The veil of objectivity: Prophecy, divination, and social inquiry. In J. Fabian (Ed.), *The words of prophets*. Cambridge, England: Cambridge University Press, in press.

Kulah, A. A. The organization and learning of proverbs among the Kpelle of Liberia. Unpublished Ph.D. dissertation, University of California, Irvine, 1973.

Labov, W., & Waletzky, J. Narrative analysis: Oral versions of personal experience. In J. Helm (Ed.), *Essays on the verbal and visual arts: Proceedings of the American Ethnological Society*. Seattle: University of Washington Press, 1967. Pp. 12–44.

Leach, E. *Political systems of Highland Burma*. Boston: Beacon Press, 1969. P. 227.

Lomax, A. Choreometrics and ethnographic filmmaking. *Filmmakers Newsletter*, 1971, **4**, 22–30.

Loud, P. & Jackson, N. *Pat Loud: A woman's story*. New York: Bantam Books, 1974.

MacDougall, D. Prospects of ethnographic film. *Film Quarterly*, 1969–70, **23**, 22.

Maranke, J. *The new witness of the Apostles*. Bocha: Mimeographed, c. 1953.

McLuhan, M. *Understanding media: The extensions of man*. New York: New American Library, 1964.

Mead, M. & MacGregor, F. C. *Growth and culture*. New York: Putnam, 1951.

Metz, C. *Film language: A semiotics of the cinema*. M. Taylor (Transl.). New York: Oxford University Press, 1974.

Moerman, M. Analysis of Lue conversation: Providing accounts, finding breaches, and taking sides. In D. Sudnow (Ed.), *Studies in social interaction*. New York: Free Press, 1972.

Murphree, M. W. *Christianity and the Shona*. London: The Athlone Press, 1969.

Pike, K. L. "Towards a Theory of the Structure of Human Behavior." In D. Hymes (Ed.), *Language in culture and society: A reader in linguistics and anthropology*. New York: Harper & Row, 1964.

Propp, V. *The morphology of the folktale*. L. Scott (Transl.). Austin: University of Texas Press, 1968 (originally published 1928).

Roberts, K. H., & Sharples, W., Jr. *A primer for filmmaking*. New York: Bobbs-Merrill, 1971.

Rouch, J. The cinema and man. *Studies in the Anthropology of Visual Communication*, 1974, **1**, 37–44.

Rundstrom, D., Rundstrom, R., & Bergum, C. Japanese tea: The ritual, the aesthetics, the way: An ethnographic companion to the film *The Path*. A Warner Modular Publication, Module 3, 1973.

Sacks, H. On the analyzability of stories by children. In J. J. Gumperz & D. Hymes (Eds.), *Directions in sociolinguistics*. New York: Holt, Rinehart, & Winston, 1972.

Sacks, H., Jefferson, G., & Schegloff, E. A simplest systematics for the organization of turn taking in conversation. *Language*, 1974, **64**, 696–735.

Schegloff, E. Sequencing in conversational openings. In J. J. Gumperz & D. Hymes (Eds.), *Directions in sociolinguistics*. New York: Holt, Rinehart, & Winston, 1972.

Schutz, A.   *Collected papers, Vol. I.* The Hague: Martinus Nijhoff, 1964.   (a)

Schutz, A.   *Collected papers, Vol. II.* The Hague: Martinus Nijhoff, 1964. Pp. 170–173.   (b)

Segall, M. H., Campbell, D. T., & Herskovits, M. J.   *The influence of culture on visual perception.* New York: Bobbs-Merrill, 1966.

Sudnow, D. (Ed.).   *Studies in social interaction.* New York: The Free Press, 1972.

Turner, R.   Words, utterances, and activities. In J. D. Douglas (Ed.), *Understanding everyday life.* Chicago: Aldine, 1970.

Walker, S. S.   *Ceremonial spirit possession in Africa and Afro-America.* Leiden: Brill, 1972.

Welmers, W. E.   Secret medicines, magic and rites of the Kpelle Tribe in Liberia. *Southwestern Journal of Anthropology,* 1949, **5,** 208–243.

Whitaker, R.   *The language of film.* Garden City: Prentice-Hall, 1970.

Whorf, B. L.   *Language, thought, and reality.* Cambridge, Mass.: MIT Press, 1956.

Worth, S., & Adair, J.   *Through Navajo eyes: An exploration in film communication and anthropology.* Bloomington: Indiana University Press, 1972.

Author Index

Numbers in *italics* refer to pages on which the complete references are listed.

206

Subject Index